海外中華古籍書志書目叢刊

加拿大多倫多大學慕氏藏書目（外一種）

2

加拿大多倫多大學東亞圖書館 編

喬曉勤 主編

國家圖書館出版社

第二册目録

2

The University of Toronto Chinese Library

———•———

Accession No. 535   Index No. - 030-cifn

Title   " Ming yüan shih kuei "
名 媛 詩 歸

<u>Classification</u> - D-68 總集-文

<u>Subject</u> - a collection of poems of famous women from the <u>Han</u> to the
<u>Ming</u> dynasty; with explanations and commentaries.

<u>References</u> - 031-bgdf 193/23.

<u>Author</u> - (默次) <u>Chung Hsing</u> 鍾 惺.

<u>Edition</u> - a Ming edition; no date.   Blocks; bamboo paper.

<u>Index</u> - a general table of contents for 36 chüan; separate list at
the beginning of each chüan.

<u>Bound in</u> 1 t'ao 10 ts'ê.

<u>Remarks</u> - a good edition; the item is complete and in good condition.

The University of Toronto Chinese Library

Accession No. 536   Index No. - 046-zzbd

Title   " Shan-ku nei chi chu "
              山 谷 内 集 註

Classification - D-38 別集-詩

Subject - an individual comprehensive collection of poetry, with

  commentaries.

References - 163-ggcz 13/7   031-bgld 15/44   012-zafk 15/16

  031-bgdf 154/11.

Author - (撰) Huang T'ing-chien 黄 庭 堅 .

Edition - a reprint of the Japanese edition; (postscriptum) dated

  Hsüan-T'ung 2/1910.   Blocks; "fên" paper.

Index - (内 集) a detailed table of contents for 20 chüan;

  (外 集) for 17 chüan; (別 集) for 2 chüan.

Bound in 2 t'ao 20 ts'ê (10-10).

Remarks - a very good modern edition; the item is new.

2

Accession No. 538   **Index No.** - 044-aoez

Title   " <u>Ch'ih</u> <u>tu</u> <u>chien</u> <u>yen</u> "
尺　牘　雋　言

Classification - D-73 總集一文

Subject - a collection of letters written by famous scholars from the
<u>Chou</u> to the <u>Yüan</u> dynasty.

References - 031-bgdf 193/18.

Author - (輯) <u>Ch'ên Ch'ên-chung</u> 陳 臣 忠.

Edition - a Ming edition; no date.   Blocks; "fên" paper.

Index - none; 12 chüan.

Bound in 1 t'ao 6 ts'ê; doubly interleaved with margins.

Remarks - a very good edition; the item is complete and in good
condition.   This work appears to have been repaired extensively
not very long ago.

Accession No. 537   Index No. – 073–hzab

Title   " Tsêng Wên-chêng kung chia shu "
               曾 文 正 公 家 書

Classification – D-43 別集一文

Subject – a collection of family letters of Tsêng Kuo-fan

References – 012-zafk 18/31.

Author – (撰) Tsêng Kuo-fan 曾 國 藩.

Edition – the "Chuan-chung-shu-chü" 傳 忠 書 局 ; dated Kua
   "chi-mao" 5/1879.   Blocks; "mao-t'ai" paper.

Index – none; 10 chüan; 家 訓 2 chüan.

Bound in 1 t'ao 12 ts'ê.

Remarks – an ordinary edition; the item is complete and in
   condition.

The University of Toronto Chinese Library

Accession No. 539   Index No. - 149-hj

Title   " Lun hêng "
                           論   衡

Classification - C-308 雜家 - 雜文

Subject - "a miscellany of short dissertations on a wide variety of
    subjects, and among others those connected with human existence
    (more particularly at that period) and the immortality of the
    soul,- the emptiness and unreality of the present life and the
    improbability of a life hereafter." (Gest No. 1539)

References - 160-lj 163-ggoz 10/6 031-bgld 13/15 037-ahhg (hsü) 5/20
    167-mhfm 16/16 030-iaff 19/1 106-gdkn 57/1 012-zafk 12/26
    031-bgdf 120/1 Gest Nos. 608 and 1539.

Author - Wang Ch'ung 王充 .

Edition - no notation; no date.   Blocks; "mao-t'ai" paper.

Index - a table of contents for 30 chüan; arranged according to
    subjects.

Bound in 1 t'ao 8 ts'ê.

Remarks - an ordinary edition; the item is complete and in good
    condition.

Accession No. 540   Index No. - 064-mqd   009-dzmq

Title
" Chi jang chi "
擊   壞   集
" I-ch'uan chi jang chi "
伊 川 擊 壞 集

Classification - D-38 別集一詩

Subject - an individual collection of poetry.

References - 160-1j 163-ggcz 13/4 031-bgld 15/38 037-ahhg 6/35;

10/16 167-mhfm 20/14 030-iaff 27/5 106-gdkn 75/12 012-zafk
15/14 031-bgdf 153/28 Gest No. 1263.

Author - Shao Yung 邵 雍 ·

Edition - apparently a Ming edition; (preface) dated Chih-P'ing 治平
"ping-wu" 3/1066.   Blocks; bamboo paper.

Index - a list of poems arranged in 20 chüan.

Bound in 1 t'ao 6 ts'ê; doubly interleaved.

Remarks - the item is complete and in very good condition.

———

Accession No. 541   **Index No.** - 030-gdhe 178-hekp

Title   " T'ang-Sung Han Liu Ou Su wên hsüan "
唐　宋　韓　柳　歐　蘇　文　選
" Han Liu Ou Su liu ta chia ku wên hsüan sui p'ing lin "
韓　柳　歐　蘇　六　大　家　古　文　選　粹　評　林

Classification - D-73 總集-文

Subject - a general collection of prose written by 6 famous scholars
    of the T'ang and Sung dynasties; with commentaries and marginal
    notes.

References - none.

Author - （選）Li Chiu-ê 李　九　我；（評）Yeh T'ai-shan 葉　台　山．

Edition - published by Li Ch'ao 李　潮；(preface) dated Wan-Li
    "ping-wu" 34/1606.   Blocks; bamboo paper.

Index - a list of prose in 8 chüan.

Bound in 2 t'ao 12 ts'ê (6-6); doubly interleaved.

Remarks - a fair edition; complete; but with a few defects.

———·———

Accession No. 542   Index No. - 067-zlci

Title   " W**ē**n hsüan Li Shan chu "
            文 選 李 善 注

Classification - D-63 總集—詩文

Subject - a general literary collection,- prose and poetry; with
     commentary.

References - Wylie's Notes page 238 160-1j   163-ggcz 16/1   031-bgld
     19/1   167-mhfm 23/1   030-iaff 38/1   106-gdkn 112/1   (#)

Author - (編) The Prince Chao Ming 昭 明 太 子 ; (注) Li Shan
     李 善 .

Edition - the "Chin-ling-shu-chü" 金 陵 書 局 ; dated T'ung-Chih
     8/1869.   Blocks; "f**ē**n" paper.

Index - separate lists of contents at the beginning of each of 60
     chüan.

Bound in 2 t'ao 10 ts'**ê** (5-5).

Remarks - a good edition; the item is complete and in very good
     condition.

     (#)   012-zafk 19/1   031-bgdf 186/1   Gest Nos. 262, 302, 572,
     and 1074.

The University of Toronto Chinese Library

Accession No. 543   Index No. - 112-fdle   128-eccg

Title   " Chu p'i tseng chu Liao chai chih i "
               碌 批 增 註 聊 齋 志 異

Classification - C-368 小說家
Subject - a collection of strange tales,- fairly-stories etc;
    with commentary.

References - 012-zafk 14/15   Gest No. 1516.

Author - P'u Sung-ling 蒲 松 齡.

Edition - the "Ch'ing-yün-lou" 青 雲 樓 ; dated T'ung-Chih
    "chi-ssŭ" 8/1869.   Blocks; "fēn" paper.

Index - a list of the stories in 16 chüan.

Bound in 2 t'ao 16 ts'ê (8-8).

Remarks - a very good edition; the item is complete and in good
    condition.

Accession No. 544   Index No. - 060-fecc

Title   " Hou Liao chai chih i t'u shuo "
            後 聊 齋 志 異 圖 説

Classification - C-368 小 説 家
Subject - a collection of short tales; with illustrations.

References - none.

Author - Wang T'ao 王 韜 .

Edition - the "Hung-wên-shu-chü" 鴻 文 書 局 ; dated Kuang-Hsü
    "hsin-mao" 17/1891.   Lithographed on "fên" paper.

Index - none; 12 chüan.

Bound in 1 t'ao 6 ts'ê; singly interleaved.

Remarks - a good modern edition; the item is complete and in good
    condition.

———— • ————

Accession No. 545   Index No. - 115-jzji

Title   " Ku yü lei pien "
                         穀 玉 類 編

Classification - C-348 類書

Subject - a general encyclopaedia under 34 classifications; the
    explanations being taken from various standard works.

References - none.

Author - (輯) Wang Chao-shu 汪 兆 舒.

Edition - the "Tzŭ-li-t'ang" 資 履 堂 ; (preface) dated Ch'ien-Lung
    "mou-yin" 23/1758.   Blocks; "mao-pien" paper.

Index - a general classified table of contents for 50 chüan.

Bound in 2 t'ao 10 ts'ê (5-5).

Remarks - an ordinary good edition; the item is complete and in
    good condition.

The University of Toronto Chinese Library

Accession No. 546   Index No. - 085-ccih

Title

" Ch'ih pei ou t'an "
池 北 偶 談

Classification - C-308 雜家 - 雜文

Subject - (Wylie) "----- is a large collection of memoranda arranged
under four divisions, treating respectively of: Court Notabilia,
Distinguished Characters, Literary Compositions, and Marvels."

References - Wylie's Notes page 169   160-1j   163-ggcz 10/9
031-bgld 13/26   012-zafk 12/34   031-bgdf 122/32.

Author - (撰) Wang Shih-chêng 王 士 禎 .

Edition - the "Wên-sui-t'ang" 文 粹 堂 ; (preface) dated K'ang-Hsi
"hsin-wei" 30/1691.   Blocks; "mao-pien" paper.

Index - separate lists of contents at the beginning of each of 26
chüan.

Bound in 1 t'ao 8 ts's.

Remarks - a good edition; the items is complete and in good condition.
Chüan 21 with a few repaired corners.

Accession No. 547   Index No. - 195-fhgd

Title   " Chi-ch'i t'ing chi "
                     結 埼 亭 集

Classification - D-33 別集 - 詩文
Subject - an individual literary collection,-prose and poetry.

References - 160-1j   012-zafk 17/26.

Author - (撰) Ch'üan Tsu-wang 全 祖 望; (校) Shih Mĕng-chiao
        史 夢 蛟 .

Edition - the "Chieh-shu-shan-fang" 借 樹 山 房; no date.
        Blocks; bamboo paper.

Index - a detailed table of contents for 38 chüan; separate list of
        contents for 10 chüan for the 經 史 問 答.

Bound in 1 t'ao 10 ts'ê.

Remarks - a good edition; complete and without defects.   012-zafk
        gives two supplements, but this item only contains one as
        mentioned in the "Index".

Accession No.   548 (a)   Index No. - 075-cfkf

Title   " Tu shih ching ch'üan "
                  杜   詩   鏡   銓

Classification - D-38 別集 - 詩

Subject - a selection of Tu Fu's 杜 甫 poems; with annotations.

References - 012-zafk 15/6   Gest No. 1111.

Author - (編輯) Yang Lun 楊 倫 ﹒

Edition - the "Wang-san-i-chai" 望 三 益 齋 ; dated T'ung-Chih
    11/1872.   Blocks; "mao-pien" paper.

Index - a table of contents for 20 chüan.

Bound in 2 t'ao 11 ts'8; with (b).

Remarks - an ordinary edition; complete and without defects.

———•—•———

Accession No.   548 (b)   Index No. - 149-ofhc   075-czhz

Title   " Tu-shu-t'ang Tu Kung-pu wên chi chu chieh "
          讀 書 堂 杜 工 部 文 集 註 解

Classification - D-43 別集一文

Subject - a collection of selections from the prose writings of
    Tu Fu 杜甫 ; with commentary and explanation.

References - Gest No. 1111.

Author - (評註) Chang Chin 張溍 .

Edition - uniform with (a).

Index - a table of contents for 2 chüan.

Bound in 1 ts'ê in 2d t'ao with (a).

Remarks - as under (a).

———•———

Accession No. 549   Index No. - 102-jgpf

Title   " <u>Chi</u> <u>fu</u> <u>ts'ung</u> <u>shu</u> "
                          畿　輔　叢　書

Classification - C-338 雜家 -叢書
Subject - a collection of reprints of 181 works on all classes of
    Chinese literature, with 9 additional works.

References - 029-pffz 515   058-jffz 庚/1   Gest No. 2.

Author - compiled by <u>Wang Hao</u> 王　灝 .

Edition - the "<u>Chien-tê-t'ang</u>" 謙　德　堂 ; dated Kuang-Hsü 5/1879.
    Blocks; "fên" paper.

Index - a classified list of the works in a separate ts'ê.

Bound in 54 t'ao 425 ts'ê.

Remarks - a fairly good modern edition; the item is complete and
    without defects.

Accession No. 550   Index No. - 037-zhif

Title   " Ta-Ch'ing hui tien "
                  大 清 會 典

Classification - B-282 政書一通制

Subject - (Gest No. 3515) " a comprehensive description of the
Chinese governmental system during the (first part of)
Ch'ing or Manchu Dynasty."

References - Wylie's Notes page 70   163-ggoz 6/3   031-bgld 8/7
012-zafk 9/5   031-bgdf 81/21   Gest Nos. 106 and 3515.

Author - an official compilation, by a commission headed by the
Imperial Princes Yün-lu 允 禄 and Yün-li 允 禮 .

Edition - a "palace" edition; (preface) dated Yung-Chêng 10/1732.
Blocks; "k'ai-hua" paper.

Index - a general table of contents for 250 chüan.

Bound in 14 t'ao 100 ts'ê.

Remarks - this is a very fine edition; and the item is complete.
A few places have been stained and page 38 in chüan 122 has been
badly ruined.

Accession No. 551   Index No. - 031-bhpc

Title   " <u>Ssŭ pu ts'ung k'an</u> "
                         四   部   叢   刊

Classification - C-338 雜家 - 叢書

Subject - a collection of reprints of 323 works in all the four
        classes of Chinese literature.

References - Gest Library.

Author - numerous; compiled by the Commerial Press of Shanghai.

Edition - the "<u>Han-fên-lou</u>" 涵 芳 樓 ; dated "jên-hsü" 1922.
        Process; "mao-pien" paper.

Index - a list of the 323 works, arranged under the four divisions
       of Chinese literature, in a separate ts'ê.

Bound in 216 t'ao 2101 ts'ê.

Remarks - a good modern edition; the item is new.

The University of Toronto Chinese Library

Accession No. 552   Index No. - 037-abho

Title   " T'ai p'ing yü lan "
太 平 御 覽

Classification - C-348 類書

Subject - a general encyclopaedia under 55 main sections; the items
of which are explained by a group of quotations taken from some
1690 works, only a small part of which are now extant.

References - Wylie's Notes page 183   160-1j   163-ggcz 10/12
031-bgld 14/50   030-iaff 20/3   106-gdkn 59/9   012-zafk 3/20
031-bgdf 135/20   Gest No. 110.

Author - compiled on order of Emperor T'ai-Tsung (Sung) by Li Fang
李 昉.

Edition - published by "Pao-shih" 鮑 氏 ; dated Chia-Ch'ing 17/1812.
Blocks; "fên" paper.

Index - a general table of the 55 sections; a detailed table of
contents (in 15 sections) for 1000 chüan.

Bound in 12 t'ao 120 ts'ê (10 each).

Remarks - one of the most famous works in the field of Chinese
literature.   The item is complete and practically without
defects.   Chüan 633-660 are replacements from another copy
printed from the same set of blocks.

Accession No. 553   Index No. - 076-hezb 012-zbik

Title   " Ch'in-ting Pa hsün wan shou shêng tien "
         欽 定 八 旬 萬 壽 盛 典
         " Pa hsün wan shou shêng tien "
         八 旬 萬 壽 盛 典

Classification - B-287 政書一典禮

Subject - a record of matters in connection with the celebration of
         Ch'ien-Lung's 80th birthday, with numerous illustrations.

References - 163-ggcz 6/4   012-zafk 9/7   031-bgdf 82/28.

Author - compiled by an Imperial Commission headed by A Kuei 阿桂.

Edition - a manuscript written on "fên" paper; (chin-piao) dated
         Ch'ien-Lung 57/1792.

Index - a table of contents for 120 chüan.

Bound in 6 t'ao 61 ts'ê (10-10-10-10-10-11).

Remarks - a very fine manuscript; the item is complete and in very
         good condition.

The University of Toronto Chinese Library

Accession No. 554   Index No. - 060-hned   030-eddc

Title   " Yü-tsuan Chou-i chê chung "
　　　　　　　御　纂　周　易　折　中

Classification - A-11 易

Subject - (Gest No. 2096) "a dissertation on the "Book of Changes",
　　based on the writings of 218 scholars from the Han to the Ming
　　period, both included."

References - 163-ggcz 1/7 031-bgld 1/24 012-zafk 1/7 031-bgdf 6/3
　　Gest No. 2096.

Author - an editorial commission headed by Li Kuang-ti 李 光 地．

Edition - a palace edition; (preface) dated K'ang-Hsi 54/1715.
　　Blocks; "k'ai-hua" paper.

Index - a general table of contents for 卷首 and 22 chüan.

Bound in 1 t'ao 10 ts'ê.

Remarks - a very fine edition indeed; the item is complete and in
　　perfect condition.

The University of Toronto Chinese Library

Accession No. 555-a   Index No. - 189-zlke   075-gzlk

Title   " Kao sêng chuan ch'u chi "
                 高　僧　傳　初　集
                 " Liang kao sêng chuan "
                 梁　高　僧　傳

Classification - C-513 釋家

Subject - a collection of biographies of famous priests covering
        the period from the Later Han to the first reign of the
        Liang Dynasty.

References - Wylie's Notes page 208 160-1j 163-ggcz 11/7
        012-zafk 14/19.

Author - (撰) Hui Chiao 慧 皎 .

Edition - no notation; (preface) dated Kuang-Hsü 10/1884.   Blocks;
        "mao-pien" paper.

Index - a table of contents for 15 chüan arranged under 10 divisions.

Bound in 1 t'ao 4 ts'ê.

Remarks - an ordinary edition; complete and without defects.

———•·•———

Accession No. 555-b   Index No. - 189-zlkz   120-ozlk

Title   " Kao sêng chuan êrh chi "
               高   僧   傳   二   集
               " Hsü kao sêng chüan "
               續   高   僧   傳

Classification - C-513 釋家

Subject - the second series of (a); covering the period from the
          Liang to the beginning of the T'ang Dynasty.

References - Wylie's Notes page 208   160-1j   012-zafk 14/19.

Author - (撰) Tao Hsüan 道 宣 ·

Edition - uniform with (a).

Index - separate lists at the beginning of each of 40 chüan.

Bound in 2 t'ao 10 ts'ê (5-5).

Remarks - as under (a).

The University of Toronto Chinese Library

Accession No. 555-c   Index No. - 189-zlkb   040-dzlk

Title   " <u>Kao sêng chuan san chi</u> "
                高　僧　傳　三　集
                " <u>Sung kao sêng chuan</u> "
                宋　高　僧　傳

<u>Classification</u> - C-513 釋家

<u>Subject</u> - the third series of (a); covering the period from the
        <u>T'ang</u> to the beginning of the <u>Sung Dynasty</u>.

<u>References</u> - Wylie's Notes page 209   160-1j   163-ggcz 11/8
        031-bgld 14/42   012-zafk 14/19   031-bgdf 145/7.

<u>Author</u> - (撰) <u>Tsan Ning</u> 贊寧 and others under Imperial order.

<u>Edition</u> - uniform with (a).

<u>Index</u> - a table of contents for 30 chüan.

<u>Bound in</u> 1 t'ao 8 ts'ê.

<u>Remarks</u> - as under (a).

Accession No. 556   Index No. - 060-hhkg   066-kghp

Title   " Yü-chih Shu li ching yün "
                御 製 數 理 精 蘊

Classification - C-138 天文算法一算書

Subject - (Gest No. 1812) "a comprehensive mathematical treatise;

   including numeration, arithmetic, theory of numbers, plane

   and solid geometry, algebra, logarithms, trigonometry, etc.;

   tables of logarithms, trigonometrical functions, factors,

   prime numbers, etc."

References - Wylie's Notes page 120   160-1j   163-ggcz 8/11

   031-bgld 11/10 012-zafk 11/5 031-bgdf 107/24 Gest No. 1812.

Author - officially compiled.

Edition - the "Chiang-ning-fan-shu" 江 甯 藩 署 ; dated Kuang-Hsü

   8/1882.   Blocks; "fên" paper.

Index - (上 編) a general table of contents for 5 chüan; detailed

   tables at the beginning of each chüan; (下 編) same for 40

   chüan; (表) in 8 chüan.

Bound in 6 t'ao 40 ts'ê (7-7-8-8-5-5).

Remarks - a fairly good edition; the item is complete and in very

   good condition.

Accession No. 557   Index No. - 075-bzgj

Title   " <u>Chu</u> <u>tzŭ</u> <u>yŭ</u> <u>lei</u> "
朱 子 語 類

<u>Classification</u> - C-13 儒家

<u>Subject</u> - a comprehensive classified collection of lectures and
sayings of <u>Chu Hsi</u> 朱 熹 .

<u>References</u> - Wylie's Notes page 85   160-1j   163-ggcz 7/4
031-bgld 9/12   030-iaff 15/12   167-mhfm 13/10   (#)

<u>Author</u> - compiled by <u>Li Ching-tê</u> 黎 靖 德 .

<u>Edition</u> - the "<u>Ying-yüan-shu-yüan</u>" 應 元 書 院 ; dated T'ung-Chih
"jên-shên" 11/1872.   Blocks; "mao-pien" paper.

<u>Index</u> - a table of contents for 140 chüan.

<u>Bound in</u> 4 t'ao 40 ts'ê (10 each).

<u>Remarks</u> - an ordinary modern edition; the item is complete and as
new.

(#) 012-zafk 10/3   031-bgdf 92/26   Gest No. 804.

26

Accession No. 558   Index No. - 154-fegn

Title   " Tzŭ chih t'ung chien "
　　　　　　　資　治　通　鑑

Classification - B-22 編年

Subject - annals of Chinese history covering a period from the
commencement of the fourth century B. C. down to the end of
the Five Dynasties.

References - Wylie's Notes page 25   160-1j   163-ggcz 4/6   031-bgld
5/18   030-iaff 7/2   037-ahhg (hsü) 14/7   106-gdkn 20/6   (#)

Author - compiled on Imperial order by Ssŭ-ma Kuang 司　馬　光;
(音註) Hu San-hsing 胡　三　省.

Edition - no notation; (preface) dated Chia-Ch'ing 21/1816.
Blocks; "fên" paper.

Index - a list of dynasties at the end of the work, with the number
of chüan for each; 294 chüan in all.

Bound in 10 t'ao 100 ts'ê (10 each).

Remarks - a good edition; the item is complete and in generally good
condition.   The following is a supplement to this work:-
" Tzŭ chih t'ung chien shih wên pien wu "
　資　治　通　鑑　釋　文　辯　誤　 (154-fegn)
by Hu San-hsing 胡三省   12 chüan

27

28

Accession No. 559   Index No. - 030-edkg   030-edzd

Title   " Chou-i chuan i ta ch'üan "
               周　易　傳　義　大　全

               " Chou-i ta ch'üan "
               周　易　大　全

Classification - A-11 易

Subject - (Gest No. 1465) "a symposium of commentaries and notes on

　　the "Book of Changes."

References - 163-ggcz 1/6   031-bgld 1/21   037-ahhg (hsü) 12/2

　　030-iaff 1/16   012-zafk 1/5   031-bgdf 5/1   Gest Nos. 553 and

　　1465.

Author - prepared by a commission headed by Hu Kuang 胡 廣 .

Edition - of the Ming period; but no date.   Blocks; "mien" paper.

Index - a table of contents for 24 chüan.

Bound in 2 t'ao 12 ts'ê.

Remarks - a very fine edition; the item is complete and in very good

　　condition with the exception of some stains.

Accession No. 560   Index No. - 196-fe

Title   " Hung pao "

鴻　苞

Classification – C-308 雜家 – 雜文

Subject – a collection of dissertations on miscellaneous subjects.

References – 012-zafk 12/17   031-bgdf 125/12   Gest No. 693.

Author – (著) T'u Lung 屠　隆 .

Edition – a Ming edition; (preface) dated "kêng-hsü" 38/1610.

Blocks; bamboo paper.

Index – a detailed table of contents for 48 chüan.

Bound in 4 t'ao 24 ts'ê (6 each).

Remarks – a fairly good edition; the item is complete and without

defects.

Accession No. 561   Index No. - 085-gzkh   085-gzch

Title   " <u>Hai-shan-hsien-kuan ts'ung shu</u> "
             海 山 儔 (仙) 館 叢 書

<u>Classification</u> - C-338 雜家 - 叢書

<u>Subject</u> - a collection of reprints of 56 miscellaneous works.

<u>References</u> - 031-bgld 13/34   012-zafk 13/16   029-pffz 325

   Gest Nos. 108 and 1649.

<u>Author</u> - (編) <u>P'an Shih-ch'êng</u> 潘 仕 成 .

<u>Edition</u> - the "<u>Hai-shan-hsien-kuan</u>" 海 山 仙 館 ; dated Tao-Kuang
   "chi-yu" 29/1849.   Blocks; "fên" paper.

<u>Index</u> - a list of the 56 works.

<u>Bound in</u> 12 t'ao 120 ts'ê (10 each).

<u>Remarks</u> - the item is complete and in good condition.

Accession No. 562   Index No. - 076-hedg   011-dgf

Title   " Ch'in-ting Ch'üan T'ang shih "
                欽 定 全 唐 詩

Classification - D-68 總集－詩
Subject - an anthology of poems of the T'ang Dynasty.

References - Wylie's Notes page 242 160-lj 163-ggcz 16/9 031-bgld
     19/32 012-zafk 19/14 031-bgdf 190/2 Gest Nos. 537, 2222, and
     2226.
Author - an Imperial commission headed by Ts'ao Yin 曹 寅 .

Edition - the "T'ung-wên-shu-chü" 同 文 書 局 ; dated Kuang-Hsü
     13/1887.   Lithographed on "fên" paper.

Index - a detailed table of contents (authors); separate lists for
     each of 32 chüan.

Bound in 4 t'ao 32 ts'ê (8 each).

Remarks - a very good edition; the item is complete and in good
     condition.

Accession No. 563   Index No. - 076-hebg   031-bgdf

Title   " Ch'in-ting Ssŭ-k'u ch'üan shu tsung mu "
           欽 定 四 庫 全 書 總 目

Classification - B-342 目錄 一 經籍

Subject - a descriptive catalogue of the Imperial Library of the
         Ch'ing Dynasty.

References - Wylie's Notes page 75   160-1j   163-ggcz 6/6
           012-zafk 9/15   Gest Nos. 316, 449 and 821.

Author - compiled on order of Emperor Ch'ien-Lung by a commission
        headed by Chi Yün 紀 昀 .

Edition - the "Kuang-tung-shu-chü" 廣 東 書 局 ; dated T'ung-Chih
         7/1868.   Blocks; "fên" paper.

Index - a general table of contents (classifications) for 200 chüan.

Bound in 12 t'ao 120 ts'ê (10 each).

Remarks - a good edition; complete and in good condition.

Accession No. 564   Index No. - 030-gjf

Title   " T'ang lei han "
                      唐 類 函

Classification - C-348 類書
Subject - an encyclopaedia under 43 main divisions; the explanations
    being selected from various works.

References - Wylie's Notes page 188   160-1j   163-ggcz 10/16
    012-zafk 13/25   031-bgdf 138/19   Gest No. 679.

Author - (彙 纂) Yü An-ch'i 俞 安 期 .

Edition - a Ming edition; (preface) dated Wan-Li "kuei-mao" 31/1603.
    Blocks; bamboo paper.

Index - a classified table of contents for 200 chüan.

Bound in 8 t'ao 40 ts'ê (5 each).

Remarks - this is a fairly good edition; and the item is complete
    and in very good condition.

Accession No. 565   Index No. - 030-bbng

Title   " Ku chin ju hsiao hsüan chang "
               古　今　濡　削　選　章

Classification - D-73 總集一文
Subject - (Gest No. 2407) "a general collection of letters written in
    the "four-six" style; the period covered being from the "Six
    Dynasties" (A.D. 222) to the Ming Dynasty (A.D. 1644)."

References - 012-zafk 19/14   031-bgdf 193/41   Gest No. 2407.

Author - (選) Li Kuo-hsiang 李 國 祥 ·

Edition - no particular notation; (preface) dated Wan-Li "hsin-ch'ou"
    29/1601.   Blocks; bamboo paper.

Index - a list of the classifications; a table of additions and
    supplements to the various chüan; a general table of contents
    for 40 chüan.
Bound in 6 t'ao 30 ts'ê (5 each).

Remarks - a fairly good edition; the item is in generally good condition
    but with a good many torn page-edges.   All the paper has been
    backed and the blank leaves found here and there indicate the
    pages missing.

Accession No. 566   Index No. - 024-zzdf

Title   " Shih tzǔ ch'üan shu "
                        十　子　全　書

Classification - C-338 雜家 一叢書
Subject - a collection of reprints of 10 philosophical works.

References - 012-zafk 13/15   029-pffz 11   058-jffz 3/10.

Author - (編) Huang P'ei-lieh 黃 丕 烈 according to 012-zafk.

Edition - the "Chü-wên-t'ang" 聚 文 堂 ; dated Chia-Ch'ing "chia-tzǔ"
     9/1804.   Blocks; "fên" paper.

Index - a list of the 10 works.

Bound in 4 t'ao 24 ts'ê (6 each).

Remarks - a good edition; the item is complete and in good condition.

The University of Toronto Chinese Library

Accession No. 567   Index No. - 134-1bcb

Title   " Chiu Wu-tai shih "
                         舊 五 代 史

Classification - B-12 正史

Subject - the official Chinese history of the Five Dynasties (old).

References - Wylie's Notes page 16 and 22   160-1j   163-ggcz 4/5

    031-bgld 5/12   012-zafk 4/6   031-bgdf 46/9   Gest No. 952.

Author - (撰) Hsüeh Chü-chêng 薛居正 and others.

Edition - the "Liu's Chia-yeh-t'ang" 劉氏嘉業堂   ; dated "hsin-yu"

    1921.   Blocks; "fên" paper.

Index - a general table of contents for 150 chüan.

Bound in 4 t'ao 32 ts'ê (8 each).

Remarks - a very good modern edition; the item is new.

The University of Toronto Chinese Library

Accession No. 568   Index No. - 075-dedd

Title   " Tung-p'o ch'üan chi "
                 東 坡 全 集

Classification - D-33 別集一詩文

Subject - an individual collection of prose; with some poetical

writings.

References - Wylie's Notes page 229   160-lj   163-ggcz 13/6   031-bgld

15/41 106-gdkn 76/12 167-mhfm 20/20 012-zafk 15/15
031-bgdf 154/1   Gest No. 652.

Author - (撰) Su Shih 蘇 軾 .

Edition - apparently a Ming edition; dated? (see under Remarks).

Blocks; bamboo paper.

Index - a detailed classified table of contents for 75 chüan.

Bound in 4 t'ao 40 ts'ê (10 each).

Remarks - as the first ts'ê containing the prefaces etc is a

replacement from a Ch'ing edition copy, there is no indication

as to the exact date of the rest of the work. One of the

catalogues referred to states that the Ming edition contains

75 chüan and later ones 115.   The item is complete and in

fairly good condition.

Accession No. 569   Index No. - 075-ifih

Title   " Ying shu yü lu "
　　　　　　　　　　　　楹　書　隅　錄

Classification - B-342 目 錄 一 經 籍
Subject - (Gest No. 2359) "a catalogue of the rare books and manuscripts
    in the library of the Yang family,- the "Hai-yüan-ko" 海 源 閣
    library."

References - 160-1j 012-zafk 9/19   Gest Nos. 984 and 2359.

Author - compiled by Yang Shao-ho 楊 紹 和.

Edition - the "Hai-yüan-ko" 海 源 閣; (postscriptum) dated "jên-tzǔ"
    1912.   Blocks; "mao-pien" paper.

Index - a general table of contents for 5 chüan arranged according to
    the 4 divisions of Chinese literature, with separate lists for
    each chüan; 續 錄 4 chüan.
Bound in 2 t'ao 12 ts'ê (6 each).

Remarks - an ordinary good edition; the item is complete and as if
    new.

————•————

Accession No. 570   Index No. - 131-kzd   096-zkzd

Title   " <u>Lin-ch'uan   chi</u> "
                          臨   川   集

                " <u>Wang   Lin-ch'uan   ch'üan   chi</u> "
                  王   臨   川   全   集

Classification - D-33 別集 - 詩文
Subject - an individual collection of prose and poetry.

References - 160-1j 163-ggcz 13/5 031-bgld 15/41 030-iaff 27/13
    037-ahhg 10/22 106-gdkn 76/10 167-mhfm 20/18 012-zafk 15/15
    031-bgdf 153/42.
Author - (撰) <u>Wang An-shih</u> 王 安 石 .

Edition - the "<u>T'ing-hsiang-kuan</u>" 聽 香 館 ; dated Kuang-Hsü 9/1883.
    Blocks; "fên" paper.

Index - a detailed table of contents (in 2 parts) for 100 chüan.

Bound in 2 t'ao 16 ts'ê (8 each).

Remarks - a good modern edition; the item is complete and in very
    good condition.

Accession No.   571-a   Index No. - 186-z1of

Title   " Hsiang-shu-chai shih chi "
                    香 樹 齋 詩 集

Classification - D-38 別集一詩

Subject - an individual collection of poetry.

References - 012-zafk 17/34   Gest No. 1565.

Author - (撰) Ch'ien Ch'ên-ch'ün 錢 陳 羣 .

Edition - no notation;(preface) dated Ch'ien-Lung 16/1751.
    Blocks; "fên" paper.

Index - a general table of contents for 18 chüan; 續 集 36 chüan.

Bound in 2 t'ao 15 ts'ê (8-7).

Remarks - a fairly good edition; the item is without defects and
    complete.

Accession No.   571-b   Index No. - 186-zlcz

Title   " Hsiang-shu-chai   wên   chi "

香 樹 齋 文 集

Classification - D-43 別集一文

Subject - an individual collection of prose.

References - 012-zafk 17/34.

Author - (撰) Ch'ien Ch'ên-ch'ün 錢 陳 羣．

Edition - uniform with (a); but dated Ch'ien-Lung "chia-shên"
29/1764.

Index - a table of contents for 28 chüan; 續 鈔 5 chüan.

Bound in 1 t'ao 9 ts'ê.

Remarks - as under (a).

———•———

Accession No. 572   Index No. - 140-ozef

Title   " Ou hsiang ling shih "
               藕　香　零　拾

Classification - C-338 雜家－叢書
Subject - a collection of reprints of 39 miscellaneous works.

References - 029-pffz 565.

Author - compiled by Miao Ch'üan-sun 繆荃孫.

Edition - published by the author; dated Hsüan-T'ung 2/1910.
    Blocks; "mao-pien" paper.

Index - a list of the 39 works.

Bound in 4 t'ao 32 ts'ê (8 each).

Remarks - an ordinary but clear-cut edition; the item is complete
    and without defects.

———•◦•———

Accession No. 573   Index No. - 064-elcz

Title   " Pao-jun-hsien wên chi "
                抱 潤 軒 文 集

Classification - D-43 別集 一文
Subject - an individual collection of prose.

References - none.

Author - Ma Ch'i-ch'ang 馬 其 昶.

Edition - no particular notation; (title-page) dated "kuei-hai" 1923.
     Blocks; "fên" paper.

Index - a detailed table of contents for 22 chüan.

Bound in 1 t'ao 4 ts'ê.

Remarks - a very good modern edition; the item is new.

The University of Toronto Chinese Library

Accession No. 574   Index No. - 039-cgkz   039-cfkz

Title   " Ts'un-yen-lou wên chi "
                     存硯 (研) 樓 文 集

Classification - D-43 別集 一文
Subject - an individual collection of prose.

References - 163-ggcz 15/12   031-bgld 18/41   012-zafk 17/20
      031-bgdf 173/48.

Author - (著) Ch'u Ta-wên 儲 大 文 .

Edition - the "Ching-yüan-t'ang" 靜 遠 堂 ; dated Kuang-Hsü 1/1875.
      Blocks; "fên" paper.

Index - a detailed table of contents for 16 chüan.

Bound in 1 t'ao 8 ts'ê.

Remarks - an ordinary edition; the item is complete and in good
      condition.

———•———

Accession No. 575   Index No. - 046-zdgc

Title   " Shan-tung t'ung chih "
                       山　東　通　志

Classification - B-192. 地理一省志
Subject - a gazeteer of the province of Shantung.

References - 163-ggcz 5/13   031-bgld 7/15   012-zafk 6/7
    031-bgdf 68/60.

Author - compiled by Yo Chün 岳濬 and others.

Edition - no particular notation; (preface) dated Ch'ien-Lung 1/1736.
    Blocks; bamboo paper.

Index - a general table of contents for 首卷 and 36 chüan.

Bound in 4 t'ao 42 ts'è (10-12-10-10).

Remarks - a standard geographical work. The edition is not very
    good; and the item appears to be complete but stained in many
    places besides a few worm-holes. The impression shows evidences
    of having been printed from old and somewhat worn-out blocks.

Accession No. 576   Index No. - 096-zzfb   067-zfbd   173-gmdz
                                                173-gmd

Title   " Wang Wên-k'o kung chi "
             王 文 恪 公 集
          " Chên-tsê hsien-shêng chi "
             震 澤 先 生 集

Classification - D-33 別集 — 詩文

Subject - an individual collection of prose and poetry.

References - 160-1j   163-ggcz 15/6   031-bgld 18/19   030-iaff 36/21

     012-zafk 16/19   031-bgdf 171/9   Gest No. 2244.

Author - (著) Wang Ao 王 鏊 .

Edition - the "San-huai-t'ang" 三 槐 堂; no date, but of the Ch'ing

     period.   Blocks; "mao-pien" paper.

Index - a table of contents for 36 chüan arranged according to

     character of composition.

Bound in 2 t'ao 12 ts'ê (6-6).

Remarks - a fairly good edition; the item is complete and in very

     good condition.

Accession No. 577   Index No. - 162-lzd   010-blzd

Title   " I-shan chi "
                        遺 山 集
                    " Yüan I-shan chi "
                    元 遺 山 集

Classification - D-33 別集 - 詩文
Subject - an individual collection of prose and poetry.

References - 160-1j 163-ggcz 14/1   031-bgld 17/1   030-iaff 33/2

    012-zafk 15/35   031-bgdf 166/7   Gest No. 1553.

Author - (撰) Yüan Hao-wên 元 好 問 .

Edition - the "Yang-ch'üan-shan-chuang" 陽 泉 山 莊; (title-page)

    dated Kuang-Hsü 8/1882.   Blocks; "fên" paper.

Index - a general table of contents for 40 chüan; 附 錄 1 chüan;

    附 錄 增 1 chüan; 補 載 1 chüan.

Bound in 2 t'ao 16 ts'ê.

Remarks - an ordinary modern edition; the item is complete and as new.

    This item also includes the following 5 separate works as

    supplements:-

        (#)

48

(#) 1. " Yüan I-shan hsien-shêng nien p'u "
元 遺 山 先 生 年 譜　　(010-blzd; 162-lzdz)

by Shih Kuo-ch'i 施 國 祁　　1 chüan

2. " Yüan I-shan hsien-shêng nien p'u "
元 遺 山 先 生 年 譜　　(010-blzd; 162-lzdz)

by Wêng Fang-kang 翁 方 綱　　1 chüan

3. " Yüan I-shan hsien-shêng nien p'u "
元 遺 山 先 生 年 譜　　(010-blzd; 162-lzdz)

by Ling T'ing-k'an 凌 廷 堪　　2 chüan

4. " I-shan hsien-shêng hsin yüah fu "
遺 山 先 生 新 樂 府　　(162-lzdz; 162-lzik)

by Yüan Hao-wên 元 好 問　　4 chüan

5. " Hsü I chien chih "
續 夷 堅 志　　(120-oohc)

by Yüan Hao-wên 元 好 問　　4 chüan

The University of Toronto Chinese Library

————•————

Accession No. 578   Index No. - 131-kzd   096-zkzz

Title   " Lin-ch'uan chi "
                          臨 川 集
                  " Wang Lin-ch'uan wĕn chi "
                  王 臨 川 文 集

Classification - D-33 別集 一 詩文

Subject - an individual collection of prose and poetry.

References - 160-lj   163-ggcz 13/5   031-bgld 15/41   030-iaff 27/13

        037-ahhg 10/22   106-gdkn 76/10   167-mhfm 20/18   (#)

Author - (撰) Wang An-shih 王 安 石 .

Edition - published by "Yin-shih" 殷 氏 ; (preface) dated Kuang-Hsü

        8/1882.   Blocks; "mao-pien" paper.

Index - a detailed table of contents for 63 chüan arranged according

        to class of composition.

Bound in 2 t'ao 10 ts'ĕ (5-5).

Remarks - the original edition of this item consists of 100 chüan, and

        this edition 63 chüan.   The material embraced is from chüan 38-

        100 of the original work and the chüan are re-numbered 1-63.   The

        item has no defects other than a large number of repaired corners.

        (#) 012-zafk 15/15 031-bgdf 153/42 Toronto No.570.

Accession No. 579   Index No. - 030-emag

Title   " Chou li chêng i "
周 禮 正 義

Classification - A-46 周 禮

Subject - a commentary and explanation of the "Chou Ritual".

References - none to this particular work.

Author - by Sun I-jang 孫 詒 讓.

Edition - no notation; dated Kuang-Hsü "i-ssŭ" 31/1905.   Type;
"fên" paper.

Index - none; 86 chüan.

Bound in 2 t'ao 20 ts'ê (10-10).

Remarks - an ordinary edition; complete and without defects.

Accession No. 580   Index No. - 072-edbk

Title   " Ch'un ch'iu Tso chuan Tu chu "
               春 秋 左 傳 杜 注

Classification - A-101 春 秋

Subject - a commentary on the "Tso chuan" commentary on the "Spring
    and Autumn Annals."

References - none to this particular work.

Author - Yao P'ei-ch'ien 姚 培 謙.

Edition - the "Chiang-nan-shu-chü" 江 南 書 局; dated Kuang-Hsü
    9/1883.   Blocks; "mao-pien" paper.

Index - a table of contents for 卷 首 and 30 chüan.

Bound in 2 t'ao 10 ts'ê (5-5).

Remarks - a very ordinary edition; the item has no defects and is
    complete.

Accession No. 581   Index No. - 076-heah   037-ahhg

Title   " Ch'in-ting T'ien-lu-lin-lang shu mu "
         欽 定 天 禄 琳 琅 書 目

Classification - B-342 目 録 一 經 籍

Subject - the Imperial catalogue of the Sung, Yüan and Ming works

    stored in the T'ien-lu-lin-lang palace during the time of

    Emperor Ch'ien-Lung.

References - 160-1j 163-ggoz 6/6   031-bgld 8/19   012-zafk 9/15

    031-bgdf 85/16   Gest No. 674.

Author - compiled on Imperial order by Yü Min-chung 于 敏 中

    and others.

Edition - the "Wang-shih" of Ch'ang-sha 長 沙 王 氏 ; dated Kuang-Hsü

    "chia-shên" 10/1884.   Blocks; "fên" paper.

Index - none; 10 chüan; 後 編 20 chüan.

Bound in 1 t'ao 10 ts'ê.

Remarks - a very good modern edition; the item is complete and as if

    new.

Accession No. 582   Index No. - 085-khbh

Title   " Han Wei Liu-ch'ao nü tzǔ wên hsüan "
          漢 魏 六 朝 女 子 文 選

Classification - D-63 總集 - 詩文

Subject - a collection of prose and poetic compositions by noted
     women between the period from the Han 漢 dynasty to the period
     of Liu-ch'ao 六朝 ; with annotations.

References - none.

Author - by Chang Wei 張 維 .

Edition - published by "Chu-shih" 朱 是 (?); dated "hsin-hai" 1911.
     Blocks; "fên" paper.

Index - separate tables of contents at the beginning of each of two
     chüan.

Bound in 1 t'ao 2 ts'ê; doubly interleaved.

Remarks - a very good modern edition; the item is complete and in
     very good condition.

Accession No. 583   Index No. - 038-fhea   061-heao

Title   " <u>Yao</u> <u>Hsi-pao</u> <u>ch'ih</u> <u>tu</u> "

姚 惜 抱 尺 牘

Classification - D-43 別 集 一 文

Subject - an individual collection of letters.

References - 012-zafk 17/41.

Author - <u>Yao Nai</u> 姚 鼐 .

Edition - the "<u>Hsiao-wan-liu-t'ang</u>" 小 萬 柳 堂 ; dated Hsüan-T'ung
        1/1909.   Blocks; "mao-pien" paper.

Index - none; 8 chüan.

Bound in 1 t'ao 4 ts'ê; doubly interleaved.

Remarks - a fair edition; complete and in very good condition.   This
        item is only a part of the several works making up the "ch'üan
        chi ".

Accession No. 584   Index No. - 075-dlpf

Title   " Sung lin ts'ung shu "
松 鄰 叢 書

Classification - C-338 雜家 一 叢書

Subject - a collection of reprints of 20 works, consisting of catalogues,
short narratives etc.

References - 029-pffz 278   058-jffz (hsü)   閏/24   Gest No. 953.

Author - compiled by Wu Ch'ang-shou 吳昌綬.

Edition - the "Shuang-chao-lou" 雙照樓; dated "ting-ssŭ" 1917.
Blocks; "fên" paper.

Index - (甲編) a list of 14 works; (乙編) a list of 6 works.

Bound in 1 t'ao 12 ts'ê.

Remarks - a good edition; the item is new.

Accession No. 585   Index No. - 061-jehc

Title   " Shên-shih-chi-chai ts'ung shu "
               慎　始　基　齋　叢　書

Classification - C-338 雜家 一 叢書

Subject - a collection of reprints of 11 works chiefly on bibliogra-
         phical subjects.

References - 029-pffz 457   Gest No. 413.

Author - compiled by Lu Ching 盧　靖.

Edition - published by the author; dated "kuei-hai" 1923.   Blocks;
         "fên" paper.

Index - a list of the 11 works.

Bound in 1 t'ao 8 ts'ê.

Remarks - a good modern edition; the item is new.

Accession No. 586   Index No. - 147-rbhd

Title   " Kuan-ku t'ang so chu shu "
              觀 古 堂 所 著 書

Classification - C-338 雜家 - 叢書

Subject - (Gest No. 1016-b) "Collection of 16 reprints of works on
     all Four Classes of Literature,-----."

References - 029-pffz 585   058-jffz 閏/59 Gest No. 1016-b.

Author - compiled by Yeh Tê-hui 葉 德 輝.

Edition - published by the author; dated Kuang-Hsü "jên-yin" 28/1902.
     Blocks; "fên" paper.

Index - a list of 8 works for the first "chi"; same for the second
     "chi".

Bound in 1 t'ao 16 ts'ê.

Remarks - an ordinary edition; the item is complete and in good
     condition with the exception that the last ts'ê is slightly
     stained.

Accession No. 587   Index No. - 147-rbhj

Title   " Kuan-ku t'ang hui k'ê shu "
             觀 古 堂 彙 刻 書

Classification - C-338 雜家一叢書

Subject - (Gest No. 1016-a) "Collection of 21 reprints of works on all
    Four Classes of Literature."

References - 029-pffz 586   Gest No. 1016-a.

Author - compiled by Yeh Tê-hui 葉 德 輝.

Edition - published by the author; dated Kuang-Hsü "jên-yin" 29/1902.
    Blocks; "fên" paper.

Index - a list of 14 works for the first "chi"; a list of 7 works for
    the second "chi".

Bound in 1 t'ao 16 ts'ê.

Remarks - an ordinary edition; the item is complete and in very good
    condition.

Accession No. 588   Index No. - 149-gj

Title   " Shuo   lei "
                              說   類

Classification - C-328 雜家－雜纂
Subject - a collection of extracts taken from standard works (chiefly
    dealing with miscellaneous sayings and narrations) of the T'ang
    and Sung authors; classified and arranged in the form of an
    encyclopaedia.

References - 012-zafk 13/5   031-bgdf 132/6.

Author - (編) Yeh Hsiang-kao 葉 向 高.

Edition - a Ming edition; no date.   Blocks; bamboo paper.

Index - a classified table of contents for 62 chüan.

Bound in 2 t'ao 20 ts'ê (10-10); singly interleaved.

Remarks - this is a fairly good edition; and the item is in good
    condition and complete with the exception that page 8 in chüan
    42 is missing.

Accession No. 589   Index No. - 149-gzgc

Title   " Shuo wên t'ung hsün ting shêng "
         說 文 通 訓 定 聲

Classification - A-161 小學 一字書
Subject - (Gest No. 52) "Commentary on the meaning of the characters
    in the Shuo wên 說文 dictionary,-----"

References - 012-zafk 3/25   Gest No. 52.

Author - compiled by Chu Chün-shêng 朱駿聲.

Edition - the "Lin-hsiao-ke" 臨嘯閣 ; dated (at the end) T'ung-Chih
    9/1870.   Blocks; bamboo paper.

Index - a general table of contents for 18 chüan, with separate
    detailed lists at the beginning of each chüan; 東 韻 1 chüan;
    說 雅 19 篇 ; 韻 準 1 chüan; 行 述 1 chüan.
Bound in 4 t'ao 32 ts'ê (8 each).

Remarks - a very useful reference work.   The item is complete and
    with no defects.

61

The University of Toronto Chinese Library

Accession No. 590   Index No. - 018-bjge   075-cazf   030-gjdc

Title

" **Fēn lei pu chu Li t'ai-po shih** "

分 類 補 註 李 太 白 詩

" **T'ang han-lin Li t'ai-po shih** "

唐 翰 林 李 太 白 詩

Classification - D-38 別 集 一 詩

Subject - an individual collection of poems; with commentaries.

References - 163-ggcz 12/4   031-bgld 15/9   037-ahhg 6/18 10/5

(hsü) 11/2   167-mhfm 19/12   030-iaff 24/7   106-gdkn 68/10

012-zafk 15/5   031-bgdf 149/16   Gest No. 1221.

Author - (of the poems) <u>Li Po</u> 李 白 ; (集 註) <u>Yang Ch'i-hsien</u>

楊 齊 賢 ; (補 註) <u>Hsiao Shih-yün</u> 蕭 士 贇 .

Edition - a Ming edition; no date.   Blocks; bamboo paper.

Index - a table of contents for 25 chüan arranged according to classes

of composition.

Bound in 2 t'ao 16 ts'è (8-8); doubly interleaved with margins.

Remarks - this is a very good edition; and the item is complete and in

good condition with the exception of a few pages at the end of the

work, which are somewhat worm-eaten.   Pages 29 and 30 in chüan

10 are hand-written.

———◆———

Accession No. 591   Index No. – 018-dze   015-dfeg   015-dfzl

Title   " Lieh-tzŭ chu "
                          列 子 註
                     " Ch'ung hsü chên ching "
                      沖 虛 真 經
(#)

Classification – C-731 道家

Subject – a work on metaphysical philosophy; one of the principal
    works of the Taoist gospel, with commentaries.

References – Wylie's Notes page 217   160-lj   012-zafk 14/32
    Toronto Nos. 26-c, 28, and 52.

Author – (解) Lu Chung-yüan 盧 重 元 .

Edition – the "Shih-yen-chai" 石 研 齋 ; dated Chia-Ch'ing 8/1803.
    Blocks; "mien" paper.

Index – none; 8 chüan.

Bound in 1 t'ao 4 ts'ê; doubly interleaved with margins.

Remarks – a good edition; the item is complete and in very good
    condition.

(#) " Ch'ung hsü chih tê chên ching "
      沖 虛 至 德 真 經

Accession No. 592   Index No. - 120-czib

Title   " Chi Wên-ta kung i chi "

紀 文 達 公 遺 集

Classification - D-33 別集 - 詩文

Subject - an individual collection of prose and poetry.

References - 012-zafk 17/37.

Author - (撰) Chi Yün 紀 昀 .

Edition - no particular notation; (preface) dated Chia-Ch'ing 17/1812.

Blocks; "mao-t'ai" paper.

Index - a detailed table of contents (prose) for 16 chüan; a detailed

table of contents (poems) for 16 chüan.

Bound in 1 t'ao 10 ts'ê.

Remarks - the item is complete and without defects.

The University of Toronto Chinese Library

Accession No. 593   Index No. - 074-zchi

Title   " Yüeh ling sui pien "
                   月 令 粹 編

Classification - B-157 時令

Subject - (Wylie) "----- is a compilation of historical memoranda for
    every day in the year ----- "

References - Wylie's Notes page 43   Gest No. 153   Toronto No. 504.

Author - by Ch'in Chia-mo 秦嘉謨.

Edition - published by the author; dated Chia-Ch'ing 17/1812.
    Blocks; "mao-pien" paper.

Index - a general table of contents for 卷首 and 24 chüan.

Bound in 1 t'ao 8 ts'ê.

Remarks - an ordinary edition; complete and without defects.

Accession No. 594   Index No. - 030-gfzz   140-fzd

Title   " T'ang Ching-ch'uan wên chi "

唐　荊　川　文　集

" Ching-ch'uan chi "

荊　川　集

Classification - D-33 別集 - 詩文

Subject - an individual literary collection,- prose and poetry.

References - 163-ggcz 15/8   031-bgld 18/28   012-zafk 16/25

031-bgdf 172/18   Toronto No. 137-d.

Author - (著) T'ang Shun-chih 唐 順 之 .

Edition - a Ming edition; (preface) dated Chia-Ching "chi-yu" 28/1549.

Blocks; bamboo paper.

Index - a detailed table of contents for 12 chüan.

Bound in 2 t'ao 12 ts'ê; doubly interleaved.

Remarks - this is a very fine edition; and the item is complete and

in practically perfect condition.

Accession No. 595   Index No. - 009-dihd

Title   " Yang-chieh-t'ang chi "
                         仰 節 堂 集

Classification - D-33 別 集 一 詩 文
Subject - an individual literary collection,- prose and poetry.

References - 163-ggcz 15/9   031-bgld 18/33   012-zafk 16/34
     031-bgdf 172/57.

Author - (撰) Ts'ao Yü-pien 曹 于 汴 .

Edition - no particular notation; (preface) dated K'ang-Hsi 2/1663.
     Blocks; "fên" paper.

Index - separate tables of contents for each of 14 chüan.

Bound in 1 t'ao 4 ts'ê.

Remarks - the item is complete and without defects.
        Hand-written pages;- first half page of first preface;
     preface (2 pages) of Lü Ch'ung-lieh 呂 崇 烈 ; the list
     (1 page) of publishers' names. According to information from
     the manuscript pages the work was published by the "Hung-yün-
     shu-yüan" 弘 運 書 院 .

67

Accession No. 596   Index No. - 167-hggb

Title   " Ch'ien Min-su kung tsou su "
               錢 敏 肅 公 奏 疏

Classification - B-72 詔令奏議 - 奏議
Subject - a collection of memorials.

References - 012-zafk 4/32.

Author - (撰) Ch'ien Ting-ming 錢 鼎 銘.

Edition - the "Ts'un-su-t'ang" 存 素 堂 ; dated Kuang-Hsü 6/1880.
    Blocks; "fên" paper.

Index - a detailed table of contents for 7 chüan.

Bound in 1 t'ao 4 ts'ê.

Remarks - a modern edition; the item is complete and in good condition.

———— • ————

Accession No. 597   Index No. - 170-hegd   120-egd

Title   " Ch'ên Tzǔ-fêng hsien-shêng wên chi "
            陳　紫　峯　先　生　文　集
            " Tzǔ-fêng chi "
            紫　峯　集

Classification - D-33 別集一詩文
Subject - an individual literary collection,- prose and poetry; with
    a "nien-p'u" 年譜 of the author.

References - 031-bgdf 176/53.

Author - (撰) Ch'ên Ch'ên 陳琛 ; (選稿) Chang Yo 張岳 .

Edition - no particular notation; dated Kuang-Hsü 17/1891.   Blocks;
    "fên" paper.

Index - a detailed table of contents for 13 chüan, arranged according
    to the class of composition.

Bound in 1 t'ao 5 ts'ê.

Remarks - a fairly good edition; the item is complete and without
    defects.

Accession No. 598   Index No. - 039-eddf   039-eddd

Title   " Mĕng   Tung-yeh   shih "
                           孟   東   野   詩
                         " Mĕng   Tung-yeh   chi "
                           孟   東   野   集

Classification - D-38 別集一詩
Subject - an individual collection of poetry.

References - 163-ggcz 12/9   031-bgld 15/20   030-iaff 25/4   106-gdkn 69/16
        167-mhfm 19/27   012-zafk 15/9   031-bgdf 150/31.

Author - (撰) Mĕng Chiao 孟 郊 .

Edition - based upon the Sung edition; no date, possibly of the early
        Ch'ing period.   Blocks; bamboo paper.

Index - a table of contents for 10 chüan.

Bound in 1 t'ao 4 ts'ĕ; doubly interleaved.

Remarks - a good edition; the item is complete and in good condition.

Accession No. 599   Index No. - 030-bze

Title   " <u>Ku</u> <u>wên</u> <u>yüan</u> "

　　　　　　　　　古　文　苑

Classification - D-63 總集 - 詩文

Subject - a general literary collection of scholars of the ancient
　　　period,- prose and poetry.

References - Wylie's Notes page 239   160-1j   163-ggcz 16/2
　　　031-bgld 19/7   030-1aff 38/8   037-ahhg (hsü) 7/18   (#)

Author - not stated.

Edition - no notation; (preface) dated Wan-Li "kuei-ssŭ" 21/1593.
　　　Blocks; bamboo paper.

Index - a table of contents for 21 chüan, arranged according to the
　　　character of composition; separate lists for each chüan.

Bound in 1 t'ao 4 ts'ê.

Remarks - the item is complete and in fairly good condition.

　　　(#) 106-gdkn 112/11   167-mhfm 23/7   012-zafk 19/2
　　　　　031-bgdf 186/28.

71

Accession No. 600   Index No. - 059-1hcb

Title   " P'êng Kang-chih kung tsou i "
                彭 剛 直 公 奏 議

Classification - B-72 詔令奏議－奏議
Subject - a collection of memorials.

References - 012-zafk 4/32.

Author - (撰) P'êng Yü-lin 彭玉麟.

Edition - no notation; dated Kuang-Hsü 17/1891.   Blocks; "fên"
    paper.

Index - a table of contents for 8 chüan.

Bound in 1 t'ao 8 ts'ê.

Remarks - an ordinary modern edition; the item is complete and without
    defects.   The following is a supplement:-
        " P'êng Kang-chih kung shih chi "
            彭 剛 直 公 詩 集
                D-38   (059-1hcb) 8 chüan.

Accession No. 601   Index No. - 067-zcjb

Title   " Wên tzǔ mêng ch'iu "
              文 字 蒙 求

Classification - A-161 小學 - 字書
Subject - a dictionary explaining the formation of more than 2,000
    characters, with variants in other styles; classified into 4
    general classes.

References - none.

Author - by Lu Yu-yün 蒙 友 筠.

Edition - published by the "Hsüeh-wu-chü" 學 務 局 ; dated Kuang-Hsü
    30/1904.   Blocks; "fên" paper.

Index - none; 4 chüan.

Bound in 1 t'ao 1 ts'ê.

Remarks - a useful reference work.   The item is new.

Accession No. 602   Index No. - 031-bfaj   031-bf

Title   " Ssŭ shu chêng mêng "
               四　書　正　蒙
               " Ssŭ shu "
               四　書

Classification - A-131 四書

Subject - a commentary on the "Four Books",- (1) "Ta-hsüeh";
    (2) "Chung-yung"; (3)"Lun-yü"; and (4) "Mêng-tzŭ".   (See
    separate notes that follow).

References - Wylie's Notes page 7   160-1j   163-ggcz 3/4   031-bgld
    4/3   167-mhfm 6/5   030-iaff 4/15   012-zafk 3/7   031-bgdf 35/21
    Gest No. 1498.

Author - by Chu Hsi 朱熹.

Edition - the "Ta-shêng-t'ang" 大盛堂; dated Tao-Kuang "mou-tzŭ"
    8/1828.   Blocks; "mien" paper.

Index - none.

Bound in 1 t'ao 8 ts'ê.

Remarks - a good edition; the item is complete and without defects.

Accession No. 602-a   Index No. - 037-zmfb   037-zm

Title   " Ta-hsüeh chang chü "
                   大　學　章　句
                  " Ta-hsüeh "
                   大　學

Classification - A-132 四書 - 大學

Subject - (Gest No. 1498-a) "a commentary on the advanced course of
    study for youths under the Chou Dynasty educational system,
    A treatise on government."

References - as under No. 602.

Author - by Chu Hsi 朱熹.

Edition - as under No. 602.

Index - none; 1 chüan.

Bound in 1/2 ts'ê with (b); in 1 t'ao with (c) and (d).

Remarks - as under No. 602.

Accession No. 602-b   Index No. - 002-chfb   002-ch

Title   " Chung-yung chang chü "

中 庸 章 句

" Chung-yung "

中 庸

Classification - A-133 四書 - 中庸

Subject - (Gest No. 1498-b) " a commentary on the "Doctrine of the Mean".

References - as under No. 602.

Author - by Chu Hsi 朱熹 .

Edition - as under No. 602.

Index - none; 1 chüan.

Bound in 1/2 ts'ä with (a); in 1 t'ao with (c) and (d).

Remarks - as under No. 602.

Accession No. 602-c   Index No. - 149-hgde   149-hg

Title   " Lun-yü chi chu "
          論 語 集 註
               " Lun-yü "
               論 語

Classification - A-134 四書 - 論語

Subject - (Gest No. 1498-c) " a commentary on the discourses of
     Confucius with his followers and others."

References - as under No. 602.

Author - by Chu Hsi 朱 熹 .

Edition - as under No. 602.

Index - none; 10 chüan.

Bound in 3 ts'ê in 1 t'ao with (a) (b) and (d).

Remarks - as under No. 602.

Accession No. 602-d   Index No. - 039-ezde   039-ez

Title   " M**ě**ng-tzǔ chi chu "
                         孟　子　集　註
                          " M**ě**ng-tzǔ "
                          孟　子

Classification - A-135 四書 - 孟子

Subject - (Gest No. 1498-d) " a commentary on the discourses of
     Mencius on political, social, and ethical subjects."

References - as under No. 602.

Author - by Chu Hsi 朱熹 .

Edition - as under No. 602.

Index - none; 7 chüan.

Bound in 4 ts'ê in 1 t'ao with (a) (b) and (c).

Remarks - as under No. 602; but with a few worm-holes at the end.

Accession No. 603   Index No. - 106-azdf   039-zfag

Title   " Po tzŭ ch'üan shu "
                百   子   全   書
                " Tzŭ shu po chia "
                子   書   百   家

Classification - C-338 雜家 - 叢書

Subject - a collection of reprints of 100 works, all of which pertain

    to the 子 部 (Class "C") of Chinese literature.

References - 029-pffz page 203   012-zafk 13/19 (?)   Gest No. 131.

Author - not stated.

Edition - the "Ch'ung-wên-shu-chü" 崇文書局; dated Kuang-Hsü

    1/1875.   Blocks; "fên" paper.

Index - a list of the 100 works.

Bound in 10 t'ao 110 ts'ê (11 each).

Remarks - an ordinary good edition; the item is complete and in perfect

    condition.

The University of Toronto Chinese Library

Accession No. 604   Index No. - 072-dic

Title   " <u>Ming hui yao</u> "
                       明 會 要

<u>Classification</u> - B-282 政書 - 通制

<u>Subject</u> - a record of the governmental affairs of the <u>Ming Dynasty</u>.

<u>References</u> - none.

<u>Author</u> - (纂) <u>Lung Wên-pin</u> 龍 文 彬 .

<u>Edition</u> - the "<u>Yung-huai-t'ang</u>" 永 懷 堂 ; dated Kuang-Hsü "ting-hai"
        13/1887.   Blocks; "mao-t'ai" paper.

<u>Index</u> - a table of contents for 80 chüan.

<u>Bound in</u> 2 t'ao 20 ts'ê (10-10).

<u>Remarks</u> - a very ordinary edition; complete and without defects.

The University of Toronto Chinese Library

Accession No. 605   Index No. - 036-cihb

Title   " To-sui-t'ang ku shih ts'un "

多 歲 堂 古 詩 存

Classification - D-38 別集一詩

Subject - a collection of ancient poems; with commentary.

References - none.

Author - (選 評) Ch'êng Shu 成 書 .

Edition - the "To-sui-t'ang"; dated Tao-Kuang "hsin-mao" 11/1831.
    Blocks; "mao-pien" paper.

Index - a table of contents for 8 chüan, arranged dynastically.

Bound in 1 t'ao 4 ts'ê.

Remarks - a very good edition; the item is complete and in very good
    condition

Accession No. 606   Index No. - 077-ahhd

Title   " Chêng-i-t'ang ch'üan shu "
                 正 誼 堂 全 書

Classification - C-338 雜家 - 叢書

Subject - a collection of reprints of 63 works chiefly consisting of
    individual literary collections; with 3 additional works.

References - 012-zafk 13/14   029-pffz 189   058-jffz 18/13.

Author - (重刊) Tso Tsung-t'ang 左 宗 棠.

Edition - published by the author; dated T'ung-Chih 5/1866.   Blocks;
    "fên" paper.

Index - a list of the 63 works.

Bound in 20 t'ao 200 ts'ê (10 each).

Remarks - this is a good modern edition; and the item is complete
    and as new.

The University of Toronto Chinese Library

Accession No. 607-a   Index No. - 162-gncg

Title   " T'ung chien chi shih pên mo "
             通 鑑 紀 事 本 末

Classification - B-32 紀事本末

Subject - (Toronto No. 217-a) "a rearrangement of the historical
    narratives of the "T'ung Chien" 通 鑑 of Ssŭ-ma Kuang 司馬光;
    which embraces the period from the 4th century down to the end
    of the Five Dynasties 五代 ."

References - Wylie's Notes page 27 163-ggcz 4/10   031-bgld 5/26
    106-gdkn 22/11 012-zafk 4/11 031-bgdf 49/1 Gest No. 403
    Toronto No. 217-a.

Author - (編輯) Yüan Shu 袁樞 ; (論正) Chang P'u 張溥 .

Edition - the "Chiang-hsi-shu-chü" 江 西 書 局 ; dated T'ung-Chih
    "kuei-yu" 12/1873.   Blocks; "fên" paper.

Index - a general table of contents for 239 chüan.

Bound in 8 t'ao 80 ts'ê (10 each).

Remarks - an ordinary edition; the item is complete and in good
    condition.

The University of Toronto Chinese Library

Accession No. 607-b   Index No. - 048-bkcg

Title   " Tso chuan chi shih pên mo "
　　　　　　　　左　傳　紀　事　本　末

Classification - B-32　紀 事 本 末

Subject - (Toronto No. 217-b) "a collection of historical narratives based upon the "Tso Chuan" 左 傳 ."

References - 163-ggcz 4/11   031-bgld 5/29   012-zafk 4/13
　　　　031-bgdf 49/32   Gest No. 851   Toronto No. 217-b.

Author - Kao Shih-ch'i 高 士 奇 .

Edition - uniform with (a).

Index - a general table of contents for 53 chüan.

Bound in 2 t'ao 12 ts'ê (6-6).

Remarks - as under (a).

Accession No. 607-c   Index No. - 040-dbcg

Title   " Sung shih chi shih pên mo "
               宋 史 紀 事 本 末

Classification - B-32 紀事本末

Subject - (Toronto No. 217-c) "a collection of historical narratives
     of the Sung Dynasty."

References - Wylie's Notes page 28   163-ggcz 4/10   031-bgld 5/27

     030-1aff 7/19 012-zafk 4/12 031-bgdf 49/8 Gest No. 851
     Toronto No. 217-c.

Author - (原 編) Fêng Ch'i 馮 琦 ; (增 訂) Ch'ên Pang-chan
     陳 邦 瞻 .

Edition - uniform with (a).

Index - a general table of contents for 109 chüan.

Bound in 4 t'ao 20 ts'ê (5 each).

Remarks - as under (a).

———•———

Accession No. 607-d   Index No. - 010-bbcg

Title   " <u>Yüan</u> <u>shih</u> <u>chi</u> <u>shih</u> <u>pên</u> <u>mo</u> "
                元 史 紀 事 本 末

Classification - B-32 紀事本末

Subject - (Toronto No. 217-d) "a collection of historical narratives

    of the <u>Yüan Dynasty</u>."

References - Wylie's Notes page 28   163-ggcz 4/10   031-bgld 5/27

    030-iaff 7/19 012-zafk 4/12 031-bgdf 49/9 Gest No. 851
    Toronto No. 217-d.

Author - （編輯）<u>Ch'ên Pang-chan</u> 陳 邦 瞻；（論正）<u>Chang P'u</u>
          張 溥．

Edition - uniform with (a); but dated T'ung-Chih "chia-hsü" 13/1874.

Index - a general table of contents for 27 chüan.

Bound in 1 t'ao 4 ts'ê.

Remarks - as under (a).

The University of Toronto Chinese Library

Accession No. 607-e   Index No. - 072-dbcg

Title   " <u>Ming shih chi shih pên mo</u> "

明 史 紀 事 本 末

Classification - B-32 紀事本末

Subject - (Toronto No. 217-e) "a collection of historical narratives
of the <u>Ming Dynasty</u>."

References - Wylie's Notes page 28   163-ggcz 4/10   031-bgld 5/29
012-zafk 4/13 031-bgdf 49/30 Gest No. 851   Toronto No. 217-e.

Author - (編輯) <u>Ku Ying-t'ai</u> 谷 應 泰 ．

Edition - uniform with (a); but dated T'ung-Chih "chia-hsü" 13/1874.

Index - a general table of contents for 80 chüan.

Bound in 4 t'ao 20 ts'ê (5 each).

Remarks - as under (a).

———•◦•———

Accession No. 608   Index No. - 051-bejm

Title   " P'ing ting Chun-ko-êrh fang lüeh "
             平 定 準 噶 爾 方 略

Classification - B-32 紀事本末

Subject - an account of the subjugation of the Chun-ko-êrh 準噶爾

tribe (of Mongolian origin) occupying the north-western frontier

of Chan̆a during the early part of the Ch'ing Dynasty.

References - 031-bgld 5/28   012-zafk 4/12   031-bgdf 49/16.

Author - compiled by an Imperial Commission headed by Fu Hêng

on order of the Emperor Ch'ien-Lung.

Edition - a "palace" edition; (preface) dated Ch'ien-Lung 35/1770.

Blocks; "k'ai-hua" paper.

Index - . general table of contents for (前編) 54 chüan; (正編)

85 chüan; (續編) 32 chüan.

Bound in 10 t'ao 100 ts'ê (10 each).

Remarks - a very fine edition; the item is complete and in perfect

condition with the exception of a few worm-holes.   This work

is quite a rare one now; and all the ts'ê are with original

covers made of yellow brocade.

Accession No. 609   Index No. - 075-cgzf   075-cgzf

Title   " Li I-shan shih chi "
                      李 義 山 詩 集
                     " Li I-shan shih chu "
                      李 義 山 詩 註

Classification - D-38 別 集 一 詩

Subject - a commentary on the poems of Li Shang-yin 李 商 隱 ；
with marginal notes.

References - 163-ggoz 12/11   031-bgld 15/23   012-zafk 15/10
031-bgdf 151/11.

Author - (箋 註) Chu Hao-ling 朱 鶴 齡 .

Edition - the "Kuang-chou-ts'ui-shu" 廣 州 倅 署 ; dated T'ung-Chih
"k'ěng-wu" 9/1870.   Blocks ; "fěn" paper.

Index - a detailed table of contents for 3 chüan.

Bound in 1 t'ao 4 ts'ě.

Remarks - an ordinary edition; complete and without defects.

———•—•———

Accession No. 610   Index No. 120-gg(zb)

Title   " Ching i k'ao "
經 義 考

Classification - B-342 目録 一 經籍

Subject - (Gest No. 46) " A catalogue of Classics; a bibliographical
study;-----."

References - 160-lj 163-ggcz 6/7 031-bgld 8/21 012-zafk 9/16
031-bgdf 85/20 Gest No. 46.

Author - compiled by Chu I-tsun 朱彝尊 .

Edition - the "Pao-shu-t'ing" 曝書亭 ; (preface) dated K'ang-Hsi
"chi-mao" 38/1699.   Blocks; "mao-pien" paper.

Index - a general table of contents for 300 chüan.

Bound in 6 t'ao 60 ts'ê (10 each).

Remarks - the item is complete and in good condition.

Accession No. 611   Index No. – 037-zhzf

Title   " Ta Ch'ing i t'ung chih "
                大　清　一　統　志

Classification – B-187 地 理 一 總 志

Subject – (Gest No. 1459) "a general "geography" of China in the
   broadest sense of the term."

References – Wylie's Notes page 43 160-1j 163-ggcz 5/10 031-bgld 7/6
   012-zafk 6/2 031-bgdf 68/12 Gest No. 1459.

Author – officially compiled.

Edition – the "Pao-shan-chai" 寶 善 齋 ; dated Kuang-Hsü "jên-yin"
   28/1902.   Lithographed on "mao-pien" paper.

Index – a table of contents for 500 chüan.

Bound in 6 t'ao 60 ts'ê (10 each).

Remarks – an ordinary edition; complete and without defects.

Accession No. 612   Index No. - 030-bbgh

Title   " Ku-chin shuo pu ts'ung shu "
               古　今　說　部　叢　書

Classification - C-338 雜家 - 叢書
Subject - a collection of reprints of some 250 works on miscellaneous
   narrations, records of marvels, and detached sayings.

References - 029-pffz 589.

Author - compiled by Wang Wên-ju 王文濡 .

Edition - published by the "Kuo-hsüeh-fu-lun-shê" 國學扶輪社;
   (preface) dated Hsüan-T'ung "kêng-hsü" 2/1910.   Type; foreign
   paper.

Index - separate list of works at the beginning of each of 10 "chi" 集 .

Bound in 5 t'ao 60 ts'ê (12 each).

Remarks - an ordinary edition; the item is new.

———•———

Accession No. 613   Index No. - 124-hgoh

Title   " Ts'ui-lang-kan kuan ts'ung shu "
                   翠 琅 玕 館 叢 書

Classification - C-338 雜家 一 叢書
Subject - a collection of reprints of 74 works on all four classes of
    literature.

References - none.

Author - (重 編) Huang Jên-hêng 黄 任 恆.

Edition - privately published; (preface) dated "ping-ch'ên" 1916.
    Blocks; "fên" paper.

Index - a list of the 74 works arranged under four classes.

Bound in 8 t'ao 80 ts'ê (10 each).

Remarks - a modern edition; the item is in good condition.   One of
    the works,- "P'u-shan-lun-hua" 浦 山 論 畫 ,- is wholly missing
    with the exception of its title-page.   It probably consists of a
    few pages only, because it is amongst a number of small works on
    a similar subject.

—•—

Accession No. 614   Index No. - 076-hebe   051-beon

Title   " Ch'in-ting P'ing ting Hui-chiang chiao ch'in ni i fang lüeh "

欽 定 平 定 回 疆 勦 捦 逆 裔 方 略

Classification - B-32 紀事本末

Subject - an account of the suppression of the Mohammedan rebels in
the Chinese Turkestan region during the period of Chia-Ch'ing
and Tao-Kuang.

References - 012-zafk 4/13.

Author - by an Imperial Commission headed by Ts'ao Chên-yung 曹 振 鏞
on order of Emperor Tao-Kuang.

Edition - a "palace" edition; (preface) dated Tao-Kuang 10/1830.
Blocks; "fên" paper.

Index - a table of contents for 卷首 and 80 chüan.

Bound in 6 t'ao 86 ts'ê (16-14-14-14-14-14).

Remarks - this item is complete, but has been very badly worm-eaten,
but it has been repaired as far as possible.

The University of Toronto Chinese Library

Accession No. 615   Index No. - 096-epzh   108-edhd

Title   " Ling-lung-shan-kuan ts'ung shu "

玲 瓏 山 館 叢 書

" I-ya-t'ang ch'üan chi "

益 雅 堂 全 集

Classification - C-338 雜家 - 叢書

Subject - a collection of reprints of 71 works chiefly on classical
    subjects.

References - none.

Author - compiled by the W&n-hsüan-lou 文 選 樓·

Edition - the "W&n-hsüan-lou"; dated "chi-ch'ou" 1889.   Blocks;
    "mao-t'ai" paper.

Index - a list of the 71 works.

Bound in 8 t'ao 48 ts'& (6 each).

Remarks - the item is complete and without defects.

Accession No. 616   Index No. - 031-hhda   010-dagf

Title   " <u>Kuo</u> <u>ch'ao</u> <u>hsien</u> <u>chêng</u> <u>shih</u> <u>lüeh</u> "
               國   朝   先   正   事   略

Classification - B-117 傳記 - 總錄

Subject - a collection of biographies of famous persons of the earlier

part of the <u>Ch'ing</u> Dynasty.

References - Gest No. 473.

Author - (纂) <u>Li Yüan-tu</u> 李 元 度.

Edition - the "<u>Hsün-kai-ts'ao-t'ang</u>" 循 陔 草 堂; dated T'ung-Chih

"ping-yin" 5/1866.   Blocks; bamboo paper.

Index - a detailed list of contents (names) for 60 chüan.

Bound in 4 t'ao 32 ts'ê (8 each).

Remarks - an ordinary edition; the item is complete and in generally

good condition.

————— • —————

Accession No. 617   Index No. - 076-hedh   010-dhcg

Title   " Ch'in-ting Kuang-lu-ssŭ tsê li "
             欽 定 光 禄 寺 則 例

Classification - B-287 政書－典禮 B-282 政書－通制

Subject - a general description of the Kuang-lu-ssŭ,- Banqueting
    Court; organization, regulations etc.

References - none.

Author - officially compiled.

Edition - an official publication; (preface) dated Hsien-Fêng 5/1855.
    Blocks; "fên" paper.

Index - a general table of contents for 90 chüan; (supplement) 14
    chüan.

Bound in 4 t'ao 54 ts'ê (16-13-13-12).

Remarks - an ordinary clear-cut edition; the item seems to be complete
    and is in very good condition.

Accession No. 618   Index No. - 085-akzf

Title   " <u>Yung-lo ta tien mu lu</u> "
                    永 樂 大 典 目 録

Classification - C-348 類書

<u>Subject</u> - (Gest No. 1711) "the index, or table of contents, of the
   comprehensive encyclopaedia with the same title."

<u>References</u> - to this work - 012-zafk 13/23   Gest No. 1711. to the
   encyclopaedia - Wylie's Notes page 186   160-1j.

<u>Author</u> - (encyclopaedia) officially compiled.

<u>Edition</u> - the "<u>Lien-yün-i</u>" 連 筠 簃; no date.   Blocks; "mao-pien"
   paper.

<u>Index</u> - in 60 chüan.

<u>Bound</u> in 2 t'ao 20 ts's (10-10).

<u>Remarks</u> - an ordinary edition; the item is complete and without
   defects.

The University of Toronto Chinese Library

Accession No. 619   Index No. - 069-hzaf

Title   " Ssŭ wên chêng t'ung "

斯　文　正　統

Classification - D-73 總集 一 文

Subject - a collection of selected prose compositions of famous scholars
   of the several dynasties, commencing with ancient times and going
   down to the beginning of the Ch'ing Dynasty.

References - 031-bgdf 194/3.

Author - (選 輯) Tiao Pao 刁 包 .

Edition - no particular notation; (preface) dated Shun-Chih "chia-wu"
   11/1654.   Blocks; bamboo paper.

Index - a table of contents for 12 chüan arranged according to
   character of composition.

Bound in 2 t'ao 12 ts'ê; doubly interleaved.

Remarks - a good edition; the item is complete and in generally good
   condition.

Accession No. 620-a   Index No. - 057-hzkb

Title   " Chang Wên-hsiang kung tsou-kao "
           張　文　襄　公　奏　稿

Classification - B-72 詔令奏議 一 奏議

Subject - (Gest No. 1045-a) "a collection of draft memorials drawn up

by Chang Chih-tung 張 之 洞.

References - Gest No. 1045-a.

Author - (編 輯) Hsü T'ung-hsin 許 同 莘.

Edition - no particular notation; dated "kêng-shên" 1920.   Type;
   "mao-pien" paper.

Index - a table of contents for 50 chüan arranged chronologically.

Bound in 3 t'ao 26 ts'ê (8-8-10).

Remarks - a modern edition; the item is new.

Accession No.   620-b   Index No. - 057-hzkb

Title   " Chang Wên-hsiang kung tien kao "
             張 文 襄 公 電 稿

Classification - B-77 詔令奏議 一 公文

Subject - (Gest No. 1045-d) "a collection of the telegraphic
    correspondence of Chang Chih-tung."

References - Gest No. 1045-d.

Author - (編 輯) Hsü T'ung-hsin 許 同 華 .

Edition - uniform with (a).

Index - a table of contents for 66 chüan arranged chronologically.

Bound in 3 t'ao 32 ts'ê (11-11-10).

Remarks - as under (a).

———◆·◆———

Accession No.   620-c   Index No. - 057-hzk'b

Title   " Chang Wên-hsiang kung han kao "
             張 文 襄 公 函 稿

Classification - D-43 別 集 一 文

Subject - (Gest No. 1045-b) "a collection of the personal correspondence
    of Chang Chih-tung."

References - Gest No. 1045-b.

Author - (編 輯) Hsü T'ung-hsin 許 同 莘.

Edition - uniform with (a).

Index - a table of contents of 6 chüan and a 續 編.

Bound in 2 ts'ê in the 1st t'ao of (d).

Remarks - as under (a).

Accession No. 620-d   Index No. - 057-hzkb

Title   " Chang Wên-hsiang kung kung tu kao "
         張 文 襄 公 公 牘 稿

Classification - B-77 詔令奏議 一 公文

Subject - (Gest No. 1045-c) "a collection of the official correspondence
    of Chang Chih-tung."

References - Gest No. 1045-c.

Author - (編 輯) Hsü T'ung-hsin 許 同 莘 .

Edition - uniform with (a).

Index - a table of contents for 28 chüan.

Bound in 2 t'ao 15 ts'ê; lst t'ao with (c).

Remarks - as under (a).

Accession No. 621   Index No.- 128-gmfd   075-fdg

Title   " Shêng hsüeh ko wu t'ung "
                    聖　學　格　物　通

Classification – C-13 儒家

Subject – (Wylie) "----, is a work after the model of the Ta hëŏ yen é,-
----.   This is divided into six sections, under the heads:
Sincerity of Intention, Singleness of Aim, Personal Cultivation,
Family Adjustment, State Government, and Pacification of the
Empire.   These several points are elaborately illustrated by (#)

References – Wylie's Notes page 87   163-ggcz 7/6   031-bgld 9/20
037-ahhg 9/11 012-zafk 10/6 031-bgdf 93/22   Gest No. 2712.

Author – (撰) Chan Jo-shui 湛 若 水．

Edition – a Ming edition; (preface) dated Chia-Ching 12/1533.
Blocks; "mien" paper.

Index – a general table of contents for 100 chüan.

Bound in 4 t'ao 24 ts'ê; singly interleaved.

Remarks – a very fine edition; the item is complete and with
practically no defects.

(#) examples from history, with a discussion of each paragraph
by the author."

The University of Toronto Chinese Library

Accession No. 622   Index No. - 140-ogfk

Title   " I hai chu ch'ên "
             藝 海 珠 塵

Classification - C-338 雜家 - 叢書
Subject - a collection of 165 reprints of a miscellaneous character.

References - Wylie's Notes page 266   012-zafk 13/14   029-pffz 567
    058-jffz 6/23.

Author - (輯) Wu Hsing-lan 吳 省 蘭 .

Edition - the "T'ing-i-t'ang" 聽 彝 堂 ; no date notation.   Blocks;
    "mao-t'ai" paper.

Index - separate lists of works for each of 8 "chi" 集 .

Bound in 8 t'ao 66 ts'ê (8-8-8-8-8-8-9-9).

Remarks - this is an ordinary edition; and the item is without
    defects.

The University of Toronto Chinese Library

Accession No. 623   Index No. - 072-hf

Title   " **Chih** **p'in** "
智   品

Classification - C-328 雜家 － 雜纂

Subject - (Gest No. 2435) "a collection of classified miscellaneous
   extracts of an informative and instructive character relating
   to incidents taking place during ancient times and down to the
   Ming Dynasty."

References - 012-zafk 13/5   031-bgdf 132/9   Gest No. 2435.

Author - (撰) **Fan Yü-hêng** 樊 玉 衡 .

Edition - no particular notation; (preface) dated "chia-yin" 1614.
   Blocks; bamboo paper.

Index - none; 13 chüan.

Bound in 2 t'ao 18 ts'ê (9-9); doubly interleaved.

Remarks - a fairly good edition; the item is complete and without
   defects.   Page 45 of chüan 10 is hand-written.

106

The University of Toronto Chinese Library

Accession No. 624   Index No. - 042-afzd

Title   " Shao-shih-shan-fang pi ts'ung "

少 室 山 房 筆 叢

Classification - C-338 雜家 - 叢書

Subject - a collection of reprints of 13 miscellaneous works by one author.

References - 163-ggcz 10/11   031-bgld 13/31   012-zafk 13/12
031-bgdf 123/28.

Author - (撰) Hu Ying-lin 胡 應 麟.

Edition - a Ming edition; (preface) dated Wan-Li "chi-ch'ou" 17/1589.
Blocks; bamboo paper.

Index - none.

Bound in 4 t'ao 17 ts's (4-5-4-4); doubly interleaved.

Remarks - a good edition; the item is complete and in very fine condition.

Accession No. 625   Index No. – 012-bfg

Title   " <u>Liu   shu   t'ung</u> "
                         六   書   通

Classification – A-161 小學 – 字書

Subject – a dictionary of Chinese characters in a variety of ancient
forms, arranged according to rhymes.

References – Wylie's Notes page 14 160-1j   012-zafk 3/22
031-bgdf 43/40   Gest Nos. 67 and 255.

Author – (撰) <u>Min Ch'i-chi</u> 閔齊伋 ; (篆訂) <u>Pi Hung-shu</u> 畢宏述

Edition – no particular notation; (preface) dated Ch'ien-Lung 60/1795.
Blocks; "mao-pien" paper.

Index – none; 10 chüan.

Bound in 1 t'ao 8 ts'ê.

Remarks – an ordinary edition; the item is complete and in generally
good condition.

Accession No. 626　　　　　Index No. - 149-gzfc

Title　　　　　" Shuo wên chieh tzǔ "
　　　　　　　　說 文 解 字

Classification - A-161 小學 - 字書

Subject - a dictionary of ancient Chinese characters arranged according
　　to radicals.

References - Wylie's Notes page 10　160-1j　163-ggcz 3/10　031-bgld 4/19
　　037-ahhg 5/15　106-gdkn 13/6　012-zafk 3/19　031-bgdf 41/2　Gest
　　No. 247.

Author - (記) Hsü Shên 許 慎 ; (校定) Hsü Hsüan 徐 鉉 .

Edition - reprinted by Ch'ên Ch'ang-chih 陳 昌 治 ; dated T'ung-Chih
　　12/1873.　　Blocks; "fên" paper.

Index - a table of contents (radical sections) for 14 chüan.　(See
　　under "Remarks".)

Bound in 1 t'ao 10 ts'ê.

Remarks - a modern edition, and a useful work for helping to decipher
　　the "seal" characters.　In some of the catalogues this work is
　　considered to be in 30 chüan; as each of the 15 chüan (chüan 15
　　not being given in the index) is in 2 sections (上 下).
　　(#)

Accession No. 627   Index No. - 082-zfm   149-fzzm

Title   " Mao shih hsüeh "
      毛　詩　學
      " Shih Mao-shih hsüeh "
      詩　毛　氏　學

Classification - A-31 詩

Subject - an explanation and commentary on the Mao Hêng
   version of the "Book of Odes".

References - none to this particular work.

Author - (著) Ma Ch'i-ch'ang 馬 其 昶.

Edition - reprinted by Chang Shih-ch'ing 張 石 卿 and others; dated
   "chia-tzŭ" 1924.   Blocks; "mao-pien" paper.

Index - none; in 30 chüan.

Bound in 1 t'ao 10 ts'ê.

Remarks - a very good modern edition; the item is new.

Accession No. 628   Index No. - 076-hehf   064-hfg(zb)

Title   " Ch'in-ting shou shih t'ung k'ao "
                欽　定　授　時　通　考

Classification - C-53 農家

Subject - a comprehensive treatise on agriculture and horticulture,
    with the various collateral branches of industrial science.
    (illustrated).

References - Wylie's Notes page 95 160-1j 165-ggoz 7/11 031-bgld 10/6
    012-zafk 10/19   031-bgdf 102/11   Gest No. 565.

Author - compiled by an Imperial Commission headed by Hung Chou 弘書
    on order of Emperor Ch'ien-Lung 乾隆.

Edition - the "Chiang-hsi-shu-chü" 江西書局; no date notation,
    but fairly recent.   Blocks; "mao-t'ai" paper.

Index - a general table of contents for 78 chüan.

Bound in 2 t'ao 24 ts'ê (12-12).

Remarks - an ordinary edition; complete and without defects.   A
    standard work on the subject.

112

—•—

Accession No. 629   Index No. - 030-bizz   030-bipf

Title   " Ku-yü-lao-jên hsiao hsia lu "
                 古 愚 老 人 消 夏 録
                 " Ku-yü ts'ung shu "
                 古 愚 叢 書

Classification - C-338 雜家 - 叢書
Subject - a collection of 15 reprints on a variety of subjects.

References - 012-zafk 13/15   029-pffz 157   058-jffz 18/71

    Gest No. 1032.

Author - (著) Wang Chi 汪 汲 .

Edition - the "Ku-yü-shan-fang" 古 愚 山 房 ; no notation as to the
    date.   Blocks; "mao-pien" paper.

Index - a list of the 15 works on the back of the title-page.

Bound in 4 t'ao 24 ts'$ (6 each).

Remarks - the item is complete and in good condition, but the paper
    is rather fragile owing to its age.

———•———

Accession No. 630   Index No. - 058-jnci   019-cif

Title   " Hui tsuan kung kuo ko "
                    彙　纂　功　過　格

Classification - C-308 雜家 - 雜文

Subject - a treatise on the personal cultivation of man,- morality
    and ethics; with explanations and examples.

References - none.

Author - not stated.

Edition - the "Lan-shih-yin-kuan" 蘭室唫館; dated Kuang-Hsü
    5/1879.   Blocks; "fên" paper.

Index - a general table of contents for 14 chüan including the leading
    and the concluding chapters.

Bound in 1 t'ao 10 ts's.

Remarks - an ordinary edition; the item is in good condition.

Accession No. 631   Index No. - 077-jccz   077-lccz

Title   " Li-tai ming jên nien p'u "
                        歷 代 名 人 年 譜

Classification - B-117 傳 記 - 總 錄

Subject - biographical sketches of notables of all dynasties;

    chronologically tabulated; the period it covers being from

    the Han 漢 down to the period of Tao-Kuang of the Ch'ing

    Dynasty.

References - 012-zafk 5/19   Gest No. 99.

Author - (撰) Wu Jung-kuang 吳 榮 光.

Edition - reprinted by Chang Yin-huan 張 陰 桓; dated Kuang-Hsü

    1/1875.   Blocks; "mao-pien" paper.

Index - none; 10 chüan.

Bound in 1 t'ao 10 ts'ê.

Remarks ,- an ordinary edition; complete and in good condition.

Accession No. 632   Index No. - 075-dez1

Title   " Tung-p'o wên hsüan "
                      東   坡   文   選

Classification - D-43 別 集 - 文

Subject - a collection of selected prose compositions of Su Shih
         蘇 軾 , better known as Su Tung-p'o.

References - 012-zafk 15/16.

Author - (編) Chung Hsing 鍾 惺 .

Edition - no particular notation; no date, but apparently sometime
         toward the close of the Ming Dynasty.   Blocks; bamboo paper.

Index - a classified table of contents for 20 chüan.

Bound in 1 t'ao 5 ts'ê.

Remarks - the impression is a very clear one; and the item is apparently
         complete and in very good condition.

Accession No. 633   Index No. - 030-bizz   030-bipf

Title   " Ku-yü-lao-jên hsiao hsia lu "
                    古 愚 老 人 消 夏 錄
                 " Ku-yü ts'ung shu "
                    古 愚 叢 書

Classification - C-338 雜家 - 叢書

Subject - "a collection of 15 reprints on a variety of subjects."

   (Toronto No. 629)

References - 012-zafk 13/15   029-pffz 157   058-jffz 18/71

   Gest No. 1032   Toronto No. 629.

Author - (著) Wang Chi 汪 汲 .

Edition - the "Erh-ming-ts'ao-t'ang" 二 銘 草 堂; no date.

   Blocks; "mao-pien" paper.

Index - a list of the 15 works on the back of the title-page.

Bound in 2 t'ao 16 ts'ê.

Remarks - the edition is an ordinary one; and the item has no defects

   and is complete.

Accession No. 634   Index No. - 040-qihe

Title   " Pao-yen-t'ang pi chi "
                         寶 顏 堂 秘 笈

Classification - C-338 雜 家 - 叢 書

Subject - a collection of reprints of more than 200 miscellaneous
    works.

References - 012-zafk 13/12   029-pffz 577   058-jffz 4/12
    Gest No. 1705.

Author - (輯) Ch'ên Chi-ju 陳 儸 儒.

Edition - the "Wên-ming-shu-chü" 文 明 書 局 ; dated Min-Kuo
    11/1922.   Lithographed on "fên" paper.

Index - a list of the works arranged under six section headings,- 正 集
    - 續 集 - 廣 集 - 普 集 - 彙 集 - 眉 公 雜 著 ; separate
    lists for each of the 6 sections.
Bound in 6 t'so 48 ts'ê (8 each).

Remarks - an ordinary edition; the item is new.

Accession No. 635   Index No. - 032-rizh   141-gljd

Title   " Hsüan-wu-shan-kuan wên chi "
                    㙔 務 山 館 文 集
                   " Yü Tê-yüan hsien-shêng chi "
                    虞 德 園 先 生 集

Classification - D-43 別 集 一 文
Subject - an individual collection of prose.

References - 012-zafk 16/35.

Author - (著) Yü Shun-hsi 虞 淳 熙 .

Edition - that of Huang Ju-hêng 黃 汝 亨 and others; (preface)
    dated T'ien-Ch'i "kuei-hai" 3/1623.   Blocks; bamboo paper.

Index - a detailed table of contents for 25 chüan arranged according
    to subjects.

Bound in 1 t'ao 6 ts'ê.

Remarks - according to 012-zafk this item should contain 8 chüan
    more on poetic writings; but this edition does not.   The item
    is in good condition.

———•———

Accession No. **636**   Index No. — **140-zcj**   **140-fcj**

Title   " **Ts'ao tzŭ hui** "

艸 (艸) 字 彙

Classification — **A-161** 小 學 一 字 書

Subject — (Gest No. 1735) "a collection of examples of the characters

as written in the "grass", or running-hand, form."

References — Gest No. 1735.

Author — (集) Shih Liang 石 梁 .

Edition — the "Ching-i-chai" 敬 義 齋 ; dated Ch'ien-Lung "mou-shên"

53/1788.   Blocks; "fên" paper.

Index — none; in 12 sections.

Bound in 1 t'ao 4 ts'ê.

Remarks — the item is complete and in perfect condition.

The University of Toronto Chinese Library

Accession No. 637   Index No. - 140-fjj1

Title   " Ts'ao yün hui pien "
             草 韻 彙 編

Classification - A-161 小學 一字書

Subject - (Gest No. 1745) "a collection of examples of the 'grass-hand'
    forms of the characters."

References - Gest No. 1745.

Author - (手輯) T'ao Nan-wang 陶 南 望 .

Edition - no notation; (preface) dated Ch'ien-Lung 20/1755.   Blocks;
    bamboo paper.

Index - for 26 chüan, arranged in the usual manner according to the
    tones and rhymes.

Bound in 1 t'ao 10 ts's.

Remarks - a very good edition; the item appears to be complete and
    is in good condition.

—•—

Accession No. 638   Index No. - 085-1hez

Title   " Chan-jan chü-shih chi "
                 湛 然 居 士 集

Classification - D-33 別集 - 詩文

Subject - an individual literary collection,- prose and poetry.

References - 160-1j   163-ggcz 14/1   031-bgld 17/1   030-iaff 33/3

   106-gdkn 94/20   012-zafk 16/1   031-bgdf 166/8.

Author - (撰) Yeh-lü Ch'u-ts'ai 耶 律 楚 材.

Edition - the "Chien-hsi-ts'un-shê" 漸 西 村 舍; (preface) dated

   "chia-wu" 1894.   Blocks; "fen" paper.

Index - separate tables of contents at the beginning of each of 14

   chüan.

Bound in 1 t'ao 6 ts'ê; singly interleaved.

Remarks - the item is in good condition and complete.

Accession No. 639   Index No. - 140-ezzd

Title   " Mao Lu-mên hsien-shêng wên chi "
                  茅 鹿 門 先 生 文 集

Classification - D-43 列 集 - 文
Subject - an individual miscellaneous collection of prose.

References - 012-zafk 16/26.

Author - (著) Mao K'un 茅 坤 .

Edition - no particular notation; (preface) dated Wan-Li "mou-tzŭ"
       16/1588.   Blocks; bamboo paper.

Index - a table of contents for 36 chüan, arranged according to
       subject matter.

Bound in 2 t'ao 12 ts's (6-6).

Remarks - a fairly good edition; the item is complete.

The University of Toronto Chinese Library

Accession No. 640   Index No. - 053-hkzd   041-kzd

Title   " K'ang Tui-shan hsien-shêng wên chi "
　　　　　康　對　山　先　生　文　集
　　　　　　" Tui-shan chi "
　　　　　　對　山　集

Classification - D-33 別 集 - 詩 文

Subject - an individual literary collection,- prose and poetry.

References - 163-ggcz 15/7   031-bgld 18/23   012-zafk 16/21
　　031-bgdf 171/34.

Author - (撰) K'ang Hai 康 海 .

Edition - that of Sun Ching-lieh 孫 景 烈 ; dated Ch'ien-Lung
　　"hsin-ssǔ" 26/1761.   Blocks; "fên" paper.

Index - a general table of contents for 10 chüan.

Bound in 1 t'ao 6 ts'ê; doubly interleaved.

Remarks - the item is complete and in perfect condition.

124

Accession No. 641   Index No. 096-zhif

Title   " Yü t'ai hsin yung chien chu "

玉　臺　新　詠　箋　註

Classification - D-68 總集一詩

Subject- a collection of commentaries and notes on "Yü t'ai hsin yung",-
being a selection of poems of scholars prior to the Liang Dynasty.

References- to the original work,- 160-1j   163-ggcz 16/1   031-bgld 19/3
030-iaff 38/4   037-ahhg 3/36   167-mhfm 23/4   106-gdkn 12/4   (#)

Author - (編) Hsü Ling 徐 陵 ; (原 注) Wu Chao-i 吳 兆 宜 ;
(刪補) Ch'êng Yen 程 琰 .

Edition - the "Tao-hsiang-lou" 稻 香 樓 ; dated Ch'ien-Lung "chia-wu"
39/1774.   Blocks; "mao-pien" paper.

Index - a detailed table of contents for 10 chüan.

Bound in 2 t'ao 12 ts'ê; doubly interleaved.

Remarks- a fairly good edition; the item is in perfect condition.

(#) 012-zafk 19/1   031-bgdf 186/7   to this work,- 031-bgdf
191/9.

———•———

Accession No. 642   Index No. - 195-fhgd

Title   " Chi-ch'i ting chi "
                   鮚 埼 亭 集

Classification - D-33 別集 - 詩文
Subject - an individual literary collection,- prose and poetry.

References - 160-1j   012-zafk 17/26   Toronto No. 547.

Author - (撰) Ch'üan Tsu-wang 全 祖 望 ; (校) Shih Mêng-chiao
         史 夢 蛟 .

Edition - the "Chieh-shu-shan-fang" 借 樹 山 房; no date.
          Blocks; bamboo paper.

Index - a detailed table of contents for 38 chüan.

Bound in 1 t'ao 12 ts'ê.

Remarks - a duplicate of No. 547; and the item is in very good
          condition.   This item does not contain either of the 2
          supplements mentioned in 012-zafk.

The University of Toronto Chinese Library

Accession No. **643**   Index No. - **212-zjdd**   **212-zjzd**

Title   " <u>Lung-ch'i ch'üan chi</u> "
龍 谿 全 集

" <u>Lung-ch'i Wang hsien-shêng ch'üan chi</u> "
龍 谿 王 先 生 全 集

Classification - D-33 列集 - 詩文

Subject - an individual collection of prose and poetry.

References - 012-zafk 16/25   031-bgdf 177/37   Cest No. 617.

Author - (撰) <u>Wang Ch'i</u> 王 畿 ; <u>Ting Pin</u> 丁 賓 .

Edition - that of <u>Hsiao Liang-kan</u> 蕭 良 幹 ; (preface) dated Wan-Li
"ting-hai" 15/1587.   Blocks; bamboo paper.

Index - a table of contents for 22 chüan. (chüan 21-22 being of a
supplementary nature).

Bound in 1 t'ao 12 ts'ê.

Remarks - the edition is a very good one; and the item is complete
and with no defects.

Accession No. 644-a   Index No. = 002-czzd

Title   " Chung-shan wên ch'ao "
                 中　山　文　鈔

Classification = D-43 別集 - 文
Subject = an individual collection of prose.

References = none.

Author = (著) Ho Yü 郝浴.

Edition = no notation; no date.   Blocks; bamboo paper.

Index = a table of contents for 4 chüan.

Bound in 2 ts's in 1 t'ao with (b), (c) and (d).

Remarks = an ordinary edition; the item is complete and without
    defects except a few worm-holes.

Accession No. 644-b   Index No. - 002-czfd

Title   " Chung-shan shih ch'ao "
中　山　詩　鈔

Classification - D-38 別集一詩
Subject - an individual collection of poetry.

References - none.

Author - (著) Ho Yü 郝浴.

Edition - uniform with (a).

Index - a table of contents for 4 chüan.

Bound in 2 ts's in 1 t'ao with (a), (c) and (d).

Remarks - as under (a).

Accession No. 644-c   Index No. - 002-czfm

Title   " Chung-shan tsou-i "
中 山 奏 議

Classification - B-72 詔令奏議 一 奏議
Subject - a collection of memorials.

References - none.

Author - (著) Ho Yü 郝浴 .

Edition - uniform with (a).

Index - a table of contents for 4 chüan.

Bound in 2 ts's in 1 t'ao with (b), (b) and (d).

Remarks - as under (a).

Accession No. **644-d**   Index No. **002-czbh**

Title   " **Chung-shan shih lun** "
中　山　史　論

Classification - B-357 史 評

Subject - discourses on Chinese history from ancient times down to
and including the Ming Dynasty.

References - none.

Author - (著) **Ho Yü** 郝 浴 .

Edition - uniform with (a).

Index - a table of contents for 2 chüan 上 下 .

Bound in 2 ts's in 1 t'ao with (a), (b) and (c).

Remarks - as under (a).

Accession No. 645   Index No. - 030-ghbe

Title   " T'ang hsien san mei chi chien chu "
               唐 賢 三 昧 集 箋 註

Classification - D-68 總集 - 詩

Subject - a collection of poems of the T'ang Dynasty; with
   annotations and marginal notes.

References - 163-ggcz 16/10   031-bgld 19/35   012-zafk 19/16
   031-bgdf 190/24   Gest No. 1500   Toronto No. 99.

Author - (選) Wang Shih-chêng 王 士 禎; (輯 註) Wu Hsüan 吳 煊
   and Hu T'ang 胡 棠.

Edition - reprinted by the "Han-mo-yüan" 翰 墨 園 ; dated Kuang-Hsü
   9/1883.   Blocks; "fên" paper.

Index - a list of authors, in 3 chüan.

Bound in 1 t'ao 6 ts'ê; doubly interleaved.

Remarks - a fairly good edition; the item is complete and as new.

Accession No. 646　　　　　　Index No. - 072-gzfp

Title　　　　　" Ch'ên-fêng-ko ts'ung shu "
　　　　　　　晨　風　閣　叢　書

Classification - C-338 雜家 一 叢書

Subject - a collection of 22 reprints of works on a variety of
　　subjects.

References - 029-pffz 366　Gest No. 1123.

Author - compiled by Shên Tsung-chi 沈 宗 畸.

Edition - that of the author; dated Hsüan-T'ung 1/1909.　Blocks;
　　"fên" paper.

Index - a list of the 22 works.

Bound in 2 t'ao 16 ts's (8-8).

Remarks - the item is new.

133

The University of Toronto Chinese Library

Accession No. 647   Index No. - 194-zzz

Title   " Kuei-ku-tzŭ "

鬼 谷 子

Classification - C-308 雜家 一 雜文

Subject - a philosophical miscellany of a semi-political character
and tinged with Taoist notations; with annotations.

References - 160-1j   163-ggcz 10/1   031-bgld 13/3   030-iaff 18/15
106-gdkn 53/3   012-zafk 12/13   031-bgdf 117/12   Toronto No. 73-a.

Author - (注) T'ao Hung-ching 陶 宏 景 ．

Edition - the "Ch'in-shih" 秦 氏 ; dated Chia-Ch'ing 10/1805.
Blocks; "fên" paper.

Index - none; 3 chüan; 篇 目 考 1 chüan; 附 録 1 chüan.

Bound in 1 t'ao 2 ts'ê; doubly interleaved with margins.

Remarks - this item is in very good condition and is complete.

Accession No. **648**   Index No. - **156-gzgb**   **075-dccd**

Title   " Chao Wên-min kung Sung-hsüeh-chai ch'üan chi "

趙 文 敏 公 松 雪 齋 全 集

" Sung-hsüeh-chai chi "

松 雪 齋 集

Classification - D-**85** 別 集 一 詩 文

Subject - an individual collection of prose and poetry.

References - 160-1j 163-ggcz 14/2 031-bgld 17/5 037-ahhg (hsü) 11/11

167-mhfm 22/4 106-gdkn 96/6 012-zafk 16/2 031-bgdf 166/36

Author - (撰) Chan Mêng-fu 趙 孟 頫 ; (校) Ts'ao P'ei-lien

曹 培 廉.

Edition - the "Ch'êng-shu-shih" 城 書 室 ; dated Kuang-Hsü 8/1882.

Blocks; bamboo paper.

Index - a table of contents for 10 chüan; 外 集 1 chüan; 續 集

1 chüan.

Bound in 1 t'ao 6 ts'ê.

Remarks - an ordinary edition; complete and in good condition.

Accession No. 649   Index No. - 167-zdib

Title   " Chin Chung-chieh kung wên chi "
               金 忠 節 公 文 集

Classification - D-43 列 集 一 文
Subject - an individual collection of prose.

References - 012-zafk 16/39.

Author - (撰) Chin Shêng 金 聲 ; (編 次) Shao Jang 邵 勷 .

Edition - the "Chia-yü-kuan-shu" 嘉 魚 官 署; dated Tao-Kuang
         "ting-hai" 7/1827.   Blocks; "fên" paper.

Index - a table of contents for 8 chüan.

Bound in 1 t'ao 4 ts'ê.

Remarks - a fairly good edition; complete and in perfect condition.

Accession No. 650   Index No. - 198-hkpf

Title   " Li lou ts'ung shu "
                麗 廔 叢 書

Classification - C-338 雜家 一 叢書
Subject - a collection of reprints of 9 miscellaneous works.

References - 029-pffz 572   Gest No. 2259.

Author - (刊) Yeh Shih 葉氏。

Edition,- that of the author; dated Kuang-Hsü "ting-wei" 35/1909.
        Blocks; "fên" paper.

Index - a list of the 9 works with names of the authors etc.

Bound in 1 t'ao 8 ts's.

Remarks - a modern edition. The item is new. 029-pffz as well as
        the Gest catalogue all mention this item as containing 8 works,
        of which 7 are in this work with 2 additional ones. This is
        undoubtedly a revised edition of a later date, as the index page
        contains the characters,- 己 未 重 編。

Accession No. 651   Index No. - 212-zfef

Title   " Lung wei pi shu "
                          龍 威 秘 書

Classification - C-338 雜 家 - 叢 書

Subject - (Gest No. 1535) "a general collection of reprints covering
    many subjects of a miscellaneous character."

References - 012-zafk 13/15   029-pffz 546   058-jffz 6/46
    Gest Nos. 17 and 1535.

Author - compiled by Ma Chün-liang 馬 俊 良.

Edition - no definite notation; apparently privately published by Ma;
    (title-page of 2d chi) dated Chia-Ch'ing 1/1796.   Blocks;
    "fên" paper.

Index - a general table of contents at the beginning of each "chi"
    for the 8 ts's contained therein; and a detailed list of contents
    at the beginning of each ts's. (last "chi" excepted)
Bound in 10 t'ao 80 ts's (8 each).

Remarks - an ordinary edition of a small size; the item appears to be
    complete and is without defects.

Accession No. 652   Index No. - 007-zbd

Title   " Erh-ch'ü chi "
                        二　曲　集

Classification - D-43 別集 - 文
Subject - an individual comprehensive literary collection,- prose.

References - 012-zafk 17/5.

Author - (撰) Li Yung 李 顒 .

Edition - reprinted by P'êng Mao-ch'ien 彭 懋 謙 ; dated Kuang-Hsü
      3/1877.   Blocks; "fên" paper.

Index - a general table of contents for 46 chüan.

Bound in 2 t'ao 16 ts's (8-8).

Remarks - this is a fairly good modern edition; and the item is
      complete and as new. The number of chüan as given in 012-zafk
      is only 22.

The University of Toronto Chinese Library

Accession No. 653   Index No. - 169-gjfh   120-olid

Title   " Yüan-wei-ts'ao-t'ang pi chi "
            閱　微　草　堂　筆　記

        " Chi Hsiao-lan hsien-shêng pi chi "
            紀　曉　嵐　先　生　筆　記

Classification - C-368 小 說 家

Subject - five collections of notes and jottings on a variety of

    subjects.

References - 012-zafk 14/10   Gest No. 3646   Toronto No. 31.

Author - (撰) Kuan-i tao jên 觀 弈 道 人 i.e. Chi Yün 紀 昀 .

Edition - the "Wang-i-shu-wu" 望 益 書 屋 ; dated Chia-Ch'ing

    "kêng-shên" 5/1800.   Blocks; "fên" paper.

Index - a general table of contents for the 5 collections in 24 chüan.

Bound in 1 t'ao 10 ts'ê.

Remarks - an ordinary edition; the item is complete and without defects.

    A duplicate of Toronto No. 31.

Accession No. 654   Index No. - 075-ilde   075-iede   075-bzbi

Title   " Ch'u-tz'ŭ chi chu "
                楚 辭 (詞) 集 注
            " Chu Wên-kung Ch'u-tz'ŭ chi chu "
                朱 文 公 楚 辭 集 注

Classification - D-14 楚 辭

Subject - (Gest No. 2239) "a collection of (84) commentaries on the
    work generally known (in English) as the 'Elegies of Ch'u';
    being a collection of poems of a semi-historical nature,
    referring to the kingdom of Ch'u."

References - Wylie's Notes page 226 160-1j 163-ggoz 12/1 031-bgld
    15/1 037-ahhg(hsü) 6/1 167-mhfm 19/1 030-iaff 23/1 (#)

Author - (集註) Chu Hsi 朱 熹 .

Edition - the "T'ing-yü-chai" 聽 雨 齋 ; no date.   Blocks; "fên"
    paper.

Index - a general table of contents for 8 chüan.

Bound in 1 t'ao 2 ts's.

Remarks- a good edition; the item is in perfect condition.   This item,
    however, does not contain the two supplementary works - 辨 證 and
    後 語 as mentioned in the catalogues.

    (#) 106-gdkn 67/1 012-zafk 15/1 031-bgdf 148/7 Gest Nos.
    580 and 2239.

———•———

Accession No. 655   Index No. – 067-zlgl

Title   " Wên hsüan pu i "
                   文　選　補　遺

Classification – D-63 總集 – 詩文
Subject – a general selection of prose and poetry of ancient scholars;
   being supplementary to the well-known work,– "Wên hsüan".

References – 163-ggcz 16/5   031-bgld 19/16   037-ahhg 10/40
   106-gdkn 115/2   012-zafk 19/5   031-bgdf 187/37   Gest No. 302.

Author – (編) Ch'ên Jên-tzŭ 陳 仁 子.

Edition – the 湖 南 edition; dated Tao-Kuang 25/1845.   Blocks;
   "mao-pien" paper.

Index – a classified table of contents for 40 chüan with the names of
   the authors.

Bound in 2 t'ao 12 ts'ê (6-6).

Remarks – an ordinary edition; complete and without defects.

Accession No. **656**   Index No. - **007-bzgz**

Title   " **Wu ta chia wên ch'ao** "

五　大　家　文　鈔　粹

Classification - **D-73** 總 集 一 文

Subject - a collection of prose compositions of five noted scholars

of the **Ming** and **Ch'ing** dynasties.

References - **none.**

Author - (選 刊) **Hsü Tê-li** 徐 德 立.

Edition - the "**Hsü's Shih-kêng-shan-fang**" 徐 氏 石 耕 山 房; dated

Kuang-Hsü "ping-wu" 32/1906.   Blocks; "mao-pien" paper.

Index - none for the collection; separate list of contents for the

work of each author.

Bound in 1 t'ao 5 ts's.

Remarks - an ordinary edition; the item is complete and in perfect

condition.   The 5 works are :-

(#)

(#) " Chên-ch'uan wên sui "   (175-gzzh)
     震 川 文 粹   D-43

     by Kuei Yu-kuang 歸有光

     " Ching-ch'uan wên sui "   (140-fzzh)
     荆 川 文 粹   D-43

     by T'ang Shun-chih 唐順之

     " Tsun-yen wên sui "   (162-ltzh)
     遵 巖 文 粹   D-43

     by Wang Shên-chung 王慎中

     " Yao-fêng wên sui "   (032-igzh)
     堯 峯 文 粹   D-43

     by Wang Yüan 汪琬

     " Wang-hsi wên sui "   (074-gjzh)
     望 溪 文 粹   D-43

     by Fang Pao 方苞

144

Accession No. 657   Index No. - 067-zjcj   067-zjd

Title   " Wên-hsi ts'un kao "
                    文 溪 存 彙
                    " Wên-hsi chi "
                    文 溪 集

Classification - D-33 別 集 一 詩 文

Subject - an individual literary collection,- prose and poetry.

References - 163-ggcz 13/20   031-bgld 16/32   012-zafk 15/30

    031-bgdf 164/2.

Author - (撰) Li Mao-ying 李 昴 英.

Edition - the "Li-chiu-yüan-t'ang" 李 久 遠 堂 ; dated Kuang-Hsü
    23/1897.   Blocks; "fên" paper.

Index - a general table of contents for 卷 首 and 20 chüan.

Bound in 1 t'ao 4 ts's.

Remarks - an ordinary edition; the item is almost new.

Accession No. 658   Index No. - 055-azbc   007-zzzb

Title   " Nien-i shih yüeh pien "
                   廿 一 史 約 編

                   " Erh-shih-i shih yüeh pien "
                   二 十 一 史 約 編

Classification - B-137 史 鈔
Subject - a condensed version of the twenty-one official dynastic

    histories of China; that is, from ancient times up to the end

    of the Yüan Dynasty; together with an additional chapter on

    matters of the Ming Dynasty.

References - 012-zafk 5/29   Toronto Nos. 368 and 421.

Author - (述) Cheng Yüan-ch'ing 鄭 元 慶 ; (鑒定) Ch'en Ch'ü-shih

    陳 瞿 石 .

Edition - the "Yü-chi-t'ing" 魚 計 亭 ; (preface) dated "ping-tzǔ"

    (? Ch'ien-Lung 21/1756).   Blocks; bamboo paper.

Index - a general table of contents for a leading chüan and 8 "pu" 部 .

Bound in 1 t'ao 8 ts'ê.

Remarks - a good edition; the item is complete and in fairly good

    condition.   The last 6 pages in the section 竹部 are for the

    most part handwritten, and appear to have been very badly damaged

    before they were repaired.

146

The University of Toronto Chinese Library

Accession No. 659   Index No. - 030-edg

Title   " Shên yin yü "
          呻 吟 語

Classification - C-13 儒家
Subject - a treatise on mental philosophy and conduct.

References - 160-lj   012-zafk 10/7   031-bgdf 96/29   Toronto Nos.
    38 and 498.

Author - (著) Lü K'un 呂坤 .

Edition - reprinted by "Lo-shih" of Nan-hai 南 海 羅 氏 ; (preface)
    dated Kuang-Hsü "mou-hsü" 24/1898.   Blocks; "mao-pien" paper.

Index - a table of contents for 6 chüan divided into 2 p'ien (内 外);
    附 錄 1 chüan.

Bound in 1 t'ao 4 ts'ê.

Remarks - an ordinary edition; the item is in very good condition
    and is complete.   A duplicate of Toronto Nos. 38 and 498.

Accession No. 660   Index No. - 009-ezge

Title   " Tso wên chia fa "

作 文 家 法

Classification - D-153 學 校 讀 本

Subject - a concise treatise on the rules of composition writing;-

construction; style etc.

References - none.

Author - (手著) Wu Tzŭ-su 吳 自 肅.

Edition - privately published; dated Ch'ien-Lung "ping-wu" 51/1786.

Blocks; "fên" paper.

Index - none; complete in 1 chüan.

Bound in 1 t'ao 2 ts'ê; doubly interleaved.

Remarks - this work was apparently written for use by some private

schools, and does not seem to have ever come into general use.

The item appears to be complete and is without defects.

———•———

Accession No. 661   Index No. - 120-czib

Title   " Chi Wên-ta kung i chi "
               紀 文 達 公 遺 集

Classification - D-33 別 集 - 詩 文
Subject - an individual collection of prose and poetry.

References - 012-zafk 17/34   Toronto No. 592.

Author - (撰) Chi Yün 紀 昀.

Edition - no particular notation; (preface) dated Chia-Ch'ing 10/1805.
    Blocks; "fên" paper.   1812?

Index - a detailed table of contents (prose) for 16 chüan; a detailed
    table of contents (poems) for 16 chüan.

Bound in 2 t'ao 18 ts'ê (8-10).

Remarks - a duplicate of Toronto No. 592.   The item is complete and
    in very good condition.

Accession No. 662   Index No. – 075–mzpf

Title   " T'an chi ts'ung shu "
               檀　几　叢　書

Classification – C–338 雜家 – 叢書
Subject – a collection of miscellaneous reprints.

References – 029–pffz 558   012–zafk 13/13   031–bgdf 134/26.

Author – (輯) Wang Cho 王 暐 ; (校) Chang Ch'ao 張 潮.

Edition – the "Hsia–chü–t'ang" 霞 舉 堂 ; (preface) dated K'ang–Hsi
          "i–hai" 34/1695.   Blocks; "fen" paper.

Index – (一 集) a list of works in 50 chüan; (二 集) same for
        50 chüan; (餘 集) for 2 chüan (上 下).

Bound in 2 t'ao 16 ts's (8–8).

Remarks – an ordinary edition; and the item is in good condition.

150

The University of Toronto Chinese Library

Accession No. 663   Index No. - 077-jcbc   077-lcbc

Title   " Li tai shih piao "
               歴 代 史 表

Classification - B-42 別 史

Subject - historical tabulations of emperors, princes, statesmen,
    important events etc covering the period from the Eastern
    Han Dynasty 東 漢 down to the Five Dynasties 五 代.

References - 160-1j   163-ggcz 4/12   031-bgld 5/33   012-zafk 4/16
    031-bgdf 50/33   Gest No. 95.

Author - (撰) Wan Ssŭ-t'ung 萬 斯 同.

Edition - the "Kuang-ya-shu-chü"; dated Kuang-Hsü 15/1889.   Blocks;
    "mao-pien" paper.

Index - a general table of contents for 59 chüan.

Bound in 1 t'ao 12 ts's.

Remarks - an ordinary edition; the item is complete and without
    defects.

151

The University of Toronto Chinese Library

Accession No. 664   Index No. - 002-cg

Title   " Chung   shuo "
                          中   説

Classification - C-13 儒 家

Subject - (Gest No. 2384) "a philosophical work of a political
    nature, on somewhat the same lines as the "Lün-Yü" 論 語 ;
    with annotations."

References - 160-1j 163-ggcz 7/2 031-bgld 9/5 106-gdkn 39/10
    012-zafk 10/2 031-bgdf 91/24 Gest Nos. 313-339(4)-381-2384
    Toronto Nos. 204 and 281.

Author - Wang T'ung 王 通 ; (注) Yüan I 阮 逸 .

Edition - the "Ching-jên-t'ang" 敬 忍 堂; no date; apparently
    of the Ming period.   Blocks; "fên" paper.

Index - a table of contents; 10 chüan.

Bound in 1 t'ao 4 ts'ê; doubly interleaved.

Remarks - a very good edition; the item is complete and without
    defects.   Pages 23 to 30 in chüan 10 are handwritten.

The University of Toronto Chinese Library

Accession No. 665   Index No. - 031-bfzd

Title   " Ssŭ shu i kuan chiang "
                 四 書 一 貫 講

Classification - A-131 四 書

Subject - an explanation and commentary on the "Four Books".

References - none to this particular work.

Author - (著) Ku T'ien-chien 顧 天 健；(鑒) Lu Chia-shu 陸 稼 書
    and Lu Hao-an 陸 蒿 菴．

Edition - the "Ch'i-hou-t'ang" 啟 後 堂；(preface) dated Ch'ien-Lung
    29/1764.   Blocks; bamboo paper.

Index - a general table of contents for (論 語) 10 chüan; (大 學)
    1 chüan; (中 庸) 1 chüan; and (孟 子) 7 chüan.

Bound in 2 t'ao 8 ts's.

Remarks - an ordinary edition; the item is complete.

Accession No. 666   Index No. - 075-dedh

Title   " Tung Chou lieh kuo chih "
东　周　列　国　志

Classification - C-368 小 说 家

Subject - (Wylie) "----- written in the form of a novel, differs
less from authentic history probably than any other in the
same category.   It embraces the period when China was divided
into a great many tributary states, and extends from the 8th
to the 3rd century B. C. when the Tsin dynasty was established."

References - Wylie's Notes page 203.

Author - (评 点) Ts'ai Hao 蔡 昊 .

Edition - the "Shu-ch'êng-shan-fang" 书 成 山 房; dated Hsien-Fêng
4/1854.   Blocks; "mao-pien" paper.

Index - a general table of contents for 108 "hui" 回 in 23 chapters.

Bound in 2 t'ao 12 ts'ê (6-6).

Remarks - an ordinary edition; the item is complete and in good
condition.

154

Accession No.　667　　　　　Index No. - 123-gzof

Title　　　　　" I-mên tu shu chi "
　　　　　　　義 門 讀 書 記

Classification - C-308 雜 家 － 雜 文

Subject - discussions and critical commentaries on a collection of
　　classical, historical and other standard works.

References - 160-1j　163-ggcz 10/5　031-bgld 13/14　012-zafk 12/22
　　031-bgdf 119/24.

Author - (撰) Ho Ch'ao 何 焯 ; (編) Chiang Wei-chün 蔣 維 鈞.

Edition - no particular notation; (preface) dated Ch'ien-Lung 34/1769.
　　Blocks; "mao-pien" paper.

Index - a list of 18 works with the number of chüan for each; 58 chüan
　　in all.

Bound in 2 t'ao 12 ts'ê.

Remarks - the item is without defects and complete.

Accession No. 668   Index No. - 039-mf

Title   " Hsüeh t'ung "
                                  學   統

Classification - B-117 傳記 一 總 録

Subject - a collection of biographies of famous philosophers and
    scholars of various dynasties beginning with Confucius and
    ending with scholars of the Ming Dynasty.

References - 012-zafk 5/16   031-bgdf 63/18.

Author - (撰) Hsiung Tz'ü-li 熊 賜 履.

Edition - no particular notation; (preface) dated K'ang-Hsi "i-ch'ou"
    24/1685.   Blocks; "fên" paper.

Index - a list of names for 53 chüan.

Bound in 2 t'ao 16 ts's.

Remarks - a good edition.   The item appears to be complete and is
    in good condition except for some stains and a few worm-holes
    which have been repaired.

The University of Toronto Chinese Library

Accession No. 669   Index No. - 106-azzc

Title   " <u>Po   tzŭ   chin   tan</u> "
                百   子   金   丹

Classification - C-328 雜家 - 雜纂
Subject - extracts from miscellaneous works covering the period from
    the <u>Chou Dynasty</u> down to the <u>Ming Dynasty</u>; with annotations.

References - 031-bgdf 132/34.

Author - (選註) <u>Kuo Wei</u> 郭 偉 ; (校訂) <u>Wang Hsing-chü</u> 王星聚

Edition - the "<u>Pan-chu-chü</u>" 版 築 居 ; no date.   Blocks; bamboo
    paper.

Index - a detailed classified table of contents for 10 chüan.

Bound in 1 t'ao 12 ts's.

Remarks - a fairly good edition; the item appears to be complete
    and is in good condition.   This edition seems to be a Ming
    one; but there is no date to identify it.

Accession No.   670   Index No. - 030-bnb1

Title   " Shih tsuan tso pien "
                      史 纂 左 編

Classification - B-137 史鈔

Subject - a collection of historical records; mainly selected
    from the official dynastic histories of China; and the period
    covered being from the Han Dynasty down to the Yüan Dynasty.

References - 012-zafk 5/28   031-bgdf 65/12   Gest No. 374.

Author - (編輯) T'ang Shun-chih 唐 順 之.

Edition - a Ming edition; (hou-hsü) dated Chia-Ching 40/1561.
    Blocks; "mien" paper.

Index - a table of contents for 142 chüan arranged under 24 categories.

Bound in 10 t'ao 100 ts'ê (10 each).

Remarks - a number of the ts'ê are with worm-holes both at the
    beginning and at the end. Pages 41-51 in chüan 50; 1-7
    in chüan 118; and page 24 in chüan 131 contain repaired
    defects, but the missing characters are not filled in.
    6 ts'ê containing chüan 7-8-61-62-63-64 are replacements
    from a different copy.

The University of Toronto Chinese Library

Accession No. 671   Index No. - 149-gg

Title   " Shuo fu "
说 郛

Classification - C-328 雜家 一 雜纂

Subject - a collection of copious extracts from a large number of
works on all classes of literature.

References - Wylie's Notes page 170 160-1j 163-ggcz 10/11
031-bgld 13/30 012-zafk 13/4 031-bgdf 123/21 Gest No. 898.

Author - （纂）Tao Tsung-i 陶 宗 儀 ；（校正）Kung Fu 龔 鈇．

Edition - the "Han-fên-lou" 涵 芬 樓 ; dated Min-Kuo 16/1927.
Type; "mao-pien" paper.

Index - a list of works for 100 chüan.

Bound in 4 t'ao 40 ts's (10 each).

Remarks - a modern edition; the item is new. This edition is
based upon the Ming manuscript copy and is therefore different
from those described in the catalogues, both in the number of
chüan and in the contents.

The University of Toronto Chinese Library

Accession No. 672   Index No. - 031-hg

Title   " Kuo yü "
                           國 語

Classification - B-52 雜史

Subject - a collection of historical narratives of the various states
    during the Ch'un-Ch'iu period (722-481 B.C.); each state being
    treated separately; with commentary.

References - Wylie's Notes page 7 160-lj 165-ggcz 4/13 031-bgld 5/34
    167-mhfm 9/20 030-iaff 8/1 012-zafk 4/17 031-bgdf 51/1 Gest
    Nos. 713 and 887.

Author - Tso-ch'iu Ming 左 邱 明; (解) Wei Chao 韋 昭 .

Edition - the "Ch'ung-wên-shu-chü" 崇 文 書 局; dated T'ung-Chih
    "chi-ssǔ" 8/1869.   Blocks; "mao-pien" paper.

Index - none; in 21 chüan; 札 記 1 chüan.

Bound in 1 t'ao 5 ts'ê.

Remarks - an ordinary edition; the item is complete and without
    defects.   The following is a supplement:-
                " Kuo yü k'ao i "
                國 語 攷 異
                                        (031-hgbg)
                                        4 chüan

        by Wang Yüan-sun 汪 遠 孫 .

160

Accession No. 673   Index No.- 033-zmez   201-zzpf

Title   " Shih-li-chü Huang-shih ts'ung shu "
               士 禮 居 黃 氏 叢 書

Classification - C-338 雜家 - 叢書

Subject - a collection of 20 reprints of a miscellaneous character.

References - 012-zafk 13/15   029-pffz 122.

Author - (編) Huang P'ei-lieh 黃 丕 烈.

Edition - the "Fei-ying-kuan" 蜚 英 館 ; dated Kuang-Hsü "ting-hai"
         13/1887.   Lithographed on "fên" paper.

Index - a list of the 20 works.

Bound in 1 t'ao 30 ts'ê (7-7-8-8).

Remarks - an ordinary edition; the item is without defects.   The
         index at the beginning of the work gives 24 titles, but 4 of
         them were not published.

Accession No. 674   Index No. - 106-dhgd

Title   " Huang ch'ao ching shih wên pien "
               皇　朝　經　世　文　編

Classification - D-73 總集 - 文

Subject - a comprehensive general collection of prose compositions
    written by scholars of the Ch'ing dynasty.

References - 012-zafk 19/31.

Author - (輯) Ho Ch'ang-ling 賀 長 齡.

Edition - the "Shuang-fêng-shu-wu" 雙 峰 書 屋; dated T'ung-Chih
    "kuei-yu" 12/1873.   Blocks; "fên" paper.

Index - a table of contents (classifications) for 120 chüan; separate
    detailed list for each class.

Bound in 8 t'ao 72 ts's. (9 each).

Remarks - an ordinary edition; complete and without defects.

Accession No. 675   Index No. - 106-dhgd

Title   " Huang ch'ao ching shih wên hsü pien "
皇　朝　經　世　文　續　編

Classification - D-73 總集 - 文

Subject - a general collection of prose compositions by Ch'ing
Dynasty scholars; being supplementary to Toronto No. 674.

References - 012-zafk 19/38.

Author - (輯) Ko Shih-chün 葛 士 濬.

Edition - the "Sao-yeh-shan-fang" 掃 葉 山 房; dated Kuang-Hsü
"ting-yu" 23/1897.   Type; "fan" paper.

Index - a classified table of contents for 120 chüan.

Bound in 2 t'ao 24 ts'ê (12-12).

Remarks - a very ordinary edition; the item is complete.

Accession No. 676　　　　　Index No. - 075-egzd

Title　　　　　" Po-chien-shan-fang chi "
　　　　　　　　柏　視　山　房　集

Classification - D-33 別 集 - 詩 文
Subject - an individual literary collection,- prose and poetry.

References - 012-zafk 18/14.

Author - (撰) Mei Tsêng-liang 梅 曾 亮.

Edition - no particular notation; dated Hsien-Fêng 6/1856.　Blocks;
　　"fên" paper.

Index - (文 集) a table of contents for 16 chüan and 續 集 1 chüan;
　　(詩 集) same for 10 chüan and 續 集 2 chüan; 駢 體 文 2 chüan.

Bound in 1 t'ao 8 ts'ê.

Remarks - an ordinary edition; the item is complete.　Page 5 of the
　　8th ts'ê is slightly defective.

Accession No. 677   Index No. - 030-bcbi   163-11dd

Title   " Shih chi nei pien "
                史 記 内 編
            " Têng Chêng-chün hsien-shêng p'i tien shih chi "
                鄧 徵 君 先 生 批 點 史 記

Classification - B-367 史 評

Subject - a commentary on selected portions of the "Shih chi",-
    the official history of China from the ancient times up to
    122 B. C.

References - none.

Author - (著) Ssŭ-ma Ch'ien 司馬遷 ; (選 評) Têng Yüan-hsi
    鄧 元 錫 .

Edition - privately published; (preface) dated Ch'ung-Chêng "chia-hsü"
    7/1634.   Blocks; bamboo paper.

Index - a table of contents for 15 chüan.

Bound in 4 t'ao 24 ts'ê; doubly interleaved.

Remarks - a very good edition; the item is complete and without
    defects with the exception that pages 70-73 in chüan 1 are
    handwritten.

Accession No. 678   Index No. - 178-hzce

Title   " Han-tzŭ yŭ p'ing "
                        韓 子 迂 評

Classification - C-43 法 家

Subject - a commentary on "Han-tzŭ",- a well-known ancient legal
     work.

References - 012-zafk 10/17   031-bgdf 101/14   Gest No. 703.

Author - (評) Mên-wu-tzŭ 門 無 子.

Edition - a Ming edition; dated Wan-Li "chi-mao" 7/1579.   Blocks;
     "mien" paper.

Index - a table of contents for 20 chüan; 附 錄 6 p'ien.

Bound in 2 t'ao 10 ts'e (5-5); doubly interleaved.

Remarks - a good edition; the item is complete, but it has been
     badly stained.

Accession No. 679   Index No. - 102-zzic

Title   " <u>Chia-tzŭ hui chi</u> "
甲 子 會 紀

Classification - B-22 編年

Subject - (Toronto No. 379) "a table of 71 Chinese Cycles (of 60 years

each, as designated by the method of 10 stems and 12 branches),

beginning with the 8th year of Huang-Ti and ending with the 42d

year of Chia-Ching; together with significant historical features

included under the respective years as well as an additional (#)

References - 012-zafk 4/10   031-bgdf 48/14   Toronto No. 379.

Author - (編 集) <u>Hsüeh Ying-ch'i</u> 薛 應 旂 .

Edition - the "<u>Hsüan-chin-ts'ao-t'ang</u>" 玄 津 草 堂 ; (preface) dated

Chia-Ching "mou-wu" 37/1558.   Blocks; "mien" paper.

Index - none; 5 chüan.

Bound in 1 t'ao 5 ts'e; doubly interleaved.

Remarks - this is a very fine edition; and the item is complete and

in perfect condition.

(#) chapter on miscellaneous related matters."

167

Accession No. 680   Index No. - 154-ibha   120-fld

Title   " Lai-ku-t'ang ch'ih-tu hsin ch'ao san hsüan chieh lin chi "
賴 古 堂 尺 牘 新 鈔 三 選 結 隣 集
" Chieh lin chi "
結 隣 集

Classification - D-73 總 集 一 文
Subject - (Toronto No. 139) "a general collection of extracts taken
    from the letters of more than 200 scholars; with marginal notes."

References - 012-zafk 19/19   Toronto No. 139.

Author - (編) Chou Tsai-chün 周 在 浚.

Edition - the "Huai-tê-t'ang" 懷 德 堂 ; dated Ch'ien-Lung "chia-hsü"
    19/1754.   Blocks; "mao-pien" paper.

Index - a detailed list of authors with their native districts for
    15 chüan (see remarks).

Bound in 2 t'ao 8 ts'ê (4-4); doubly interleaved.

Remarks - the item is complete and in good condition.   The work
    itself is in 16 chüan; but the last is not given in the index.

Accession No. 681   Index No. - 010-bhcz

Title " Yüan ch'ao ming ch'en shih lüeh "

元 朝 名 臣 事 略

Classification - B-117 傳 記 一 總 録

Subject - a collection of biographies of 46 high ministers and
officials of the Yüan Dynasty.

References - Wylie's Notes page 35 163-ggcz 5/4 031-bgld 6/14
106-gdkn 27/19 012-zafk 5/12 031-bgdf 58/4 Gest No. 2009.

Author - (撰) Su T'ien-chio 蘇 天 爵 .

Edition - based upon the Chü-chên-pan 聚 珍 版 ; (preface) dated
Ch'ien-Lung "chia-wu" 39/1774. Blocks; "t'u-fên" paper.

Index - a list of names for 15 chüan.

Bound in 1 t'ao 4 ts'ê.

Remarks - the item appears to be complete and is in generally good
condition,- some stains and a part of page 22 in chüan 4 missing.

Accession No. 682   Index No. - 077-lccz   077-jccz

Title   " Li-tai ming ch'ên chuan chieh lu "
           歷 代 名 臣 傳 節 錄

Classification - B-117 傳記 - 總錄

Subject - a collection of biographical sketches of famous officials
           and eminent ministers of the period extending from the Han down
           to and including the Ming dynasty.

References - Gest No. 1511.

Author - (錄 訂) Hsiao P'ei-yüan 蕭 培 元 ; (增 輯) Ch'ung Hou
           崇 厚 .

Edition - the "Yün-yin-t'ang" 雲 陰 堂 ; (preface) dated T'ung-Chih
           "kêng-wu" 9/1870.   Blocks; "fên" paper.

Index - a list of names in 30 chüan, arranged chronologically.

Bound in 1 t'ao 10 ts'ê.

Remarks - the item is complete and almost new.

170

The University of Toronto Chinese Library

Accession No. 683   Index No. - 149-1zeh

Title   " Chu tzŭ pa ts'ui "

諸 子 拔 萃

Classification - C-328 雜家 - 雜纂

Subject - a collection of extracts taken from various philosophical
works; with commentaries.

References - 031-bgdf 132/23.

Author - (評選) Li Yün-hsiang 李 雲 翔 ; (叅閱) T'ang Chieh-yüan
唐 捷 元 ; (較梓) T'ang Chien-yüan 唐 建 元 .

Edition - a Ming edition; (preface) dated T'ien-Ch'i 7/1627.   Blocks;
bamboo paper.

Index - a table of contents for 8 chüan under 26 categories.

Bound in 2 t'ao 16 ts's; doubly interleaved.

Remarks - a very good edition; the item is complete and in practically
perfect condition.

Accession No. 684   Index No. - 152-ezd 067-zobd 170-hzzd

Title   " Hsiang-shan chi "
                         象　山　集
                      " Wên-an kung chi "
                         文　安　公　集
          (#)

Classification - D-33 別 集 一 詩 文
Subject - an individual miscellaneous collection of prose and poetry.

References - 160-1j 163-ggcz 13/15 037-ahhg 10/24; (hsü) 19/1
    167-mhfm 21/16 030-iaff 30/17 106-gdkn 86/16 012-zafk 15/25
    031-bgdf 160/6 Gest No. 414.
Author - (撰) Lu Chiu-yüan 陸 九 淵 ; (點 次) Li Fu 李 紱 .

Edition - the "Ta-ju-chia-miao" 大 儒 家 廟 ; dated T'ung-Chih
    "hsin-wei" 10/1871.   Blocks; "mao-t'ai" paper.

Index - a classified table of contents for 36 chüan; 附 錄 1 chüan;
    陸 氏 家 制 1 chüan.

Bound in 1 t'ao 10 ts'ê.

Remarks - an ordinary edition; the item is complete and in fairly
    good condition.

          (#)   " Lu-tzŭ wên chi "
                         陸 子 文 集

Accession No. 685   Index No. - 085-hpd   156-ghpb

Title   " Ch'ing-hsien chi "
                        清　獻　集
                     " Chao Ch'ing-hsien kung chi "
                        趙　清　獻　公　集

Classification - D-33 別　集 - 詩　文
Subject - an individual literary collection,- prose and poetry.

References - 163-ggcz 13/2   031-bgld 15/34   167-mhfm 20/12
     030-iaff 26/18   106-gdkn 74/8   012-zafk 15/14   031-bgdf 152/47.

Author - (撰) Chao Pien 趙　抃.

Edition - reprinted by Yang Chun 楊　準 ; (preface) dated Chia-Ching
     "jên-hsü" 41/1562.   Blocks; bamboo paper.

Index - a detailed table of contents (in 2 parts) for 10 chüan.

Bound in 1 t'ao 4 ts'ê.

Remarks - a very good edition; the item is complete and without
     defects except some repaired worm-holes.

173

Accession No. 686   Index No. - 073-fzeg

Title   " Shu yen ku shih ta ch'üan "
               書 言 故 事 大 全

Classification - C-348 類 書

Subject - an encyclopaedia covering miscellaneous subjects.

References - none.

Author - (集) Hu Chi-tsung 胡 繼 宗 ; (解) Ch'ên Wan-chih
         陳 玩 直.

Edition - a Ming edition; (preface) dated "chi-ch'ou" (? Wan-Li
         17/1589).   Blocks; "mien" paper.

Index - a table of contents for 12 chüan.

Bound in 2 t'ao 12 ts's; doubly interleaved.

Remarks - this is a very good edition; and the item is complete and
         without defects with the exception of some stains and a few
         repaired worm-holes.

The University of Toronto Chinese Library

Accession No. 687   Index No. - 044-aozk

Title   " Ch'ih-tu ch'ing lien "

尺 牘 青 蓮

Classification - D-75   總集一文

Subject - a classified collection of phrases and expressions suitable in letter-writing, taken from various sources.

References - none.

Author - (纂) Ho Wei-jan 何 偉 然.

Edition - privately published; no date.   Blocks; "mao-pien" paper.

Index - a general table of contents (classifications) for 12 chüan.

Bound in 1 t'ao 10 ts'e; singly interleaved.

Remarks - a good edition; the item is complete and in very good condition.

Accession No. 688-a   Index No. - 162-fzk

Title   " Ni ch'ên chuan "

逆 臣 傳

Classification - B-117 傳記 - 總錄

Subject - (Gest No. 2235-b) "a collection of biographies of Ming
officials who accepted office under the Ch'ing Dynasty and
later rebelled."

References - Wylie's Notes page 58 160-1j 012-zafk 5/17
Gest No. 2235-b.

Author - not stated; prepared by the State Historiographer's office.

Edition - the "Pan-sung-chü-shih" 半 松 居 士 ; no date.   Blocks;
"mao-pien" paper.

Index - a list of 24 names in 4 chüan.

Bound in 2 ts's in 1 t'ao with (b).

Remarks - an ordinary edition; the item is complete and without
defects.

The University of Toronto Chinese Library

Accession No. 688-b   Index No. - 154-ezk

Title   " Erh ch'ên chuan "
貳　臣　傳

Classification - B-117 傳 記 一 總 録

Subject - (Gest No. 2235-a) "a collection of biographies of officials
who served under both the Ming and Ch'ing dynasty."

References - Wylie's Notes page 38   160-1j   012-zafk 5/17

Gest No. 2235-a.

Author - as under (a).

Edition, - uniform with (a).

Index - a list of 120 names in 12 chüan.

Bound in 6 ts'ê in 1 t'ao with (a).

Remarks - as under (a).

Accession No. 689   Index No. - 140-dzjg

Title   " Chieh-tzŭ-yüan hua chuan "
                芥 子 圓 畫 傳

Classification - C-223 藝 術 - 書 畫

Subject - an illustrated work on Chinese painting, consisting of
   4 "chi",- the first on Landscape drawing; the second on
   Epidendrum, Bamboo, Peach, and Chrysanthemum; the third on
   Flowers, Birds, Human Figures, and Buildings; and the fourth
   on Portrait Painting and the Human Figure.

References - Wylie's Notes page 155 160-1j   012-zafk 11/21
   Gest No. 709.

Author - of the 一 二 三 集 - Wang Kai 王 槩 ; of the 四 集 -
   Ting Kao 丁 皋 .

Edition - the first 集 with the designation 本 衙 藏 版; the
   second and third 書 業 堂 ; and the fourth 抱 青 閣 ;
   latest date Chia-Ch'ing 23/1818.   Blocks; "fèn" paper.

1-3 集 Kai Hsi B.t. 1679 (First Ed. 1701?)

Index - (一 集) separate detailed tables of contents for each of 5
   chüan; (二 集) a general table of contents for 4 sections in 8
   ts's, with detailed list for each ts's; (三 集) for 4 ts's (#)
Bound in 1 t'ao 15 ts's.

Remarks - the item appears to be complete and is in very good condition.
   There is a short supplement to this work entitled:-
        " Chieh-tzŭ-yüan t'u chang hui tsuan "
          芥 子 圓 圖 章 會 纂
        by Li Yü 李 漁 .   (140-dzjk)
                                            C-233

   (#) and a 卷 末 ; (四 集) for 4 chüan.

The University of Toronto Chinese Library

Accession No. 690   Index No. - 020-cdgb

Title   " Pao Hsiao-su kung tsou i "
             包 孝 肅 公 奏 議

Classification - B-72 詔令奏議 - 奏議
Subject - a collection of memorials.

References - 163-ggcz 5/1   031-bgld 6/3   167-mhfm 9/26   030-iaff 8/17
      106-gdkn 25/5   012-zafk 4/28   031-bgdf 55/19.

Author - (撰) Pao Chêng 包 拯．

Edition - the "Hsing-hsin-ko" 省 心 閣; (preface) dated T'ung-Chih
      2/1863.   Blocks; "fân" paper.

Index - a table of contents for 10 chüan.

Bound in 1 t'ao 4 ts'ê.

Remarks - the item is complete and in perfect condition.

—————•—————

Accession No. 691   Index No. - 106-agke

Title   " Po chia chai ch'i "
                      百   家   摘   奇

Classification - C-328 雜家 － 雜纂
Subject - a collection of extracts taken from various philososphical
        works.

References - none.

Author - (編) Liu Mêng-lei 劉孟雷 ; (校輯) Hsü Shou-ch'ien
        徐守謙.

Edition - no particular notation; (preface) dated Wan-Li "mou-hsü"
        26/1598.   Blocks; bamboo paper.

Index - none; 4 chüan.

Bound in 1 t'ao 2 ts'e.

Remarks - the edition is a very good one; and the item is in practically
        perfect condition.   This work can not be found in the catalogues,
        nor has it a table of contents; and therefore it is difficult to
        state whether it is complete or not, although it appears to be.

Accession No. 692   Index No. - 149-gzgm

Title   " Shuo wên t'ung chien "
              說 文 通 檢

Classification - A-161 小 學 一 字 書
Subject - an index to the "Shuo wên chieh tzŭ" 說 文 解 字
    (Toronto No. 626).

References - 012-zafk 3/26   Toronto No. 626.

Author - (編) Li Yung-ch'un 黎 永 椿.

Edition - the "Ch'ung-wên-shu-chü" 崇 文 書 局 ; dated Kuang-Hsü
    2/1876.   Blocks; "fên" paper.

Index - none; in 16 chüan.

Bound in 1 t'ao 2 ts'ê.

Remarks - a very useful work; complete and almost new.

Accession No. 693   Index No. - 140-peez   140-pzed

Title   " Su p'ing Mêng-tzŭ "
                蘇 評 孟 子
          " Su Lao-ch'üan p'i p'ing Mêng-tzŭ chên pên "
          蘇 老 泉 批 評 孟 子 真 本

Classification - A-135 四 書 - 孟 子
Subject - a commentary on the "Mêng-tzŭ",- the philosophy of Mencius.

References - 012-zafk 3/7   031-bgdf 37/1.

Author - by Su Hsün 蘇 洵 .

Edition - the "Shên-i-t'ang" 慎 詒 堂 ; dated Chia-Ch'ing "kuei-hai"
      8/1803.   Blocks; bamboo paper.

Index - none; 2 chüan 上 下 .

Bound in 1 t'ao 2 ts'ê ;doubly interleaved.

Remarks - a very good edition; the item is complete and in perfect
      condition.

182

Accession No. 694   Index No. - 077-acf

Title   " Chêng tzǔ lüeh "
                正 字 略

Classification - A-151 小 學 一 字 書
Subject - a dictionary of Chinese characters; giving the correct
    and incorrect forms together with necessary explanations.

References - none.

Author - by Wang Yün 王 筠 .

Edition - no particular notation; (postscriptum) dated Tao-Kuang
    13/1833.   Blocks; "fên" paper.

Index - none; in 1 chüan arranged according to the number of strokes.

Bound in 1 t'ao 2 ts'ê; doubly interleaved.

Remarks - the item is apparently complete and without defects.

Accession No.   695   Index No. - 085-ihkd

Title   " Hsiang-ch'i-lou ch'üan shu "
             湘　綺　樓　全　書

Classification - C-338 雜 家 － 叢 書

Subject - a collection of 19 works mostly commentaries on classical
    works.

References - none.

Author - by Wang K'ai-yün 王 闓 運 ; of the 王 志 - Ch'en Chao-k'uei
    陳 兆 奎.

Edition - published at various places and at different times; latest
    date Hsüan-T'ung "hsin-hai" 3/1911.   Blocks; "mao-pien" paper.

Index - a list of the 19 works.

Bound in 10 t'ao 83 ts's (9-10-10-8-6-8-9-7-8-8).

Remarks - an ordinary edition; the item is new.

184

Accession No.   696   Index No. - 146-zic

Title   " Hsi hu chih "
                     西   湖   志

Classification - B-207 地 理 - 山 川

Subject - (Gest No. 1532) "a general topography of the "West Lake"

   region near Hangchow ; including chapters on the scenery;

   sea-walls; bridges; gardens and pavilions; monasteries and

   temples; shrines; monuments; antiquities; famous men; literature;

   paintings; etc.; etc. (illustrated)".

References - Wylie's Notes page 55   031-bgld 7/23   012-zafk 8/8

   031-bgdf 76/40   Gest No. 1532   Toronto No. 232.

Author - (總 修) Fu Wang-lu 傅 王 露 .

Edition - the "Liang-chê-yen-i-tao-k'u" 兩 浙 鹽 驛 道 庫 ; dated

   Yung-Chêng 9/1731.   Blocks; "mao-pien" paper.

Index - a general table of contents for 48 chüan.

Bound in 4 t'ao 20 ts's (5 each).

Remarks - this is a very fine edition; and the item is complete and

   in very good condition with the exception of some stains and a

   few repaired blemishes.

Accession No. 697   Index No. - 128-gzzb

Title   " Shêng mên shih-liu tzǔ shu "

聖 門 十 六 子 書

Classification - C-13 儒 家

Subject - a collection of miscellaneous records of 16 disciples of

Confucius; including sections on biographical sketches;

activities and sayings; records of descendants, etc.

References - 012-zafk 10/11.

Author - (校刊) Fêng Yün-yüan 馮 雲 鵷 .

Edition - the "Ch'ang-p'ing-shu-yüan" 昌 平 書 院 ; dated Tao-Kuang

"jên-ch'ên" 12/1832.   Blocks; "mao-pien" paper.

Index - a list of 16 names.

Bound in 2 t'ao 12 ts'ê (6-6); doubly interleaved.

Remarks - a fairly good edition; the item is complete and without

defects.

Accession No. 698   Index No. - 076-hezh   037-zhff

Title   " Ch'in-ting Ta-Ch'ing lü li "
                    欽 定 大 清 律 例

Classification - B-302 政書 - 法令

Subject - a collection of law codes and administrative regulations
    of the Ch'ing Dynasty.

References - Wylie's Notes page 71   163-ggcz 6/5   031-bgld 8/16
    012-zafk 9/14   031-bgdf 82/49.

Author - compiled by an Imperial Commission on order of Emperor
    Ch'ien-Lung 乾隆 .

Edition - a palace edition; (preface) dated Ch'ien-Lung 5/1740.
    Blocks; "fan" paper.

Index - a general table of contents for 47 chüan; separate list for
    each of the 47 chüan.

Bound in 2 t'ao 20 ts'e (10-10).

Remarks - a good edition; the item is complete.

Accession No.   699-a   Index No. - 105-dzjj

Title   " Kuei-ssŭ lei kao "
                          癸 巳 類 稿

Classification - C-308 雜 家 － 雜 文
Subject - (Gest No. 2074) "a "miscellany",- being critical notes
    on a variety of unrelated subjects."

References - 160-1j   163-ggcz 10/5   012-zafk 12/24   Gest Nos 424
    and 2074.

Author - by Yü Chang-hsieh 俞 正 燮.

Edition - the "Ch'iu-jih-i-chai" 求 日 益 齋 ; dated Tao-Kuang
    13/1833.   Blocks; bamboo paper.

Index - a table of contents for 15 chüan.

Bound in   1 t'ao 8 ts's.

Remarks - an ordinary edition; the item is complete and in good
    condition.

Accession No.   699-b   Index No. - 105-dzcj

Title   " Kuei-ssŭ ts'un kao "
                  癸 巳 存 稿

Classification - C-308 雜 家 - 雜 文
Subject - a continuation and supplement to (a).

References - 160-lj.

Author - by Yü Chêng-hsieh 俞 正 燮 .

Edition - no particular notation; dated Kuang-Hsü "chia-shên"
    10/1884.   Blocks; bamboo paper.

Index - a table of contents for 15 chüan.

Bound in 1 t'ao 6 ts'ê.

Remarks - as under (a).

Accession No. 700   Index No. – 067-zdba 057-haed 037-aed

Title   " Wên-chung kung T'ai-yo Chang hsien-shêng wên chi "
文 忠 公 太 岳 張 先 生 文 集
" Chang T'ai-yo chi "
張 太 岳 集

Classification – D-33 別 集 － 詩 文

Subject – an individual literary collection,– prose and poetry.

References – 031-bgdf 177/68   Gest No. 1069.

Author – (著) Chang Chü-chêng 張 居 正 .

Edition – the "Kuang-ch'ing-t'ang" 廣 慶 堂 ; (preface) dated Wan-Li
"jên-tzŭ" 40/1612.   Blocks; bamboo paper.

Index – a detailed table of contents for 47 chüan.

Bound in 2 t'ao 12 ts's (6-6).

Remarks – a very good edition; the item is complete and practically
without defects.

Accession No.   701   Index No. - 074-gjdz   074-gjd

Title   " Wang-hsi hsien-shêng ch'üan chi "
               望 溪 先 生 全 集
               " Wang-hsi chi "
               望 溪 集

Classification - D-33 別 集 - 詩 文
Subject - an individual collection of prose and poetry; mainly the
    former.

References - 163-ggcz 15/18   012-zafk 17/19   031-bgdf 173/48
    Toronto No. 55.

Author - Fang Pao 方 苞 ;（重 編）Tai Chün-hêng 戴 鈞 衡.

Edition - no particular notation; (preface) dated Hsien-Fêng 1/1851.
    Blocks; "mao-pien" paper.

Index - a table of contents for 18 chüan; 集 外 文 10 chüan;
    集 外 文 補 遺 2 chüan; 年 譜 2 chüan.

Bound in 2 t'ao 16 ts'ê (8-8).

Remarks - an ordinary edition; the item is complete. A few pages
    have been bound in wrong order, but this has not been corrected,
    as it will mar the writing on the page-edges.

Accession No. 702   Index No. - 103-in

Title   " I yao "
                                  疑　耀

Classification - C-308 雜 家 - 雜 文
Subject - a collection of disquisitions and discussions on miscel-
    laneous unrelated subjects.

References - 160-1j   163-ggcz 10/4   031-bgld 13/12   012-zafk 12/21
    031-bgdf 119/6.

Author - (著) Li Chih 李 贄 ; (訂) Chang Hsüan 張 萱.

Edition - a Ming edition; (preface) dated Wan-Li "mou-shên" 36/1608.
    Blocks; bamboo paper.

Index - separate table of contents for each of 7 chüan.

Bound in 1 t'ao 6 ts'ê; doubly interleaved.

Remarks - the edition is a very good one; and the item is in generally
    good condition,- a few repaired defects.   The last chüan is
    incomplete; some pages are missing from the end.

Accession No. 703   Index No. - 061-egzz 037-zzeg 077-jzch

Title   " Hsing-li ta fang shu "
                       性 理 大 方 書
                     " Ta fang hsing-li ch'üan shu "
                       大 方 性 理 全 書
        (#)

Classification - C-13 儒 家

Subject - (Gest No. 1761) "a collection of the principal writings
          on mental philosophy."

References - to the 性 理 大 全 書 ;- Wylie's Notes page 85   160-1j
          163-ggcz 7/5   031-bgld 9/18   037-ahhg (hsü) 16/10   030-iaff 15/18
          (##)
Author - by an Imperial Commission headed by Hu Kuang 胡 廣 ;
          (校 正) Li T'ing-chi 李 廷 機 .

Edition - the "Li Hung-yü" 李 洪 宇 ; (preface) dated Yung-Lo
          13/1415.   Blocks; bamboo paper.

Index - a general table of contents for 70 chüan.

Bound in 2 t'ao 18 ts'ê (9-9).

Remarks - this is a very fine edition; and the item is complete and
          in excellent condition.   Apparently this book is the same in
          all respects as the one with the title 性 理 大 全 書.

The University of Toronto Chinese Library

Accession No. 704-a   Index No. - 128-gilo

Title   " Shêng yü kuang hsün "
               聖   諭   廣   訓

Classification - C-13 儒 家

Subject - (Gest No. 1479) " an expansion of the so-called "Sacred
   Edict", being a collection of short explanatory homilies on
   the sixteen maxims contained therein."

References - Wylie's Notes page 87   160-1j （聖諭） 031-bgld 9/21
   012-zafk 10/8 031-bgdf 94/2 Toronto No. 96   Gest No. 1479.

Author - of original - the Emperor K'ang-Hsi 康 熙 . of the
   expansion - the Emperor Yung-Chêng 雍 正 .

Edition - officially published; no date.   Blocks; "fên" paper.

Index - none; 1 chüan.

Bound in 1 ts'ê in 1 t'ao with (b).

Remarks - a clear-cut large-sized edition; the item is complete and
   with no defects other than a few repaired worm-holes.

Accession No. 704-b   Index No. - 128-gilc

Title   " Shêng yü kuang hsün chih chieh "

聖 諭 廣 訓 直 解

Classification - C-13 儒 家

Subject - an explanation of (a), in ordinary spoken language.

References - 012-zafk 10/8   Toronto No. 97.

Author - of original - the Emperor K'ang-Hsi 康 熙 . of the

expansion - the Emperor Yung-Chêng 雍 正 .

Edition - uniform with (a); but (preface) dated Yung-Chêng 2/1724.

Index - a table of the 16 maxims.

Bound in 2 ts'ê in 1 t'ao with (a).

Remarks - as under (a); but with some stains.

Accession No. 705   Index No. - 162-1n1c

Title   " Tao tsang chi yao "
               道   藏   輯   要

Classification - C-338 雜 家 - 叢 書
Subject - a comprehensive collection of reprints of Taoist and
    related works.

References - 029-pffz 427.

Author - (輯) Chiang Yüan-t'ing 蔣 元 庭 according to 029-pffz.

Edition - the "Ch'êng-tu-êrh-hsien-an" 成 都 二 仙 庵; dated
    Kuang-Hsü "ping-wu" 32/1906.   Blocks; "mien" paper.

Index - a list of the works in 28 集 .

Bound in 24 t'ao 245 ts'ê.

Remarks - the item is apparently complete and in very good condition.

Accession No. 706   Index No. - 053-1dfb

Title   " Kuang k'uai shu wu shih chung "
               廣 快 書 五 十 種

Classification - C-338 雜 家 - 叢 書
Subject - a collection of 50 reprints cheifly consisting of
    miscellaneous narrations and sayings. (incomplete)

References - 029-pffz 510   012-zafk 13/12   031-bgdf 134/18.

Author - (編) Ho Wei-jan 何 偉 然 ; (定) Wu Ts'ung-hsien
    吳 從 先 .

Edition - a Ming edition; (preface) dated "chi-ssǔ" (? Ch'ung-Chêng
    2/1629).   Blocks; bamboo paper.

Index - a list of 50 works in 50 chüan.

Bound in 2 t'ao 17 ts'ê (8-9); doubly interleaved.

Remarks - this item is incomplete; it contains only the first 27
    works.   A very good edition; clear and in excellent condition.

—————•—————

Accession No. 707   Index No. - 162-ggkp

Title   " Lien yün i ts'ung shu "
               連 筠 簃 叢 書

Classification - c-338 雜家 - 叢書
Subject - a collection of 12 reprints of miscellaneous works.

References - 029-pffz 372   058-jffz 7/25   012-zafk 13/15.

Author - (撰) Yang Shang-wen 揚 尚 文.

Edition - the "Yang-shih" of Ling-shih 靈 石 揚 氏 ; dated
     Tao-Kuang "mou-shên" 28/1848.   Blocks; "fên" paper.

Index - a list of the 12 works.

Bound in 6 t'ao 30 ts'ê (5 each).

Remarks - a good edition; the item is complete and in very fine
     condition.

Accession No.   708   Index No. - 123-gfec

Title   " Ch'ün shu chih yao "

羣 書 治 要

Classification - C-328 雜家 - 雜纂

Subject - selected portions of the Classics and other important historical writings, with commentaries, showing the cause of the rise and fall of each previous emperor as a warning to the succeeding rulers.

References - 163-ggcz 10/10   012-zafk 13/3   Gest No. 766.

Author - compiled on Imperial order by Wei Chêng 魏 徵.

Edition - published in Japan; (original preface) dated T'ien-Ming 天 明 7/629.   Blocks; Japanese paper. (actually published in 1857)

Index - a general table of contents for 50 chüan.

Bound in 4 t'ao 47 ts'ê (11-12-12-12).

Remarks - a very good edition; the item is without defects.

———•———

Accession No. 709   Index No. - 120-ofeg

Title   " <u>Hsü</u> <u>Tzǔ</u> <u>chih</u> <u>t'ung</u> <u>chien</u> "

續　資　治　通　鑑

Classification - B-22 編 年

Subject - a supplement to <u>Ssǔ-ma Kuang's</u> 司 馬 光 " <u>Tzǔ chih t'ung</u>

<u>chien</u>", continuing the records through the <u>Sung</u> and <u>Yüan</u>

dynasties.

References - 163-ggcz 4/9   012-zafk 4/11   Gest No. 75.

Author - (撰) <u>Pi Yüan</u> 畢 沅.

Edition - the "<u>Tê-yü-t'ang</u>" 德 裕 堂; (preface) dated Chia-Ch'ing

6/1801.   Blocks; "mao-pien" paper.

Index - a chronological table of contents for 220 chüan.

Bound in 8 t'ao 80 ts'ê (10 each).

Remarks - this is a very good edition; and the item is complete and

without defects except some stains.

Accession No. 710   Index No. - 075-dhh   024-zhdh

Title   " Tung-hua lu "

東 華 錄

" Shih-ch'ao Tung-hua lu "

十 朝 東 華 錄

Classification - B-22 編 年

Subject - annals of the Ch'ing, or Manchu Dynasty, from its

    establishment up to and including the Hsien-Fêng period.

References - 160-1j   012-zafk 4/11   Gest No. 1508.

Author - of the first 9 "ch'ao"- Wang Hsien-ch'ien 王 先 謙;

    of the 10th "ch'ao" - P'an I-fu 潘 頤 福.

Edition - the "Shan-ch'êng-t'ang" 善 成 堂; dated Kuang-Hsü

    "ting-hai" 13/1887.   Blocks; "fên" paper.

Index - a table of chapter dates for - (a) T'ien-Ming 天 命 4 chüan

    T'ien-Ts'ung 天 聰 11 chüan Ch'ung-Tê 崇 德 8 chüan   (b)

    Shun-Chih 順 治 36 chüan (c) K'ang-Hsi 康 熙 110 chüan (#)

Bound in 24 t'ao 140 ts'ê.

Remarks - the item is complete and without defects.

    (#)   Yung-Chêng 雍 正 26 chüan Ch'ien-Lung 乾 隆 120 chüan

        Chia-Ch'ing 嘉 慶 50 chüan Tao-Kuang 道 光 60 chüan

        Hsien-Fêng 咸 豐 69 chüan.

Accession No.   711   Index No. - 001-zbgz   037-znzg

Title   " I ch'ieh ching yin i "
                一 切 經 音 義

               " Ta tsang yin i "
                大 藏 音 義

Classification - C-513 釋 家

Subject - (Wylie) "---- is an explanation of all the foreign
   technical terms found in the works translated from the
   Sanscrit, with an examination of the correct sounds."

References - Wylie's Notes page 211   163-ggcz 11/8   120-gndb
   5/17   030-iaff 22/2   Gest No. 59-a.

Author - (撰) Hui-lin 慧 琳 .

Edition - the "Haku-ren-sha" 白 蓮 社 ; dated Gembun 3/1738.
   Blocks; Japanese paper.

Index - none; 100 chüan.

Bound in 6 t'ao 55 ts'ê (10-9-9-9-9-9).

Remarks - a good edition; complete and without defects.   The
   following is a supplement:-
        " Hsü I ch'ieh ching yin i "
          續 一 切 經 音 義   (120-ozbg)

        by Hsi-lin 希 麟   10 chüan

203

Accession No. 712   Index No. - 060-hlbz   030-bzhn

Title   " Yü hsüan Ku wên yüan chien "
              御　選　古　文　淵　鑒

Classification - D-73 總 集 一 文

Subject - a general collection of prose compositions by famous
    scholars, officials etc., beginning from the time of the
    Tso-chuan, down to the end of the Sung Dynasty; with
    commentaries.

References - Wylie's Notes page 241   160-lj   163-ggcz 16/9
    031-bgld 19/31   012-zafk 19/14   031-bgdf 190/1 Gest No. 170.

Author - compiled on Imperial order by Hsü Ch'ien-hsüeh 徐 乾 學．

Edition - a palace edition; (preface) dated K'ang-Hsi 24/1658.
    Blocks; "k'ai-hua" paper.

Index - separate lists of contents for each of 64 chüan.

Bound in 4 t'ao 32 ts'ê (8 each).

Remarks - a very good edition; the item is complete and in fairly
    good condition with the exception of some stains. Some of the
    characters in the top marginal notes have been cut off evidently
    at the time the work was repaired.

—●—

Accession No. 713   Index No. – 076-hebb   030-bbkf   031-kfdc

Title   " Ch'in-ting Ku chin T'u shu chi ch'êng "
　　　　　　欽　定　古　今　圖　書　集　成

Classification – C-348　類　書
Subject – a comprehensive Chinese encyclopaedia.

References – 160-1j (hsü)   Gest Nos. 1 and 1028.

Author – compiled on Imperial order by a commission headed by
　　Chiang T'ing-hsi 蔣 廷 錫·

Edition – no particular notation; no date.   Type; foreign and "fên"
　　paper.   (see under Remarks)

Index – a general table of contents for 6 編 divided into 32 典 ,
　　6109 部 and 10,000 chüan. a detailed table of contents for the
　　same.   The index itself in 40 chüan.
Bound in 164 boxes in 1640 ts'ê.

Remarks – on the whole the item is complete and in good condition.
　　Chüan 342 - 343 in 閨 媛 典 are missing.   In box no. 8, the
　　second ts'ê is missing, and in its place is found a duplicated
　　ts'ê of another section.   The Index (box no. 1) is of a dif-
　　ferent edition from the rest of the work.   It is from the   (#)

(#) lithographed edition of the "T'ung-wên-shu-chü"

同 文 書 局 ; and is dated Kuang-Hsü "chia-shên"
10/1884.

The University of Toronto Chinese Library

Accession No. 714   Index No. - 060-hezb   039-zbhh

Title   " Yü-ting Tzŭ shih ching hua "
               御 定 子 史 精 華

Classification - C-348 類書

Subject - (Toronto No. 471) "an encyclopaedia of selected phrases
    from various philosophical and historical works under 30 main
    classifications and about 280 sub-divisions."

References - Wylie's Notes page 188   160-lj   163-ggoz 10/16
    031-bgld 14/17 012-zafk 13/26 031-bgdf 136/21 Gest No. 291
    Toronto No. 471.

Author - compiled on order of Emperor K'ang-Hsi by an Imperial
    Commission headed by the two Imperial princes Yün-lu 允 祿
    and Yün-li 允 禮, and Chang T'ing-yü 張 廷 玉.

Edition - based upon the "palace" edition; (preface) dated Yung-Chêng
    5/1727.   Blocks; "fên" paper.

Index - a general table of contents for 160 chüan.

Bound in 6 t'ao 48 ts'ê (8 each).

Remarks - a fairly good edition; the item is complete and in generally
    good condition,- some worm-holes.

————•————

Accession No. 715   Index No. - 013-cebz

Title   " Ts'ê fu yüan kuei "
                        册　府　元　龜

Classification - C-348 類書

Subject - (Gest # 615) "Historical compendium in the form of an
    encyclopaedia embracing the details of all state matters
    from the earliest times, 600 years in all, chronologically
    arranged, in 31 sections,------."

References - Wylie's Notes page 183 160-1j 163-ggoz 10/16
    031-bgld 14/6 012-zafk 13/21 031-bgdf 135/22 Gest Nos. 615
    and 2460.

Author - (撰) Wang Ch'in-jo 王 欽 若 and Yang I 楊 億.

Edition - no particular notation; (preface) dated Ch'ien-Lung
    "chia-hsü" 19/1754.   Blocks; "mien" paper.

Index - a table of contents for 1,000 chüan.

Bound in 32 t'ao 160 ts'ê (5 each).

Remarks - a well-known standard work; the item is apparently complete,
    and in good condition on the whole, though with some stains and
    worm-holes.   Some of the ts'ê appear to be replacements from
    another copy printed from the same blocks.

Accession No. 716   Index No. - 037-zziz   140-izzf

Title   " Ta fang wan wên i t'ung "
               大 方 萬 文 一 統

Classification - D-73 總 集 一 文
Subject - a general collection of prose.

References - Gest No. 2484.

Author - (編纂) Li T'ing-chi 李 廷 機.

Edition - the "Chien-i-shu-lin" 建邑 書 林 ; no date, but
          apparently of the Wan-Li period.   Blocks; bamboo paper.

Index - a subject and author table of contents for 22 chüan.

Bound in 1 t'ao 8 ts'ê.

Remarks - a very good edition; the item is apparently complete, but
          with a few repaired defects and some stains.

Accession No. 717   Index No. - 024-bh1d

Title   " Shêng-an i chi "

升 菴 遺 集

Classification - D-33 別 集 － 詩 文

Subject - an individual literary collection,- prose and poetry.

References - 012-zafk 16/22.

Author - (著) Yang Shên 楊 慎.

Edition - a Ming edition; (preface) dated Wan-Li "ping-wu" 34/1606.
   Blocks; "mien" paper.

Index - a classified table of contents for 26 chüan.

Bound in 1 t'ao 4 ts's.

Remarks - a good edition; the item is complete and in generally
   good condition.

210

The University of Toronto Chinese Library

Accession No. 718   Index No. - 030-gdbz   031-bzgz

Title   " T'ang Sung ssǔ ta chia wên hsüan "
           唐 宋 四 大 家 文 選

Classification - D-73 總 集 一 文

Subject - a collection of prose compositions of four noted scholars
   of the T'ang and Sung periods, i.e., Han Yü 韓愈，
   Liu Tsung-yüan 柳宗元, Ou-yang Hsiu 歐陽修，and
   Su Shih 蘇軾 ; together with commentaries.

References - none.

Author - (評閱) Ku Hsi-ch'ou 顧錫疇；(選輯) Kuei Yu-kuang
   歸有光.

Edition - no particular notation; (preface) dated Ch'ung-Chêng
   "hsin-wei" 4/1631.   Blocks; bamboo paper.

Index - (韓文) a table of contents for 8 chüan; (柳文) same
   for 8 chüan; (歐文) 10 chüan; (蘇文) 16 chüan.

Bound in 3 t'ao 24 ts'ê (8-6-10).

Remarks - the item is complete and without defects.

211

—●—

Accession No. 719   Index No. - 076-hebf   031-bfz

Title   " Ch'in-ting Ssŭ-shu wên "
                       欽 定 四 書 文

Classification - D-73 總集 - 文 A-131 四書
Subject - a general collection of critical prose compositions on
    the "Four Books" written by scholars from the period of
    Ch'êng-Hua (Ming) to the period of Ch'ien-Lung (Ch'ing).

References - 031-bgld 19/34   012-zafk 19/15   031-bgdf 190/19.

Author - compiled by an Imperial Commission headed by Fang Pao 方苞
    on order of Emperor Ch'ien-Lung.

Edition - a "palace" edition; dated Ch'ien-Lung 5/1740.   Blocks;
    bamboo paper.

Index - separate tables of contents for each of the 5 main sections;
    contents not divided into chüan.

Bound in 4 t'ao 16 ts's (4 each).

Remarks - this is a very fine edition; and the item is complete and
    in very good condition.

The University of Toronto Chinese Library

———◆—◆———

Accession No. 720   Index No. - 067-zlci

Title   " Wên hsüan Li Shan chu "
                  文　選　李　善　註

Classification - D-63 總集 － 詩文
Subject - a general literary collection,- prose and poetry; with
    commentary.

References - Wylie's Notes page 238   160-1j   163-ggcz 16/1
    031-bgld 19/1   167-mhfm 23/1   030-iaff 38/1   106-gdkn 112/1
    (#)
Author - (撰) The Prince Chao Ming 昭 明 太 子; (注) Li Shan
    李善 .

Edition - the "Hai-lu-hsien" 海 錄 軒 ; (preface) dated Ch'ien-Lung
    37/1772.   Blocks; "mao-t'ai" paper.

Index - a general table of contents for 60 chüan.

Bound in 1 t'ao 6 ts'ê.

Remarks - the item is complete and without defects.

    (#) 012-zafk 19/1   031-bgdf 186/1   Gest Nos. 262, 302, 572
    and 1074   Toronto No. 542.

———◆———

Accession No. **721**   Index No. - **140-khjo**

Title   " **P'êng-lai hsien chih** "
                         蓬 莱 縣 志

Classification - **B-194** 地 理 一 別 志
Subject - a gazeteer of the **P'êng-lai** District in the province of
   Shangtung.

References - **012-zafk 7/9.**

Author - (撰) **Wang Wên-tao** 王 文 燾 and others.

Edition - an official publication; (preface) dated Tao-Kuang 19/1839.
   Blocks; "mao-pien" paper.

Index - a table of contents for 14 chüan.

Bound in **1 t'ao 8 ts'ê.**

Remarks - an ordinary edition; the item is in good condition.

214

———•———

Accession No. 722   Index No. - 060-gzze   070-zamz

Title   " Hsü Wên-ch'ang p'ing hsüan Fang Chêng-hsüeh wên chi "

徐 文 長 評 選 方 正 學 文 集

Classification - D-43 別 集 一 文

Subject - an individual collection of prose; with commentary.

References - none to this edition.

Author - by Fang Hsiao-ju 方 孝 儒 ; (評 選) Hsü Wei 徐 渭 ;

(閱) Yü Yün-hsieh 俞 允 諧 .

Edition - a Ming edition; no date notation.   Blocks; bamboo paper.

Index - a table of contents for 11 chüan.

Bound in 1 t'ao 8 ts'ê; doubly interleaved.

Remarks - this is a good edition; and the item is apparently
complete and without defects.

———•———

Accession No. **723**   Index No. - **072-zg1**

Title   " **Jih** **shê** **pien** "
                            日　涉　編

Classification - **B-157**　時　令
Subject - (Gest No. 2486) "in general, a collection of poems having
   for their subject the "seasons", and matters connected therewith."

References - 012-zafk 5/31   031-bgdf 67/6   Gest No. 2486.

Author - (編輯) **Ch'ên Chieh** 陳垯 .

Edition - no notation; (preface) dated Wan-Li "hsin-hai" 39/1611.
   Blocks; "mien" paper.

Index - none; 12 chüan.

Bound in 1 t'ao 12 ts'ê.

Remarks - a fairly good edition; the item is complete and without
   important defects.

The University of Toronto Chinese Library

Accession No. 724   Index No. - 007-zcgg   123-gdm

Title   " Erh-ju-t'ing Ch'ün fang p'u "
　　　　　　　　二 如 亭 群 芳 譜
　　　　　　　　" Ch'ün fang p'u "
　　　　　　　　群 芳 譜

Classification - C-283 譜 錄 - 草 木

Subject - a herbarium under 12 heads,- the Heavens, the Year, Grains,
　　Vegetables, Fruits, Tea and Bamboo, Mulberry, Hemp and Grass-
　　cloth Plants, Medicinal Plants, Trees, Flowers, Shrubs, and
　　Birds and Fishes; the chief portion of which consists of
　　extracts from preceding authors, ancient and modern, regarding (#)

References - Wylie's Notes page 152 160-1j 012-zafk 12/10
　　031-bgdf 116/38   Gest No. 863   Toronto No. 466.

Author - (纂輯) Wang Hsiang-chin 王 象 晋 .

Edition - no particular notation; (postscriptum) dated T'ien-Ch'i
　　"hsin-yu" 1/1621.   Blocks; bamboo paper.

Index - a general table of "classifications" with the number of
　　chüan for each; separate lists for each ts'ê.

Bound in 2 t'ao 20 ts'ê (10 each).

Remarks - a fairly good edition; complete and with no defects.

　(#)   the various productions of the garden and field; and the
　　details relate mainly to the medicinal virtues of the different
　　objects.

217

The University of Toronto Chinese Library

Accession No.   725   Index No. - 106-zzzf

Title   " Pai Hsiang-shan shih chi "
               白 香 山 詩 集

Classification - D-38 別 集 － 詩
Subject - an individual literary collection,- poetry.

References - 163-ggcz 12/10   031-bgld 15/22   012-zafk 15/10
     031-bgdf 151/4   Gest Nos. 275 and 2082.

Author - by Po Chü-i 白 居 易 ; (編 訂) Wang Li-ming 汪 立 名.

Edition - the "I-yü-ts'ao-t'ang" 一 隅 草 堂 ; (preface) dated
     K'ang-Hsi "kuei-wei" 42/1703.   Blocks; bamboo paper.

Index - a detailed table of contents for 40 chüan, including 長 慶
     20 chüan, 後 集 17 chüan, 別 集 1 chüan, 補 遺 2 chüan.

Bound in 1 t'ao 10 ts'ê.

Remarks - the item is complete and in generally good condition.

218

The University of Toronto Chinese Library

Accession No. 726   Index No. - 061-dphh   040-cid

Title   " Chung-hsien Han wei wang An-yang chi "
               忠 獻 韓 魏 王 安 陽 集

Classification - D-33 別 集 - 詩 文

Subject - an individual miscellaneous collection of prose and poetry.

References - 160-1j   031-bgld 15/32   030-iaff 26/12   106-gdkn 73/12
    012-zafk 15/13   031-bgdf 152/27   Gest Nos. 600 and 1591.

Author - Han Ch'i 韓 琦. 10081015

Edition - the "Chou-chin-t'ang" 晝 錦 堂 ; (preface) dated
    Ch'ien-Lung "jên-ch'ên" 37/1772.   Blocks; "fên" paper.

Index - a general table of contents for all prefaces etc., and 50
    chüan; a detailed table of contents for 50 chüan.

Bound in 1 t'ao 10 ts'ê.

Remarks - an ordinary edition; the item is in good condition.

Accession No.   727   Index No. - 170-hppf

Title   " T'ao-lu ts'ung k'o "
                        陶　盧　叢　刻

Classification - C-338 雜家 － 叢書
Subject - a collection of 29 miscellaneous reprints.

References - 029-pffz 364.

Author - <u>Wang Shu-nan</u> 王　樹　枏．

Edition - privately published; latest date 1919.   Blocks; "fên"

    paper.

Index - a list of works for the 初集 ; a separate list for the 二集

Bound in 8 t'ao 75 ts'ê (8-9-10-11-10-11-9-7).

Remarks - a good modern edition; the item is as new.   In the last

    t'ao 4 ts'ê are replacements from another copy.

Accession No. 728   Index No. - 149-hehg

Title   " Lün Mèng ching i "
                 論 孟 精 義

Classification - A-134 四 書 一 論 語 A-135 四 書 一 孟 子
Subject - a collection of commentaries, by ancient scholars, on the
    "Lün-yü",- the Confucian Analects, and "Mèng-tzŭ",- the
    Philosophy of Mencius.

References - 163-ggcz 3/5   031-bgld 4/4   030-iaff 4/14   012-zafk 3/7
    031-bgdf 35/24.
Author - (撰) Chu Hsi 朱 熹 .

Edition - no particular notation; no date, possibly of the Ch'ien-Lung
    period.   Blocks; "mao-pien" paper.

Index - a list of the commentators with compiler's notes; "Lün-yü"
    in 20 chüan; "Mèng-tzŭ" 14 chüan.

Bound in 2 t'ao 13 ts'è (6-7).

Remarks - a very good edition; the item is complete and without
    defects.

The University of Toronto Chinese Library

Accession No. 729   Index No. - 196-feih

Title   " Hung-pao chieh lu "
                        鴻苞 節 錄

Classification - C-308 雜家 - 雜文
Subject - a "miscellany" on a variety of unrelated subjects.

References - Gest No. 2027.

Author - (著) T'u Lung 屠 隆 ; (編) T'u Chi-lieh 屠 繼 烈.

Edition - the "Pao-yen-chai" 保硯齋 ; dated Hsien-Fêng 7/1857.
    Blocks; "fên" paper.

Index - a general table of contents for 10 chüan.

Bound in 2 t'ao 10 ts'ê (5-5).

Remarks - a very good edition; the item is complete and in perfect
    condition.

The University of Toronto Chinese Library

Accession No. **730**   Index No. - **060-gzzz   060-gzzd**

Title   " **Hsü Wên-ch'ang wên chi** "

徐 文 長 文 集

Classification - **D-33** 別 集 － 詩 文

Subject - **an individual literary collection,- prose and poetry.**

References - **012-zafk 16/30   031-bgdf 178/42   Gest No. 1245.**

Author - **Hsü Wei** 徐 渭 •

Edition - **an undated Ming edition.   Blocks; bamboo paper.**

Index - **a table of contents for 30 chüan.**

Bound in **2 t'ao 15 ts's (8-7); doubly interleaved.**

Remarks - **the item is in fairly good condition and complete.**

Accession No. 731   Index No. - 072-dhao   072-dzao

Title   " <u>Ming hsien ch'ih tu</u> "
                          明   賢   尺   牘
                        " <u>Ming jên ch'ih tu hsüan</u> "
                          明   人   尺   牘   選

<u>Classification</u> - D-73 總 集 - 文

<u>Subject</u> - a collection of letters of noted scholars of the Ming
    Dynasty.

<u>References</u> - 012-zafk 19/19.

<u>Author</u> - (同 輯) <u>Wang Yüan-hsün</u> 王 元 勳 and <u>Ch'êng Hua-lu</u> 程 化 騄

<u>Edition</u> - the "<u>Yü-yüan</u>" 榆 園 ; dated Kuang-Hsü "kêng-tzŭ" 26/1900.
    Blocks; "fên" paper.

<u>Index</u> - a list of names for 4 chüan.

<u>Bound in</u> 1 t'ao 4 ts'ê; doubly interleaved.

<u>Remarks</u> - an ordinary edition; the item is complete.

224

———•———

Accession No. **732**   Index No. – 076-heah   037-ahhg

Title   " Ch'in-ting T'ien-lu-lin-lang shu mu "
　　　　　欽　定　天　禄　琳　琅　書　目

Classification – B-342 目錄 － 經籍

Subject – the Imperial catalogue of the Sung, Yüan and Ming works

stored in the T'ien-lu-lin-lang palace during the time of

Emperor Ch'ien-Lung.

References – 160-1j 163-ggoz 6/6 031-bgld 8/19 012-zafk 9/15

031-bgdf 85/16 Gest No. 674 Toronto No. 581.

Author – compiled on Imperial order by Yü Min-chung 于 敏 中

and others.

Edition – no particular notation; (postscriptum) dated Kuang-Hsü

10/1884.   Blocks; "fēn" paper.

Index – none; 10 chüan; 後 編 20 chüan.

Bound in 2 t'ao 10 ts'ê (5-5).

Remarks – a duplicate of Toronto No. 581.   The item is complete and

in perfect condition.

Accession No. 733   Index No. - 019-cchp

Title   " Kung-shun-t'ang ts'ung shu "
                    功 順 堂 叢 書

Classification - C-338 雜家 - 叢書
Subject - a collection of 18 miscellaneous reprints.

References - 012-zafk 13/18   029-pffz 197.

Author - (編) P'an Tsu-yin 潘 祖 蔭.

Edition - no particular notation; no date.   Blocks; "fên" paper.

Index - a list of the 18 works.

Bound in 2 t'ao 24 ts'ê (12-12).

Remarks - the item is complete and in good condition.

The University of Toronto Chinese Library

Accession No. **734**   Index No. - **064-hghl   085-fccd**

Title   " **Shou-ching-t'ang i shu** "
授 經 堂 遺 書
" **Hung Pei-chiang hsien-shêng i chi** "
洪 北 江 先 生 遺 集

Classification - **C-338** 雜 家 - 叢 書
Subject - a collection of miscellaneous reprints.

References - **012-zafk 13/15   029-pffz 309.**

Author - (著) <u>Hung Liang-chi</u> 洪 亮 吉 .

Edition - a reprint by the "<u>Shou-ching-t'ang</u>" 授 經 堂 ; dated
Kuang-Hsü "ting-ch'ou" 3/1877.   Blocks; "fên" paper.

Index - a list of works with the number of chüan.

Bound in **12 t'ao 84 ts'ê (7 each).**

Remarks - the item is complete and in good condition.

Accession No. **735**   Index No. - **007-zzbb   055-abb**

Title   " **Erh-shih-ssŭ shih** "
                        二 十 四 史

                      " **Nien-ssŭ shih** "
                        廿 四 史

Classification - **B-12** 正 史

Subject - (Gest No. 1521) "the twenty-four (24) officially approved

   and authorized standard dynastic histories of China."

References - **Wylie's Notes page 15   160-1j   163-ggcz 4/1   031-bgld 5/1**

   Gest No. 1521   Numerous in all catalogues for the several
   separate histories.

Author - various for the different histories; the collection edited

   by an Imperial commission headed by **Prince Hung Chou** 弘 晝 .

Edition - a "palace" edition; (preface) dated Ch'ien-Lung 12/1747.

   Blocks; "t'ai-hsi-lien" paper.

Index - a list of chapter headings at the beginning of each history.

Bound in 84 t'ao 378 ts'ê.

Remarks - the item is apparently complete and in good condition.

   The section on the Five Dynasties (old) appears to be a

   replacement from another copy, for the ts'ê are 1/2

   inch shorter.

The University of Toronto Chinese Library

Accession No. 736   Index No. - 007-zzbb   055-abb

Title   " Êrh-shih-ssŭ shih "
           二 十 四 史
          " Nien-ssŭ shih "
          廿 四 史

Classification - B-12 正 史

Subject - (Gest No. 1521) "the twenty-four (24) officially approved
   and authorized standard dynastic histories of China."

References - Wylie's Notes page 15 160-1j 163-ggcz 4/1 031-bgld 5/1

   Gest No. 1521 Toronto No. 735. Numerous in all catalogues for
   the several separate histories.

Author - various for the different histories; the collection edited

   by an Imperial commission headed by Prince Hung Chou 弘 晝 .

Edition - the "Han-fên-lou" 涵 芬 樓 , or The Commercial Press;

   dated "ping-ch'ên" 1916.   Process; "fên" paper.

Index - a list of chapter headings at the beginning of each history.

Bound in 78 t'ao 711 ts'ê.

Remarks - a modern edition; the item is new.

Accession No. 737   Index No. - 072-echd   060-lhgk

Title   " Ch'un-tsai-t'ang ch'üan shu "
                 春　在　堂　全　書
                 " Tê-ch'ing Yü Yin-fu so chu shu "
                 德　清　俞　蔭　甫　所　著　書

Classification - C-338 雜家 - 叢書

Subject - (Gest No. 1655) "an individual literary collection,-
    both prose and poetry,- on a variety of subjects in all
    classes of literature."

References - 012-zafk 13/18   029-pffz 294   Gest No. 1655.

Author - Yü Yüeh 俞 樾.

Edition - privately published; dated T'ung-Chih 10/1871.   Blocks;
    "mao-t'ai" paper.

Index - a list of the 21 works.

Bound in 8 t'ao 72 ts's.

Remarks - the item is apparently complete and in good condition.

The University of Toronto Chinese Library

Accession No. **738**   Index No. – **096-zfzd**

Title   " Yü-han-shan-fang chi i shu "
              玉 函 山 房 輯 佚 書

Classification – **C-338** 雜 家 － 叢 書
Subject – a collection of reprints of a large number of short works
    in all four classes of Chinese literature.

References – **029-pffz 176   012-zafk 13/16   Gest No. 620.**

Author – compiled by **Ma Kuo-han** 馬 國 翰.

Edition – that of "Li-shih" 李 氏 ; dated Kuang-Hsü 15/1889.
    Blocks; "mao-pien" paper.

Index – a list of the 33 "classifications"; separate table of
    contents at the beginning of each class; 玉 函 山 房 目 耕 帖
    31 chüan.
Bound in **10** t'ao **80** ts'ê.

Remarks – an ordinary edition; the item is in good condition and
    apparently complete.

231

———•———

Accession No. 739   Index No. - 031-hhdp

Title   " <u>Kuo-ch'ao</u> <u>ch'i</u> <u>hsien</u> <u>lei</u> <u>chêng</u> <u>ch'u</u> <u>pien</u> "
          國　朝　耆　獻　類　徵　初　編

Classification - B-117 傳記一總錄

Subject - (Gest No. 1522) "a comprehensive collection of
     biographies of noted persons of the Ch'ing Dynasty
     period from the commencement until the 30th year of
     Tao-Kuang,- i.e., from 1616 to 1850 A. D."

References - 012-zafk 5/22   Gest No. 1522.

Author - (撰) <u>Li Huan</u> 李　桓 .

Edition - that of "<u>Li-shih</u>" 李　氏 ; (title-page) dated Kuang-Hsü
     "chia-shên" 10/1884.   Blocks; "mao-pien" paper.

Index - a general table of sections; a table of chapter headings
     for 204 and 484 chüan (in 20 chüan); 20 miscellaneous chüan,-
     making 720 chüan in all.
Bound in 32 t'ao 294 ts'ê.

Remarks - this item is apparently complete and with no important
     defects.

Accession No. 740   Index No. - 076-hedg   011-dgz

Title   " Ch'in-ting Ch'üan T'ang wên "
                    欽　定　全　唐　文

Classification - D-73 總集 - 文

Subject - a compenhensive general collection of prose writings of
    Emperors, famous scholars, etc of the T'ang Dynasty.

References - 160-1j 012-zafk 19/15   Gest No. 861.

Author - compiled by an Imperial commission headed by Tung Kao 董誥.

Edition - apparently based upon the "palace" edition; dated Chia-Ch'ing
    23/1818.   Blocks; "fên" paper.

Index - a list of names in 1,000 chüan arranged chronologically;
    detailed table of contents at the beginning of each chüan.

Bound in 30 t'ao 240 ts'ê (8 each).

Remarks - a fairly good edition; the item is complete and without
    defects.

—•—

Accession No. 741   Index No. - 060-hdgn   162-gnio

Title   " <u>Yü-p'i T'ung chien chi lan</u> "
　　　　　　　御　批　通　鑑　輯　覽

Classification - B-22 編年

<u>Subject</u> - a record of important historical events, covering the
　　period from the <u>Emperor Fu-Hsi</u> down to and including the
　　<u>Ming Dynasty</u>.

<u>References</u> - 160-1j   163-ggcz 4/9   031-bgld 5/24   012-zafk 4/12
　　031-bgdf 47/57   Gest No. 905.

<u>Author</u> - compiled on order of <u>Emperor Ch'ien-Lung</u> by a commission
　　headed by <u>Fu Hêng</u> 傅　恒 .

<u>Edition</u> - officially published; (preface) dated Ch'ien-Lung "ting-hai"
　　32/1767.   Blocks; "fên" paper.

<u>Index</u> - a general table of contents for 120 chüan arranged
　　chronologically.

<u>Bound in</u> 8 t'ao 58 ts'ê (8-7-7-7-7-7-8-7).

<u>Remarks</u> - the item is complete and in good condition except for
　　some slight stains and a few worm-holes.

Accession No.   742   Index No. - 123-gf(zb)d   046-zh(zb)d

Title   " Ch'ün   shu   k'ao   so "
               群   書   考   索

               " Shan-t'ang   k'ao   so "
               山   堂   考   索

Classification - C-348 類書
Subject - a general encyclopaedia, with copious literary references.

References - 160-1j   163-ggcz 10/14   031-bgld 14/10   037-ahhg 9/41
    (hsü) 17/9   167-mhfm 17/8   030-iaff 20/8   106-gdkn 60/8
    012-zafk 13/22   031-bgdf 135/44   Gest No. 1466.
Author - (編輯) Chang Ju-yü 章 如 愚 .

Edition - the "Shên-tu-chai" 慎 獨 齋 ; dated Chêng-Tê 正 德
    "mou-ch'ên" 3/1508. (See end of chüan 10 of the 前 集)
    Blocks; bamboo paper.

Index - (前集) a list of 15 main headings; a detailed table of
    contents for 66 chüan; (後集) 9 main headings and 65 chüan;
    (續集) 17 main headings and 56 chüan; (列集) 11 main   (#)
Bound in 8 t'ao 64 ts'ê (8 each).

Remarks - with the exception of some stains, this item is in quite
    good condition. Whole of chüan 21 in 前集 is handwritten.
    The 5th t'ao containing 8 ts'ê is apparently a replacement from
    another copy printed with the same set of blocks on different
    paper and possibly at an earlier period.

    (#)   headings and 25 chüan.

235

Accession No. 743   Index No. - 072-dozz

Title   " Ming ming ch'ên yen hsing lu "
                明 名 臣 言 行 錄

Classification - B-117 傳記 - 總錄
Subject - a collection of biographical sketches of famous ministers
     and officials of the Ming Dynasty.

References - none.

Author - (編輯) Hsü K'ai-jên 徐 開 任.

Edition - no particular notation; (preface) dated K'ang-Hsi "hsin-yu"
     20/1681.   Blocks; bamboo paper.

Index - a list of names in 95 chüan.

Bound in 4 t'ao 20 ts'ê (5 each).

Remarks - this is a fairly good edition; and the item is complete
     and in perfect condition.

The University of Toronto Chinese Library

Accession No. **744**   Index No. - **010-bzzk**

Title   " <u>Yüan shih Ch'ang-ch'ing chi</u> "

元 氏 長 慶 集

Classification - **D-33** 別集 - 詩文

Subject - **an individual literary collection,- prose and poetry.**

References - **163-ggcz 12/10   031-bgld 15/22   037-ahhg 10/12**

106-gdkn 70/13   030-iaff 25/8   167-mhfm 19/32   (#)

Author - (著) <u>Yüan Chên</u> 元 稹 · 779-831

Edition - **a Ming edition; (preface) dated Wan-Li "chia-ch'ên"**

32/1604.   Blocks; bamboo paper.

Index - **a table of contents for 60 chüan;** 補 遺 **6 chüan.**

Bound in **2 t'ao 10 ts'ê; doubly interleaved.**

Remarks **- this is a very good edition; and the item is complete;**

and in generally good condition.

(#)   012-zafk 15/10   031-bgdf 151/1   Gest No. 275-a

Accession No. 745   Index No. - 106-zzzk

Title   " Po shih Ch'ang-ch'ing chi "
                   白 氏 長 慶 集

Classification - D-33 別 集 - 詩文
Subject - an individual collection of prose and poetry mainly
    the latter.

References - 163-ggez 12/10   031-bgld 15/22   037-ahhg 10/11
    030-iaff 25/9   167-mhfm 19/33-34   012-zafk 15/10   (#)

Author - (著) Po Chü-1 白居易 .

Edition - no particular notation; no date, but apparently same as
    given in No. 744.   Blocks; bamboo paper.

Index - a table of contents for 71 chüan.

Bound in 4 t'ao 26 ts's (7-7-6-6); doubly interleaved.

Remarks - this item is complete and in generally good condition.

    (#) 031-bgdf 151/2   Gest No. 275-b.

Accession No. 746   Index No. - 053-hicf

Title   " K'ang-Hsi tzŭ tien "
              康　熙　字　典

Classification - A-161 小學 一 字書

Subject - the standard dictionary of the Chinese language, with
    the characters arranged according to the 214 radicals.

References - Wylie's Notes page 10   160-1j   163-ggcz 3/13
    031-bgld 4/24   012-zafk 3/22   031-bgdf 41/50   Gest Nos. 306 and
    906.

Author - compiled by an Imperial commission headed by Chang Yü-shu
    張　玉　書．

Edition - a "palace" edition; (preface) dated K'ang-Hsi 55/1716.
    Blocks; "t'ai-hsi-lien" paper.

Index - a table of the 214 radicals in 12 "chi" 集 ; separate list
    at the beginning of each "chi"; 補 遺 12 "chi".

Bound in 6 t'ao 40 ts'ê (8-6-6-6-6-8).

Remarks - this is a very good edition; and the item is complete and
    without defects.   The paper is rather fragile owing to its age.

Accession No. 747   Index No. - 162-1bhd

Title   " <u>Tao-ku-t'ang ch'üan chi</u> "
道 古 堂 全 集

Classification - D-33 别 集 - 詩 文
Subject - an individual collection of prose and poetry.

References - none.

Author - (撰) <u>Hang Shih-chün</u> 杭 世 駿.

Edition - the "<u>Wang's Chên-ch'i-t'ang</u>" 汪 氏 振 綺 堂 ; dated
Kuang-Hsü "mou-tzǔ" 14/1888.   Blocks; "mao-pien" paper.

Index - a general table of contents for 16 ts'ê; separate tables
of contents for (文 集) 48 chüan; (詩 集) 26 chüan;
(集 外 文) 1 chüan; (集 外 詩) 1 chüan.
Bound in 2 t'ao 16 ts'ê (8 each).

Remarks - the item is complete and in very good condition.

Accession No. 748   Index No. - 040-dzn

Title   " <u>Sung wên kuei</u> "
                宋　文　歸

Classification - D-73 總集 一 文
Subject - a general collection of prose compositions of famous
         scholars of the <u>Sung Dynasty</u>; with commentaries.

References - 012-zafk 19/11   031-bgdf 193/24.

Author - (評選) <u>Chung Hsing</u> 鍾惺.

Edition - the "<u>Chi-hsien-t'ang</u>" 集賢堂; no date, but of the
         Ming period.   Blocks; bamboo paper.

Index - a list of names for 20 chüan; separate detailed table of
        contents at the beginning of each chüan.

Bound in 4 t'ao 40 ts'ê (10 each).

Remarks - the item is complete and without important defects.
          The paper has been backed.

Accession No. 749   Index No. - 018-bhcz

Title   " Ch'ieh-wên-chai wên oh'ao "
切 問 齋 文 鈔

Classification - D-73 總集 一文
Subject - a general collection of miscellaneous prose writings.
Essays by 清 scholars on political economic social problems
H 252

References - 012-zafk 19/22.

Author - (輯) Lu Yao 陸 燿 .

Edition - no particular notation; dated Ch'ien-Lung "i-wei" 40/1775.
Blocks; "fên" paper.

Index - a general table of "classifications" for 30 chüan; separate
detailed tables of contents at the beginning of each chüan.

Bound in 1 t'ao 10 ts'ê.

Remarks - a fairly good edition; complete and in perfect condition.

---•---

Accession No. 750   Index No. - 007-zehp

Title   " Erh-ssŭ-t'ang ts'ung shu "
                   二　思　堂　叢　書

Classification - C-338 雜 家 一 叢 書
Subject - a collection of reprints of 6 general works.

References - 058-jffz (hsü)   閏/50.

Author - (著) Liang Chang-chü 梁 章 鉅 .

Edition - the "Chê-chiang-shu-chü" 浙 江 書 局; dated Kuang-Hsü
    1/1875.   Blocks; "fên" paper.

Index - a list of the 6 works at the back of the title-page.

Bound in 2 t'ao 16 ts'ê (8-8).

Remarks - a modern edition; the item is new.

Accession No.　751　　　　Index No. - 030-bced

Title　　　　　　　" Shih chi p'ing lin "
　　　　　　　　　史　記　評　林

Classification - B-367 史評

Subject - commentaries on the "Shih Chi" 史記 of Ssŭ-ma Ch'ien
　　司　馬　遷 .

References - 012-zafk 9/29　Gest Nos. 81 and 358.

Author - (輯校) Ling Chih-lung 凌稚隆 ; (增補) Li Kuang-chin
　　李光縉 .

Edition - no particular notation; (preface) dated Wan-Li 5/1577.
　　Blocks; bamboo paper.

Index - a table of contents for 130 chüan.

Bound in 4 t'ao 24 ts'ĕ (6 each).

Remarks - the item contains a number of repaired "age" defects;
　　and it is not quite complete,- chüan 91 and 123 missing.
　　Manuscript pages:- 凡例 , 姓氏 , 書目 in the 1st ts'ĕ;
　　chüan 15 page 34; and whole of chüan 37-38-39.

244

The University of Toronto Chinese Library

Accession No. 752   Index No. - 085-kfed

Title   " Han shu p'ing lin "

汉 书 评 林

Classification - B-367 史 评

Subject - commentaries on the "Han shu" 汉 书 ,- History of the

Former Han Dynasty,- of Pan Ku 班 固 .

References - 012-zafk 9/29   Gest Nos. 82 and 701.

Author - (辑 校) Ling Chih-lung 凌 稚 隆 .

Edition - no particular notation; (preface) dated Wan-Li "kuei-wei"

11/1583.   Blocks; bamboo paper.

Index - a table of contents for 100 chüan.

Bound in 4 t'ao 20 ts'è (5 each).

Remarks - the item is complete and in generally good condition.

Accession No.   753   Index No. - 140-ozjh

Title   " I wên lei chü "
                        藝 文 類 聚

Classification - C-348 類書
Subject - a general encyclopaedia, with copious literary references.

References - 160-1j   163-ggcz 10/11   031-bgld 14/2   037-ahhg 9/48
      106-gdkn 59/3   030-iaff 20/1   167-mhfm 17/1   012-zafk 13/20
      (#)
Author - (撰) Ou-yang Hsün 歐 陽 詢 .

Edition - a reprint by the "Hung-ta-t'ang" 宏 達 堂 ; dated
      Kuang-Hsü "chi-mao" 5/1879.   Blocks; "fên" paper.

Index - a classified table of contents for 100 chüan.

Bound in   4 t'ao 32 ts'ê (8 each).

Remarks - a well-known standard work of this class; the item is
      complete and with no defects.

      (#) 031-bgdf 135/4   Gest No. 289.

246

Accession No. 754-a   Index No. - 067-zfae

Title   " Wên chang chêng tsung "
             文 章 正 宗

Classification - D-63 總集 — 詩文

Subject - (Gest No. 1540) "a general collection of prose compositions
      and poems, written during the period from ancient times down to
      the Sung Dynasty."

References - 160-1j   163-ggcz 16/4   031-bgld 19/13   037-ahhg 3/41
      (hsü) 7/9   167-mhfm 23/24   012-zafk 19/4   031-bgdf 187/18 (#)

Author - edited by Chên Tê-hsiu 真 德 秀 .

Edition - no particular notation; (preface) dated Ch'ien-Lung
      "ting-hai" 32/1767.   Blocks; bamboo paper.

Index - a detailed table of contents for 30 chüan.

Bound in 2 t'ao 20 ts'ê (10-10).

Remarks - an ordinary good edition; the item is complete and in
      perfect condition.

   (#) Gest Nos. 582, 599 and 1540   Toronto No. 803(d).

Accession No. 754-b   Index No. - 120-ozfa

Title   " Hsü Wên chang chêng tsung "
               續　文　章　正　宗

Classification - D-73 總集 一 文

Subject - a continuation and supplement to (a).

References - see under (a).

Author - edited by Chên Tê-hsiu 真 德 秀 .

Edition - uniform with (a); but dated Ch'ien-Lung "chia-wu" 39/1774.

Index - a detailed table of contents for 12 chüan.

Bound in 1 t'ao 10 ts'ê.

Remarks - as under (a).

The University of Toronto Chinese Library

Accession No.   755   Index No. - 031-bbeg

Title   " **Ssŭ-liu fa hai** "
               四 六 法 海

Classification - D-73 總集一文
Subject - a general collection of ancient prose compositions in
        the "four-six" style.

References - 160-1j   031-bgld 19/28   012-zafk 19/12   031-bgdf 189/32.

Author - (論次) <u>Wang Chih-chien</u> 王志堅．

Edition - no particular notation; (preface) dated T'ien-Ch'i 7/1627.
        Blocks; bamboo paper.

Index - a detailed table of contents for 12 chüan.

Bound in 2 t'ao 12 ts'ê (6-6).

Remarks - the item is complete and in generally good condition.

Accession No. 756   Index No. — 030-gdzz   030-gdzg

Title   " T'ang Sung shih ta chia ch'üan chi lu "
　　　　唐　宋　十　大　家　全　集　錄
　　　　" T'ang Sung ta chia ch'üan chi lu "
　　　　唐　宋　大　家　全　集　錄

Classification — D-63 總集 — 詩文 C-338 雜家 — 叢書

Subject — a collection of miscellaneous prose and poetic works of
　　10 noted scholars of the T'ang and Sung dynasties.

References — 029-pffz 320.

Author — (錄) Ch'u Hsin 儲 欣 .

Edition — the "Sung-lin-t'ang" 松 鱗 堂 ; (preface) dated K'ang-Hsi
　　44/1705.　　Blocks; "mao-pien" paper.

Index — a general table of contents of the 10 works, with separate
　　lists at the beginning of each.

Bound in 4 t'ao 40 ts'$ (10 each).

Remarks — a fairly good edition; complete and without defects.

Accession No.   757   Index No.   - 062-nzlf

Title   " Tai   shih   i   shu "
                          戴 氏 遺 書

Classification - C-338 雜家 - 叢書
Subject - a collection of 13 miscellaneous reprints.

References - 029-pffz 560.

Author - (撰) Tai Chên 戴 震 .

Edition - privately published; (preface) dated Ch'ien-Lung 43/1778.
    Blocks; "mao-pien" paper.

Index - none.

Bound in   4 t'ao 22 ts'è (6-4-6-6).

Remarks - the item is complete and in perfect condition.

Accession No. 758   Index No. - 010-dibc   030-bcec

Title   " Kuang-Hsü T'ai-chou fu chih "
               光 緒 台 州 府 志

Classification - B-194 地理 - 別志
Subject - a "gazeteer" of T'ai-chou-fu during the period of Kuang-Hsü;
    now called Lin-hai-hsien 臨 海 縣 in the province of Chê-chiang.

References - none.

Author - (纂) Wang Chou-yao 王 舟 瑤 and Mao Tsung-ch'êng 毛 宗 澄;
    (校) Wang P'ei-yao 王 佩 瑤.

Edition - printed by the "T'ai-chou-lü-Hang-t'ung-hsiang-hui"
    台 州 旅 杭 同 鄉 會; (postscriptum) dated "ping-yin"
    1926.   Type; "mao-pien" paper.

Index - a general table of contents for 100 chüan.

Bound in 6 t'ao 60 ts'ê (10 each).

Remarks - a modern edition; the item is as new.

Accession No. 759   Index No. - 120-gnne

Title   " Ching chi chuan ku "
               經　籍　籑　詁

Classification - A-156 小學 - 訓詁

Subject - a dictionary of Chinese characters arranged according to
     rhymes, with explanations taken from various classical works.

References - 012-zafk 3/19   Gest No. 826.

Author - (譔集) Yüan Yüan 阮 元 .

Edition - the "Yüan's Hsiao-lang-hsüan-hsien-kuan" 阮氏小琅嬛僊館;
     (preface) dated Chia-Ch'ing "mou-wu" 3/1798.   Blocks; "fēn"
     paper.

Index - a table of the 5 tones and 106 finals in 106 chüan; separate
     detailed lists at the beginning of each chüan.

Bound in 6 t'ao 48 ts'ē (10-7-7-8-9-7).

Remarks - the item is complete and in good condition.

The University of Toronto Chinese Library

Title   " Hui k'o shu mu "

彙 刻 書 目

Classification - B-342 目錄 - 經籍

Subject - a list of "ts'ung-shu" 叢書 ,- collection of reprints,- with tables of contents, etc of the various collections.

References - Wylie's Notes page 76   012-zafk 9/19   Gest Nos. 419 and 1088.

Author - Ku Hsiu 顧 修 according to Wylie's Notes.

Edition - the "Fu-ying-shu-chü" 福 瀛 書 局 ; dated Kuang-Hsü 15/1889.   Blocks; "mao-pien" paper.

Index - tables of contents at the beginning of each of 20 sections.

Bound in 2 t'ao 20 ts's (10-10).

Remarks - a useful reference work; the item is complete.

The University of Toronto Chinese Library

Accession No. 761   Index No. - 073-fg   073-fdk

Title   " Shu-ching "
                書   經
              " Shu chi chuan "
                書   集   傳

Classification - A-21 書

Subject - (Gest No. 3658) "a commentary on the so-called "Canon of
    History" (Wylie- Book of Government); containing the historical
    remains of the Yü 虞 , Hsia 夏 , Shang 商 , and Chou 周
    dynasties, and covering the period from about 2357 B. C. to 721
    B. C."

References - Wylie's Notes page 3   163-ggcz 1/10   031-bgld 2/4
    037-ahhg 5/3 (hsü) 8/10   167-mhfm 2/11   030-iaff 1/25   (#)

Author - Ts'ai Ch'ên 蔡 沉 .

Edition - no particular notation; no date, but of the earlier part
    of the Ming Dynasty.   Blocks; "mien" paper.

Index - none; in 6 chüan.

Bound in 2 t'ao 8 ts'è (5-3).

Remarks - this is a very good edition indeed; and the item is complete
    and in perfect condition.

    (#) 012-zafk 1/16   031-bgdf 11/20   Gest Nos. 1731 and 3658.

Accession No.   762   Index No. - 011-dbbb

Title " Ch'üan shang-ku san-tai Ch'in Han San-kuo Liu-ch'ao wên "
全 上 古 三 代 秦 漢 三 國 六 朝 文

Classification - D-63 總集一詩文
Subject - a comprehensive collection of prose and poetic writings
of more than 3,000 authors of the period from the beginning
of Chinese history down to the end of the six dynasties.

References - 012-zafk 19/28   058-jffz 15/2   Gest No. 158.

Author - (編) Yen K'o-chün 嚴 可 均 .

Edition - the "Kuang-ya-shu-chü" 廣 雅 書 局 ; dated Kuang-Hsü
"kuei-ssŭ" 19/1893.   Blocks; "fên" paper.

Index - a general list of the 15 sub-divisions of the work in
altogether 740 chüan; a separate list at the beginning of each
sub-division.
Bound in 10 t'ao 100 ts'ê (10 each).

Remarks - the item is complete and without defects.

Accession No. 763   Index No. - 001-bhff

Title   " San-kuo liang-Chin Nan-pei-ch'ao wên hsüan "

三 國 兩 晉 南 北 朝 文 選

Classification - D-63 總 集 - 詩 文

Subject - a general collection of prose and poetic writings of
famous scholars and officials covering the period from the
beginning of San-kuo 三 國 down to the end of Nan-pei-ch'ao
or Liu-ch'ao 六 朝 .

References - 012-zafk 19/9.

Author - (仝 選) Ch'ien Shih-hsing 錢 士 馨 and Lu Shang-lan
陸 上 瀾 .

Edition - an undated Ming edition.   Blocks; bamboo paper.

Index - separate tables of contents for the 12 different kingdoms
and reigns; 附 輯 1 chüan.

Bound in 2 t'ao 12 ts'ê (6-6).

Remarks - a good edition; complete and in perfect condition.

Accession No.   764   Index No. - 031-hhzb   046-zbfd

Title   " Kuo-ch'ao Shan-tso shih ch'ao "
             國 朝 山 左 詩 鈔

Classification - D-68 總集 - 詩

Subject - a general collection of poems written by scholars of the
    province of Shangtung of the Ch'ing Dynasty.

References - 012-zafk 19/20   Gest No. 183.

Author - compiled by Lu Chien-tsêng 盧見曾.

Edition - the "Ya-yü-t'ang" 雅雨堂 ; dated Ch'ien-Lung "mou-yin"
    23/1758.   Blocks; "mao-pien" paper.

Index - a list of names for 60 chüan.

Bound in 2 t'ao 20 ts'ê (10-10).

Remarks - the item is complete and in good condition.

The University of Toronto Chinese Library

Accession No.   765-a   Index No. - 085-zge

Title   " <u>Shui   ching   chu</u> "
                 水   經   注

Classification - B-197 地理 一 河渠

<u>Subject</u> - a commentary on the "<u>Shui ching</u>",- the so-called
   <u>Water Classic</u>, an ancient work on the water-courses of
   China.

<u>References</u> - Wylie's Notes page 53 160-1j   163-ggcz 5/13
   031-bgld 7/17 037-ahhg 8/36 (hsü) 15/10 106-gdkn 33/1 (#)

<u>Author</u> - of original - <u>Sang Ch'in</u> 桑 欽 ; of this work - <u>Li Tao-yüan</u>
   酈 道 元 .

<u>Edition</u> - no particular notation; (preface) dated Wan-Li "i-yu"
   13/1585.   Blocks; bamboo paper.

<u>Index</u> - a table of contents for 40 chüan.

<u>Bound in</u> 2 t'ao 14 ts'8; 2nd t'ao with (b).

<u>Remarks</u> - a very good edition; the item is complete and in perfect
   condition.

   (#)   030-iaff 12/1   167-mhfm 11/12   012-zafk 8/1
         031-bgdf 69/1   Gest No. 342.

Accession No. 765-b   Index No. - 046-zgg

Title   " Shan hai ching "
                     山 海 經

Classification - C-368 小 說 家

Subject - an ancient work containing curious descriptions of the
        hills and rivers.

References - Wylie's Notes page 43   160-1j   163-ggcz 11/5   031-bgld
        14/33   167-mhfm 17/19   030-iaff 21/17   106-gdkn 64/6   (#)

Author - (傳) Kuo P'o 郭 璞 .

Edition - uniform with (a).

Index - a list of chapter headings for 18 chüan.

Bound in 2 ts'ê in 2nd t'ao of (a).

Remarks - as under (a).

    (#)   012-zafk 14/12   031-bgdf 142/1   Gest No. 1497.

Accession No. 766   Index No. - 075-hdck

Title   " Chih-wu ming shih t'u k'ao "
               植 物 名 實 圖 考

Classification - C-283 譜録 一 草木
Subject - (Gest No. 1432) "an encyclopaedia of trees and plants;
    containing descriptions and illustrations of some 1714 and
    838 varieties."

References - 160-1j   012-zafk 12/10   Gest Nos. 520 and 1432.

Author - (著) Wu Ch'i-chün 吳其濬.

Edition - the "Chün-wên-shu-chü" 濬文書局 ; (preface) dated
    Kuang-Hsü "kêng-ch'ên" 6/1880.   Blocks; "fên" paper.

Index - a table of contents for 38 chüan arranged according to
    classes of grains, vegetables, grasses, fruits, and trees;
    and the same for 22 chüan for the "Ch'ang-pien".   (#)
Bound in 6 t'ao 40 ts'ê (7-6-6-7-7-7).

Remarks - a useful reference work.   The item is complete and in
    practically perfect condition.

    (#)   A detailed list of contents at the beginning of each chüan.

The University of Toronto Chinese Library

Accession No.   767   Index No. - 075-kfdf

Title   " Yüeh lü ch'üan shu "
             樂　律　全　書

Classification - A-141 樂

Subject - a collection of 11 works on music and its related subjects
   of measurements, mathematical calculations, rhythmic dancing;
   calendar calculations etc, with numerous illustrations.

References 160-1j   163-ggcz 3/8   031-bgld 4/13   030-iaff 4/22
   029-pffz page 508   012-zafk 3/15   031-bgdf 38/20 Gest No. 278.

Author - (撰) Chu Tsai-yü 朱 載 堉.

Edition - a Ming edition; (preface) dated Wan-Li 12/1584. Blocks;
   "mien" paper.

Index - none for the collection; 030-iaff mentions 47 chüan for
   the whole work.

Bound in 6 t'ao 40 ts'ê (7-6-6-8-6-7); doubly interleaved.

Remarks - this is a good edition; and the item is complete but with
   some slight repaired worm-holes. The number of chüan as given
   in 030-iaff is in accord with that of this item, though
   differing from the other catalogues.

Accession No. 768   Index No. - 031-bf

Title   " <u>Ssŭ</u> <u>shu</u> "
                            四 書

Classification - A-131 四書

Subject — a commentary on the "<u>Four Books</u>",- (1) "<u>Ta-hsüeh</u>";

(2) "<u>Chung-yung</u>"; (3) "<u>Lun-yü</u>"; and (4) "<u>Mêng-tzŭ</u>".

(See separate notes that follow).

References - Wylie's Notes page 7   160-1j   163-ggcz 3/4   031-bgld

4/3   167-mhfm 6/5   030-1aff 4/15   012-zafk 3/7   (#)

Author - <u>Chu Hsi</u> 朱熹.

Edition - a "Korean" edition; dated "Kêng-wu" 1870.   Blocks; Korean

paper.

Index - none.

Bound in 5 t'ao 16 ts'ê (2-3-4-4-3).

Remarks - this is a very good edition; and the item is complete

and in perfect condition.   The first 2 works,- the "<u>Ta-hsüeh</u>"

and "<u>Chung-yung</u>",- are replacements from a different copy and

the size of the ts'ê is smaller.

(#) 031-bgdf 35/21 Gest No. 1498 Toronto No. 602.

Accession No.   768-a   Index No. - 037-zmfb   037-zm

Title   " <u>Ta-hsüeh chang chü</u> "
                        大   學   章   句

                            " <u>Ta-hsüeh</u> "
                              大   學

Classification - A-132 四書-大學

Subject - (Gest No. 1498-a) "a commentary on the advanced course of
    study for youths under the <u>Chou Dynasty</u> educational system; a
    treatise on government."

References - as under No. 768.

Author - <u>Chu Hsi</u> 朱 熹 .

Edition - as under No. 768.

Index - none; 1 chüan.

Bound in 1 ts'ê in 1 t'ao with (b).

Remarks - as under No. 768.

Accession No.   768-b   Index No. - 002-chfb   002-ch

Title   " Chung-yung chang chü "
                中　庸　章　句
               " Chung-yung "
                中　　庸

Classification - A-133 四書 - 中庸

Subject - (Gest No. 1498-b) "a commentary on the "Doctrine of the
    Mean" .

References - as under No. 768.

Author - Chu Hsi 朱熹 .

Edition - as under No. 768.

Index - none; 1 chüan.

Bound in 1 ts'ê in 1 t'ao with (a).

Remarks - as under No. 768.

Accession No. 768-c   Index No. - 149-hgde   149-hg

Title   " Lun-yü chi chu "
                         論 語 集 註
                          " Lun-yü "
                         論 語

Classification - A-134 四 書 - 論 語

Subject - (Gest No. 1498-c) "a commentary on the discourses of
      Confucius with his followers and others."

References - as under No. 768.

Author - Chu Hsi 朱 熹 .

Edition - as under No. 768.

Index - none; 20 chüan.

Bound in 2 t'ao 7 ts'ê (3-4).

Remarks - as under No. 768.

Accession No. 768-d   Index No. - 039-ezde   039-ez

Title   " **Mĕng-tzŭ chi chu** "
                  孟   子   集   註

               " **Mĕng-tzŭ** "
                  孟   子

Classification - **A-135** 四 書 - 孟 子

Subject - (Gest No. 1498-d) "a commentary on the discourses of
     Mencius on political, social, and ethical subjects."

References - as under No. 768.

Author - **Chu Hsi** 朱 熹 .

Edition - as under No. 768.

Index - none; 14 chüan.

Bound in 2 t'ao 7 ts'ĕ (4-3).

Remarks - as under No. 768.

The University of Toronto Chinese Library

Accession No. 769   Index No. - 120-gfmz

Title   " Ching tien shih wên "
       經 典 釋 文

Classification - A-137 羣 經 總 義

Subject - a collection of explanative commentaries on the Classics
and related works.

References - 163-ggcz 3/2   031-bgld 3/22   037-ahhg 3/17   167-mhfm 6/1
012-zafk 3/1   031-bgdf 33/5   Gest No. 35.

Author - (撰) Lu Yüan-lang 陸 元 朗 .

Edition - the "Ch'ung-wên-shu-chü" 崇 文 書 局 ; dated T'ung-Chih
8/1869.   Blocks; "fên" paper.

Index - a table of contents for 30 chüan (given at the end of chüan 1);
攷 證 1 chüan.

Bound in 2 t'ao 12 ts'ê (6-6).

Remarks - this is a very useful reference work and the item is
complete and in good condition.

The University of Toronto Chinese Library

Accession No. 770   Index No. -040-dbbl

Title   " Sung ssŭ-liu hsüan "
         宋　四　六　選

Classification - D-73 總集 一文

Subject - a collection of selected prose compositions in the "four-six" style by scholars of the Sung Dynasty.

References - 012-zafk 19/24.

Author - (編) P'êng Yüan-jui 彭元瑞 and Ts'ao Chên-yung
    曹振鏞 .

Edition - no particular notation; dated Ch'ien-Lung "i-wei" 40/1775. Blocks; "mao-pien" paper.

Index - a table of chapter headings for 24 chüan.

Bound in 2 t'ao 12 ts'ê (6-6).

Remarks - the item is complete and in good condition,- two defective pages at the end of last ts'ê.

Accession No. 771   Index No. - 067-zfim

Title   " Wĕn chang pien t'i "
文　章　辨　體

Classification - D-63 總集 - 詩文

Subject - a general collection of miscellaneous prose and poetic

writings of scholars from ancient times down to the beginning

of the Ming Dynasty; with commentaries.

References - 012-zafk 19/7   031-bgdf 191/29   Gest No. 327.

Author - (編集) Wu No 吳　訥 .

Edition - a Ming edition; dated (at the end of chüan 50) Chia-Ching

34/1555.   Blocks; "mien" paper.

Index - a general table of contents for 50 chüan and 外 集 5 chüan;

detailed lists for the same.

Bound in 2 t'ao 12 ts'ĕ (6-6).

Remarks - this is a very good edition; and the item is complete

and without defects except some stains.

der

Accession No. 772   Index No. - 120-mb

Title   " I shih "
                         繹 史

Classification - B-32 紀事本末

Subject - (Gest No. 671) "Complete records of Chinese history from
        the remotest times to the end of the Ch'in Dynasty (206 B.C.)
        -----."

References - Wylie's Notes page 28   163-ggoz 4/11   031-bgld 5/29
        012-zafk 4/13   031-bgdf 49/31   Gest No. 671   Toronto No. 227.

Author - Ma Su 馬驌.

Edition - no notation; (preface) dated K'ang-Hsi 9/1670.   Blocks;
        bamboo paper.

Index - a general table of contents for 160 chüan.

Bound in 4 t'ao 24 ts'8 (6 each).

Remarks - a duplicate of Toronto No. 227.   The item is complete and
        in very good condition.

Accession No.   773   Index No. - 031-bfj(zb)

Title   " <u>Ssŭ-shu lei k'ao</u> "
               四 書 類 考

Classification - A-131 四書

<u>Subject</u> - a collection of extracts taken from more than 300 standard
   works in explanation of certain characters and terms that are
   used in the "<u>Four Books</u>".

<u>References</u> - 012-zafk 3/13.

<u>Author</u> - (撰) <u>Ch'ên Yǔ-ku</u> 陳愚谷.

<u>Edition</u> - that of the author; dated Chia-Ch'ing "hsin-yu" 6/1801.
   Blocks; "mien" paper.

<u>Index</u> - a list of "classifications" for 30 chüan; separate tables
   of contents at the beginning of each chüan.

<u>Bound in</u> 2 t'ao 18 ts'ê (9-9).

<u>Remarks</u> - this is a very useful work; and the item is apparently
   complete, but stained and worm-eaten in places. The
   important defects have been repaired.

Accession No. 774   Index No. - 080-1hjc

Title   " Yü t'ang yün t'ung "
               毓   堂   韻   同

Classification - A-161 小 學 - 字 書

Subject - a collection of characters, arranged according to rhymes,
    together with their synonyms.

References - none.

Author - (輯) Chao Chiao 趙 校 .

Edition - the "Tsun-i-t'ang" 遵 一 堂 ; dated Tao-Kuang 1/1821.
    Blocks; "fên" paper.

Index - none.

Bound in 1 t'ao 5 ts'ê.

Remarks - the item is complete and without defects.

Accession No. 775   Index No. - 039-gbcd

Title   " <u>Sun   K'o-chih   chi</u> "
                          孫　可　之　集

Classification - D-43 别 集 - 文
Subject - an individual literary collection,- prose.

References - 031-bgld 15/24   037-ahhg (hsü) 6/13   030-iaff 25/15

    106-gdkn 70/19   167-mhfm 19/38   012-zafk 15/11   031-bgdf 151/20.

Author - (撰) <u>Sun Ch'iao</u> 孫　樵 .   ϑ.867

Edition - the "<u>Tu-yu-yung-shu-chai</u>" 讀 有 用 書 齋; dated Kuang-Hsü
    "ping-tzŭ" 2/1876.   Blocks; "mao-pien" paper.

Index - a classified table of contents for 10 chüan.

Bound in 1 t'ao 1 ts'ê.

Remarks - the item is complete and in good condition.

The University of Toronto Chinese Library

Accession No. 776   Index No. - 189-zedd   060-hhjd

Title   " <u>Kao</u> <u>Tsung</u> <u>Shun</u> <u>Huang-ti</u> <u>Yüan-ming-yüan</u> <u>t'u</u> <u>yung</u> "

高 宗 純 皇 帝 圓 明 園 圖 詠

" <u>Yü-chih</u> <u>Yüan-ming-yüan</u> <u>t'u</u> <u>yung</u> "

御 製 圓 明 園 圖 詠

Classification - D-38 別 集 - 詩

Subject - a collection of poems written by the <u>Emperor Ch'ien-Lung</u>

in description and praise of the <u>Yüan-ming-yüan</u>,- the Old Summer

Palace which was burned during the reign of <u>Hsien-Fêng</u> by the

foreign allied forces; with illustrations and commentaries.

References - 012-zafk 17/1.

Author - (註) <u>O Êrh-t'ai</u> 鄂 爾 泰 and others.

Edition - the "<u>Shih-yin-shu-wu</u>" of Tientsin 天 津 石 印 書 屋 ; dated

Kuang-Hsü 13/1887.   Lithographed on "fên" paper.

Index - separate lists of contents for each of 2 chüan 上 下 .

Bound in 1 t'ao 2 ts'ê.

Remarks - the item is complete but with some stains.

Accession No. 777   Index No. - 146-zhc

Title   " Hsi yü chi "
                      西   域   記

Classification - B-227 地理 - 外記
Subject - a record and description of the Mohammedan regions along
    the western frontier of China.

References - 012-zafk 8/27.

Author - (著) Ch'i-shih-i 七 十 一.

Edition - no notation; (preface) dated "chia-hsü" 1874.   Blocks;
    "mao-t'ai" paper.

Index - a list of chapter headings for 8 chüan.

Bound in 1 t'ao 4 ts'ê; doubly interleaved.

Remarks - the item is complete and without defects.

Accession No. 778   Index No. - 042-zmne

Title   " Hsiao-hsüeh tsuan chu "
小　學　纂　註

Classification - C-13 儒家

Subject - a commentary on the "Lesser Learning",- a hand-book for
the instruction of youth.

References - 012-zafk 10/3   031-bgdf 95/20.

Author - (纂註) Kao Yü 高 愈 .

Edition - the "Chê-chiang-shu-chü" 浙 江 書 局 ; dated T'ung-Chih
11/1872.   Blocks; "fên" paper.

Index - a table of contents for 6 chüan divided into 2 "p'ien" 內 外 .

Bound in 1 t'ao 2 ts'ê.

Remarks - an ordinary edition; the item is complete.

Accession No.   779   Index No. - 030-bfj

Title   " <u>Ku shih yüan</u> "
                           古   詩   源

Classification - D-68 總集－詩

Subject - a collection of selected poems and songs of the period
    from ancient times down to the end of the <u>Liu-ch'ao</u>,- the
    six dynasties; with annotations.

References - none.

Author - (選) <u>Shên Tê-ch'ien</u> 沈 德 潛．

Edition - reprinted by the "<u>Ssǔ-hsien-shu-chü</u>" 思 賢 書 局 ; dated
    Kuang-Hsü 17/1891.   Blocks; "fên" paper.

Index - none; in 14 chüan arranged chronologically.

Bound in 1 t'ao 4 ts'ê.

Remarks - an ordinary edition; the item is complete and as if new.

The University of Toronto Chinese Library

Accession No. 780   Index No. - 001-bzhz

Title   " San-yü-t'ang jih chi "
               三 魚 堂 日 記

Classification - B-107 傳記 - 獨錄
Subject - a collection of personal diaries of Lu Lung-ch'i dating
    from the 5th to the 31st year of K'ang-Hsi.

References - 012-zafk 5/24.

Author - Lu Lung-ch'i 陸 隴 其 ; (校刊) Liu Shu-fang 柳 樹 芳.

Edition - the "Chê-chiang-shu-chü" 浙 江 書 局 ; dated T'ung-Chih
    "kêng-wu" 9/1870.   Blocks; "mao-pien" paper.

Index - a list of contents (years) for 10 chüan.

Bound in 1 t'ao 4 ts'ê.

Remarks - the item has no defects and is complete.

Accession No. 781   Index No. - 031-bfgc

Title   " Ssŭ-shu   shuo   yo "
                       四 書 說 約

Classification - A-131 四書

Subject - a collection of explanative and commentatorial notes on the "Four Books".

References - none.

Author - (著) Lu Shan-chi 鹿 善 繼 .

Edition - the "Liu-yü-ts'ao-t'ang" 留 餘 草 堂; dated "hsin-yu" 1921.   Blocks; "mao-pien" paper.

Index - none.

Bound in 1 t'ao 4 ts'ě.

Remarks - an ordinary edition; complete and in perfect condition.

The University of Toronto Chinese Library

Accession No. 782   Index No. - 030-em

Title   " <u>Chou li</u> "
                          周   禮

<u>Classification</u> - A-46 禮 - 周禮

<u>Subject</u> - a commentary and explanation of the "<u>Chou Ritual</u>", which -
    "consists of an elaborate detail of the various officials under
    that dynasty with their respective duties."

<u>References</u> - Wylie's Notes page 4 160-1j 163-ggcz 2/4 031-bgld 2/24
    037-ahhg 1/4 7/3 (hsü) 2/14 167-mhfm 4/1 030-iaff 2/10 (#)

<u>Author</u> - (注) <u>Chêng Hsüan</u> 鄭 玄 ; (音 義) <u>Lu Tê-ming</u> 陸 德 明 .

<u>Edition</u> - the "<u>Ch'ung-wên-shu-chü</u>" 崇 文 書 局 ; dated T'ung-Chih
    7/1868. Blocks; "fên" paper.

<u>Index</u> - a table of chapter headings for 12 chüan.

<u>Bound in</u> 1 t'ao 6 ts'ê.

<u>Remarks</u> - an ordinary edition; the item is complete.

(#) 106-gdkn 6/3   012-zafk 2/8
     031-bgdf 19/1   Gest Nos. 516 and 2475.

Accession No. 783   Index No. - 106-dhgd

Title   " Huang ch'ao ching shih wên pien "
               皇　朝　經　世　文　編

Classification - D-73 總集 - 文

Subject - (Gest No. 1129) "a general collection of the prose literary

    productions of writers of the Ch'ing Dynasty period."

References - 012-zafk 19/31   Gest No. 1129.

Author - compiled by Ho Ch'ang-ling 賀 長 齡 .

Edition - no particular notation; dated Tao-Kuang "ting-hai" 7/1827.

    Blocks; bamboo paper.

Index - a general table of contents for 120 chüan; detailed list at

    the beginning of each chüan.

Bound in 8 t'ao 64 ts'ê (8 each).

Remarks - the item is complete, but with a number of repaired worm-

    holes.

The University of Toronto Chinese Library

Accession No. 784   Index No. - 067-zzhz

Title   " Wên hsin tiao lung "
            文　心　雕　龍

Classification - D-93 詩 文 評
Subject - the earliest "critique on poetry and literature" now extant.

References - Wylie's Notes page 244 160-1j 163-ggcz 16/10 031-bgld
    20/1 030-iaff 39/25 106-gdkn 118/1 167-mhfm 24/1 (#)

Author - (著) Liu Hsieh 劉 勰 .

Edition - no particular notation; no date, but of the Ming period.
    Blocks; bamboo paper.

Index - a table of contents for 10 chüan.

Bound in 1 t'ao 4 ts'ê; doubly interleaved.

Remarks - this is a good edition; and the item is complete.

  (#) 012-zafk 20/1 031-bgdf 195/1 Gest No. 172
      Toronto No. 29.

Accession No.   785   Index No. - 031-czjh

Title   " Hui wên lei chü "
                          回　文　類　聚

Classification - D-68^63 總集 - 詩
Subject - a collection of miscellaneous palindromes and acrostics.

References - 163-ggcz 16/4   031-bgld 19/13   012-zafk 19/3

    031-bgdf 187/13.

Author - (纂 次) Sang Shih-ch'ang 桑 世 昌; of the 續編 -

    Chu Hsiang-hsien 朱 象 賢.

Edition - the "Lin-yü-t'ang" 麟 玉 堂 ; (postscriptum) dated

    "jên-shên" 1872.   Blocks; "fên" paper.

Index - a general table of contents for (原 編) 4 chüan; (另 編)

    1 chüan; (續 編) 10 chüan.

Bound in 1 t'ao 4 ts'ê.

Remarks - this item is complete and in good condition.

The University of Toronto Chinese Library

Accession No. 786   Index No. - 031-bfce

Title   " <u>Ssŭ-shu tzŭ ku</u> "
                   四 書 字 詁

Classification - A-131 四 書

Subject - a comprehensive collection of explanations, taken from various sources, on a selection of characters from the "<u>Four Books</u>".

References - 012-zafk 3/13.

Author - (撰) <u>Tuan Ê-t'ing</u> 段 諤 廷 .

Edition - privately published; dated "Hsien-Fêng 7/1857.   Blocks; "mao-pien" paper.

Index - an index of the characters arranged according to the radicals; a detailed table of contents for 78 chüan.

Bound in 2 t'ao 16 ts'ê (8-8).

Remarks - this is a useful reference work.   The item is complete and without defects.

Accession No. 787   **Index No.** - 040-eked   040-ekej

Title   " <u>Ting-an ch'u chi</u> "
               定 盦 初 集

              " <u>Ting-an ch'u kao</u> "
             定 盦 初 稿

Classification - D-43 別 集 一 文
Subject - an individual literary collection,- prose.

References - 012-zafk 18/23.

Author - (撰) <u>Kung Tzŭ-chên</u> 龔 自 珍．

Edition - no particular notation; dated T'ung-Chih 7/1868.   Blocks;
   "fên" paper.

Index - a table of contents for 3 chüan; (續集) same for 4 chüan.

Bound in 1 t'ao 3 ts'ê.

Remarks - the item is complete and in perfect condition.

Accession No. 788   Index No. - 075-ehlf   070-zehd

Title   " Po-t'ang i shu "

　　　　　　　柏　堂　遺　書

　　　　" Fang Po-t'ang ch'üan chi "

　　　　方　柏　堂　全　集

Classification - D-33 別集 - 詩文 C-308 雜家 - 雜文

Subject - a miscellaneous collection of writings.

References - 012-zafk 13/19   029-pffz page 148   Gest No. 2937.

Author - (撰) Fang Tsung-ch'êng 方 宗 誠.

Edition - the "Chih-hsüeh-t'ang" 志 學 堂 ; (chia chuan) dated

　　　Kuang-Hsü 15/1889.   Blocks; "mao-pien" paper.

Index - a general list of the several works; with separate lists

　　　for some of them.

Bound in 4 t'ao 16 ts'ê (4 each).

Remarks - this item is complete and in good condition. Both 012-zafk

　　　and 029-pffz classify this item as a "ts'ung shu", but according

　　　to the Gest Library Catalogue, that classification is incorrect,

　　　for the work is not a "collection of reprints" at all, and it

　　　should be classified under "pieh chi" and "tsa wên". (#)

(#)   This statement is quite true, hence our
adoption to the same change in classification.

288

Accession No. 789   Index No. - 031-bffe

Title   " Ssŭ shu tien ku pien chêng "
               四   書   典   故   辨   正

Classification - A-131 四書
Subject - a collection of disquisitions on certain parts of the
     "Four Books".

References - none.

Author - (著) Chou Ping-chung 周 柄 中.

Edition - the "Shang-ch'i-ko" 賞 奇 閣 ; dated T'ung-Chih "ping-yin"
     5/1866.   Blocks; "mao-pien" paper.

Index - a detailed table of contents for 20 chüan; 附 錄 1 chüan.

Bound in 1 t'ao 5 ts'ê.

Remarks - an ordinary edition; complete and without defects.

Accession No. 790   Index No. - 165-mc

Title   " Shih ming "
                                釋   名

Classification - A-156 小學 - 訓詁

Subject - an explanative dictionary of terms and words arranged
      under 27 main headings.

References - 160-lj 163-ggcz 3/9 031-bgld 4/16 106-gdkn 12/8
      167-mhfm 7/4 012-zafk 3/18 031-bgdf 40/10 Gest No. 634.

Author - (撰) Liu Hsi 劉 熙 .

Edition - a Ming edition; undated.   Blocks; bamboo paper.

Index - a table of contents for 8 chüan.

Bound in 1 t'ao 2 ts'ê; doubly interleaved.

Remarks - a good edition; the item is complete.   There are 9
      manuscript pages,- page 8 of chüan 7 to the end of chüan 8.

Accession No. 791   Index No. - 149-obzj

Title   " Tu shih fang yü chi yao "
         讀 史 方 輿 紀 要

Classification - B-187 地 理 - 總 志

Subject - (Wylie) "----- a record of geographical changes which
    have taken place in China from the earliest times down to
    the 17th century, intended as a guide to the perusal of
    the native histories."

References - Wylie's Notes page 63   160-1j   163-ggcz 5/9
    012-zafk 6/2   Gest Nos. 455 and 1874.

Author - (輯 著) Ku Tsu-yü 顧 祖 禹 .

Edition - the "Fu-wên-ko" 數 文 閣 ; no date.   Blocks; "mao-pien"
    paper.

Index - a general table of contents for 130 chüan; 輿 圖 4 chüan.

Bound in 8 t'ao 72 ts'ê (9 each).

Remarks - this is an important work; the item is complete and in
    generally good condition.   The first 9 ts'ê are shorter in
    length, and apparently replacements from another copy printed
    from the same blocks.

Accession No. 792   Index No. - 037-abgh   163-ghee

Title   " T'ien-hsia chün kuo li ping shu "
               天 下 郡 國 利 病 書

Classification - B-187 地理一總志

Subject - (Gest No. 456) "Work on the Geographical Economics of all
   provinces in China."

References - 160-1j   163-ggoz 5/9   012-zafk 6/2   Gest Nos.
   456 and 1874.

Author - (撰) Ku Yen-wu 顧 炎 武.

Edition - the "T'ung-hua-shu-wu" 桐華書屋 ; dated Kuang-Hsü
   "chi-mao" 9/1883.   Blocks; "mao-pien" paper.

Index - a general table of contents for 120 chüan.

Bound in 6 t'ao 50 ts'8 (8-8-9-8-8-9).

Remarks - this item is complete and in very good condition.

The University of Toronto Chinese Library

Accession No. 793   Index No. - 149-obhz

Title   " Tu shih sui chin hsiang chu "
               讀 史 碎 金 詳 註

Classification - C-348 類 書 B-367 史 評

Subject - Chinese history in rhyme; from the period of the "San Huang"

三 皇 down to, and including, the Ming Dynasty; with detailed

commentary.

References - 012-zafk 13/30   Gest No. 1277-b.

Author - (編 輯) Hu Wên-ping 胡 文 炳.

Edition - privately published; (preface) dated Kuang-Hsü 1/1875.

Blocks; "fên" paper.

Index - a table of contents for 80 chüan; arranged chronologically.

Bound in 10 t'ao 80 ts'ê (8 each).

Remarks - the item is complete and in good condition,- some stains.

Accession No. 794   Index No. - 149-gj

Title   " Shuo   Sung "
                      說   嵩

Classification - B-207 地 理 － 山 川

Subject - (Gest No. 115) "Description and historical account of a
    famous mountain Sung 嵩 in Honan province,-----."

References - 012-zafk 8/8   031-bgdf 76/32   Gest No. 115.

Author - (撰) Ching Jih-chên 景 日 珍.

Edition - the "Yo-shêng-t'ang" 嶽 生 堂 ; (preface) dated K'ang-Hsi
    58/1719.   Blocks; "mao-pien" paper.

Index - a detailed table of contents; 32 chüan.

Bound in 1 t'ao 10 ts'ê.

Remarks - this is a good edition; and the item is complete and
    without defects.

The University of Toronto Chinese Library

Accession No.   795   Index No. - 031-bfgb

Title   " <u>Ssǔ</u> <u>shu</u> <u>ching</u> <u>shih</u> <u>chai</u> <u>chêng</u> "
                四 書 經 史 摘 證

Classification - A-131 四 書
Subject - a collection of extracts taken from the "<u>Four Books</u>"
    with historical notes in elucidation.

References - none.

Author - (輯著) <u>Sung Chi-t'ung</u> 宋 繼 種·

Edition - the "<u>Kuang-chou-chiang-chün-shu</u>" 廣 州 將 軍 署; dated
    Kuang-Hsü "i-hai" 1/1875.   Blocks; "fên" paper.

Index - a general table of contents for 7 chüan.

Bound in 1 t'ao 4 ts'ê.

Remarks - a modern edition; the item is complete.

Accession No. 796   Index No. - 030-fhcp

Title   " Chih-chin-chai ts'ung shu "
                     咫 進 齋 叢 書

Classification - C-338 雜家 - 叢書
Subject - a collection of reprints of 35 miscellaneous works.

References - 029-pffz 313   058-jffz 7/42.

Author - (編刊) Yao Chin-yüan 姚觀元.

Edition - that of the author; dated Kuang-Hsü 9/1883.   Blocks;
    "fên" paper.

Index - a list of the 35 works in 3 "chi" 集 ; separate tables
    at the beginning of each "chi".

Bound in 4 t'ao 24 ts'ê (6 each).

Remarks - a modern edition; the item is as new.

Accession No. 797   Index No. - 031-bfde

Title   " <u>Ssŭ-shu</u> <u>chi</u> <u>chu</u> <u>chih</u> <u>chieh</u> <u>shuo</u> <u>yo</u> "
四 書 集 註 直 解 說 約

Classification - A-131 四 書

Subject - an explanation of the "<u>Four Books</u>"; together with detailed
marginal commentaries.

References - none.

Author - (著) <u>Chang Chü-chêng</u> 張 居 正 ; (閱) <u>Ku Tsung-mêng</u>
顧 宗 孟 .

Edition - the "<u>Pa-ch'i-ching-chêng-shu-yüan</u>" 八 旗 經 正 書 院;
no date notation, but of the Kuang-Hsü period.   Blocks;
"mao-pien" paper.

Index - none; 27 chüan.

Bound in 2 t'ao 12 ts'ê (6-6).

Remarks - this is a fairly good edition; and the item is complete
and in perfect condition.

Accession No.   798   Index No. - 030-czfa

Title   " <u>Ming jên shu cha</u> "
                    名 人 書 扎

Classification - D-73 總集 - 文

Subject - reproduction of a collection of holographic letters of
   noted persons.

References - none.

Author - compiled by <u>Hsieh Ch'ao</u> 謝 超 .

Edition - the "<u>Pan-chiang-shu-wu</u>" 半 江 書 屋 ; dated Kuang-Hsü
   "ting-hai" 13/1889.   Lithographed on foreign paper.

Index - none.

Bound in 1 t'ao 3 ts'ê.

Remarks - this is a very ordinary edition; and the item is without
   defects.

The University of Toronto Chinese Library

Accession No. 799   Index No. - 113-elk

Title   " Shên sêng chuan "
                                  神   僧   傳

Classification - C-513 釋 家

Subject - a collection of biographical sketches of 208 famous
Buddhist priests covering the period from the Later Han
Dynasty down to and including the first part of the Yüan
Dynasty.

References - 012-zafk 14/20   031-bgdf 145/18.

Author - not stated.

Edition - published by the Buddhist priest Ch'ing-ho 青 河 ; no date
notation, but possibly of the Chia-Ching period.   Blocks;
"mien" paper.

Index - a list of names in 9 chüan.

Bound in 1 t'ao 10 ts'ê; doubly interleaved with margins.

Remarks - this is a very good edition; and the item is in generally
good condition.   This work only contains 207 biographies, the
last one being missing.   In order to conceal the trace of this
defect, the last name in the index has been cut off.

Accession No. 800   Index No. - 077-d1   030-gfzd

Title   " Wu pien "
                              武 編
        " T'ang Ching-ch'uan hsien-shêng tsuan chi Wu pien "
          唐 荆 川 先 生 纂 輯 武 編

Classification - C-33 兵 家

Subject - a treatise on military affairs in the various phases of
    the subject.

References - 163-ggcz 7/9   031-bgld 9/27   012-zafk 10/14
    031-bgdf 99/19.

Author - (編) T'ang Shun-chih 唐 順 之.

Edition - the "Man-shan-kuan" 曼 山 館 ; no date; but of the Ming
    period.   Blocks; bamboo paper.

Index - (前 集) Separate tables of contents at the beginning of
    each of 6 chüan; (後 集) same for 6 chüan.

Bound in 1 t'ao 12 ts'ê.

Remarks - this item is complete and in generally good condition,-
    some minor defects and a few stains.

300

The University of Toronto Chinese Library

Accession No. 801　　　　Index No. - 005-ag

Title　　　　　　" Chiu　t'ung "
　　　　　　　　　九　　通

Classification - B-42 別 史　　B-282 政書 - 通制

Subject - (Gest No. 446) "Collection of 9 Complete works on History,
　　Biography, Legislation, Constitution, State Economics, etc.,---."

References - 160-1j　029-pffz 20　058-jffz 2/61-62-63　Gest No. 466.

Author - various.

Edition - the "Chê chiang-shu-chü" 浙 江 書 局 ; dated Kuang-Hsü
　　"ping-shên" 22/1896.　　Blocks; "mao-pien" paper.

Index - separate for the different works.

Bound in 9 boxes 1,000 ts'ê.

Remarks - the item is complete and in perfect condition.　The
　　following is a list of the 9 works;-

　　　1.　T'ung　tien　　　　　(162-gf)　B-282
　　　　　通　　典　　　　　　200 chüan

　　　　　by Tu Yu 杜 佑

(#)

(#) 2. " T'ung chih " (162-gc) B-42
通 志 200 chüan

by Chêng Ch'iao 鄭 樵

3. " Wên hsien t'ung k'ao " (067-zpg(zb) B-282
文 獻 通 考 348 chüan

by Ma Tuan-lin 馬 端 臨

4. " Hsü T'ung tien " (120-ogf) B-282
續 通 典 150 chüan

Compiled on order of Emperor Ch'ien-Lung

5. " Hsü T'ung chih " (120-ogc) B-42
續 通 志 640 chüan

As under No. 4.

6. " Hsü Wên hsien t'ung k'ao " (120-ozpg) B-282
續 文 獻 通 考 250 chüan

As under No. 4

7. " Huang-ch'ao T'ung tien " (106-dhgf) B-282
皇 朝 通 典 100 chüan

As under No. 4

8. " Huang-ch'ao T'ung chih " (106-dhgc) B-282
皇 朝 通 志 126 chüan

As under No. 4

9. " Huang-ch'ao Wên hsien t'ung k'ao " (106-dhzp) B-282
皇 朝 文 獻 通 考 300 chüan

As under No.4.

302

Accession No. 802   Index No. - 075-czdb

Title   " Li Wên-chung kung ch'üan chi "
               李 文 忠 公 全 集

Classification - D-43 別集 - 文
Subject - an individual collection of miscellaneous writings, -
     memorials, letters, telegrams, etc.

References - Gest No. 431.

Author - by Li Hung-chang 李 鴻 章 ；(編 錄) Wu Ju-lun 吳 汝 綸

Edition - no particular notation; (title-page) dated Kuang-Hsü
     "i-ssǔ" 31/1905.   Blocks; "mao-pien" paper.

Index - a list of 8 works with the number of chüan; separate detailed
     tables of contents at the beginning of each chüan of the several
     works.
Bound in 1 box 100 ts'ê.

Remarks - an ordinary edition; the item is complete and has no
     defects.

303

Accession No. 803-a   Index No. - 146-zzzd   109-ezdb

Title   " Hsi-shan wên chi "
               西 山 文 集

               " Chên Wên-chung kung wên chi "
               真 文 忠 公 文 集

Classification - D-43 別集 - 詩文

Subject - an individual collection of miscellaneous prose with

   some poetic writings.

References - 160-1j   163-ggcz 13/18   031-bgld 16/26   037-ahhg

   (hsü) 11/10   030-iaff 31/3   012-zafk 15/28   031-bgdf 162/14
Gest No. 1177.
Author - Chên Tê-hsiu 真 德 秀 · 1178 1235

Edition - no particular notation; no date.   Blocks; "mao-pien"

   paper.

Index - a detailed table of contents for 55 chüan; 年 譜 1 chüan;

   心 經 1 chüan; 政 經 1 chüan.

Bound in 30 ts'ê in 1 box with (b) (c) and (d).

Remarks - an ordinary edition; the item is complete and in good

   condition.

Accession No. 803-b   Index No. - 149-ofc

Title   " <u>Tu   shu   chi</u> "
                          讀　書　記

Classification - C-13 儒家

Subject - (Wylie) "It treats chiefly of mental philosophy, and the
    character and doings of eminent ministers from the Hëa down
    to the time of the Five dynasties."

References - Wylie's Notes page 86   160-1j   163-ggcz 7/5   031-bgld
    9/14   037-ahhg (hsü) 5/9   167-mhfm 13/12   030-iaff 15/14 (#)

Author - (撰) <u>Chên Tê-hsiu</u> 真 德 秀 .

Edition - uniform with (a); but dated T'ung-Chih 3/1864.

Index - a general table of contents for 40 chüan.

Bound in 30 ts'ê in 1 box with (a) (c) and (d).

Remarks - as under (a).

    (#) 106-gdkn 40/18   012-zafk 10/4   031-bgdf 92/42
         Gest No. 2028.

Accession No. 803-c   Index No. - 037-zmcg

Title   " Ta-hsüeh yen i "
                              大　學　衍　義

Classification - C-13 儒 家

Subject - (Gest No. 831-a) "Exemplifications from history of the
    doctrines of the "Great Learning", i.e. Ta Hsüeh 大 學 ."

References - Wylie's Notes page 86   163-ggcz 7/4   031-bgld 9/14
    037-ahhg (hsü) 16/8   167-mhfm 13/12   030-iaff 15/15   (#)

Author - (撰) Chên Tê-hsiu 真 德 秀 .

Edition - uniform with (a).

Index - a table of contents for 43 chüan.

Bound in 10 ts'ê in 1 box with (a) (b) and (d).

Remarks - as under (a).

    (#) 012-zafk 10/4   031-bgdf 92/40   Gest No. 831-a.

Accession No. 803-d   Index No. - 067-zfae

Title   " Wên chang chêng tsung "
               文　章　正　宗

Classification - D-63 總集 - 詩文
Subject - (Gest No. 1540) "a general collection of prose compositions
    and poems, written during the period from ancient times down to
    the Sung Dynasty."

References - 160-1j   163-ggcz 16/4   031-bgld 19/13   037-ahhg 3/41
    (hsü) 7/9   167-mhfm 23/24   012-zafk 19/4   031-bgdf 187/18 (#)

Author - edited by Chên Tê-hsiu 真德秀.

Edition - uniform with (a); but dated T'ung-Chih "chia-tzǔ" 3/1864.

Index - a table of contents for 30 chüan; 續集 12 chüan.

Bound in 30 ts'ê in 1 box with (a) (b) and (c).

Remarks - as uner (a).

(#) Gest Nos. 582, 599 and 1540   Toronto No. 754.

Accession No. 804   Index No. - 076-hezb   072-zblh

Title   " Ch'in-ting Jih hsia chiu wên k'ao "
           欽 定 日 下 舊 聞 考

Classification - B-194 地 理 一 別 志

Subject - (Gest No. 1381) "a general and detailed archaeological
    and historical description of Peking,- its environs and depen-
    dencies.   An extension and amplification of the "Jih hsia
    chiu wên".

References - Wylie's Notes page 44   160-1j   163-ggcz 5/12
    031-bgld 7/12   012-zafk 6/7   031-bgdf 68/41   Gest No. 1381.

Author - a commission headed by Yü Min-chung 于 敦 中.

Edition - a "palace" edition; undated, but apparently of the
    Ch'ien-Lung period.   Blocks; "t'ai-hsi-lien" paper.

Index - a table of contents for 160 chüan.

Bound in 2 boxes 24 ts'ê (12-12).

Remarks - a very good edition; the item has no defects and is
    complete.

Accession No. 805   Index No. - 040-ekh

Title   " Tsung ching lu "
                         宗   鏡   録

Classification - C-513 釋 家

Subject - a large thesaurus of Buddhist doctrine, in which the

various points of the system are discussed.

References - Wylie's Notes page 212   Gest No. 373.

Author - compiled by the Buddhist priest Chih-chio 智 覺.

Edition - a "palace" edition; (preface) dated Yung-Chêng 12/1734.

Blocks; "k'ai-hua" paper.

Index - none; 100 chüan.

Bound in 2 boxes 20 ts'ê.

Remarks - a very fine edition indeed; the item is complete and in

perfect condition.

Accession No. 806   Index No. - 007-zzbb   055-abb

Title   " Êrh-shih-ssŭ shih "
                  二   十   四   史

                 " Nien-ssŭ shih "
                  廿   四   史

Classification - B-12 正史

Subject - (Gest No. 1521) "the twenty-four (24) officially approved

   and authorized standard dynastic histories of China."

References - Wylie's Notes page 15 160-1j 163-ggcz 4/1 031-bgld 5/1

   Gest No. 1521 Toronto Nos. 735 and 736 Numerous in all   (#)

Author - various for the different histories; the collection edited

   by an Imperial Commission headed by Prince Hung Chou 弘 晝 .

Edition - the "Tsu-ku-t'ang" 胙 古 堂 ; dated T'ung-Chih 8/1869.

   Blocks; "fên" paper.

Index - a list of chapter headings at the beginning of each history.

Bound in 24 boxes in 850 ts'ê.

Remarks - a very good edition; the item is complete and in perfect

   condition.

   (#)   catalogues for the several separate histories.

Accession No. 807   Index No. - 030-bzce

Title   " Ku-hsiang-chai hsiu chên shih chung "
          古 香 齋 袖 珍 十 種

Classification - C-338 雜家 一叢書
Subject - a collection of reprints of 10 standard works.

References - 029-pffz 156   058-jffz 5/1.

Author - not stated.

Edition - the "San-shih-yu-san-wan-chüan-t'ang" 三十有三萬卷堂;
          dated Kuang-Hsü 8/1882.   Blocks; "fên" paper.

Index - none.

Bound in 2 boxes 322 ts'ê.

Remarks - a very good small edition; the item is as new.

311

Accession No. 808   Index No. - 017-ffgg

Title   " Han hai "
                          函 海

Classification - C-338 雜家 - 叢書
Subject - a collection of 159 reprints on a variety of subjects.

References - 012-zafk 13/15   029-pffz 288   Gest No. 2362.

Author - compiled by Li T'iao-yüan 李 調 元.

Edition - the "Lo-tao-chai" 樂 道 齋 ; dated Kuang-Hsü "jên-wu"

  8/1882.   Blocks; "mao-t'ai" paper.

Index - a list of the 159 works arranged in 40 "han" 函 .

Bound in 20 t'ao 160 ts'è in 1 box.

Remarks - the item is complete and in good condition.

The University of Toronto Chinese Library

Accession No. 809   Index No. - 170-mjbz

Title   " Sui-yüan san-shih-liu chung "
               隨 圜 三 十 六 種

Classification - C-338 雜家 - 叢書

Subject - a collection of 36 reprints mainly consisting of prose

    and poetic writings.

References - 029-pffz 543.

Author - by Yüan Mei 袁枚 and others.

Edition - the "Chi-ch'êng-t'u-shu-kung-ssŭ" 集成圖書公司;

    dated "mou-shên" 1908.   Type; "fên" paper.

Index - a list of the 36 works.

Bound in 1 box 50 ts'ê.

Remarks - the item is complete and without defects.   The character

    "liu" 六 is omitted from the title given in 029-pffz.

The University of Toronto Chinese Library

Accession No. 810   **Index No.** - 059-1dad   030-bc

Title   " Ying Sung po na pên Shih chi "
影　宋　百　衲　本　史　記

Classification - B-12 正史

Subject - (Gest No. 910) "History of ancient China from the time
of Emerpor Huang-Ti (B. C. 2697-2597) up to the reign of
Emperor Wu Ti (B. C. 140-86) of the Han Dynasty."

References - Wylie's Notes page 15   160-1j   163-ggcz 4/1   031-bgld 5/1
037-ahhg 5/21 8/2 (hsü) 4/1 14/1   167-mhfm 8/1   030-iaff 6/1 (#)

Author - (撰) Ssŭ-ma Ch'ien 司　馬　遷 .

Edition - a "process" (?) reproduction from several Sung editions,
printed on "fên" paper.

Index - none; in 130 chüan.

Bound in 1 box 24 ts'ĕ.

Remarks - a good edition; the item is in perfect condition.

(#) 106-gdkn 18/1   012-zafk 4/1   031-bgdf 45/4

Gest Nos. 73, 910, 1706 and 1707.

———•———

Accession No. 811   **Index No.** - 039-mfch

Title   " Hsüeh ching t'ao yüan "
學　津　討　原

Classification - C-338 雜家 - 叢書
Subject - a collection of reprints of 172 standard works of all
classes.

References - 160-1j 029-pffz 533   058-jffz 6/8   012-zafk 13/15.

Author - (編) Chang Hai-p'êng 張 海 鵬.

Edition - the "Han-fên-lou" 涵 芬 樓; no notation as to the date,
but fairly modern.   Process (?); "mao-pien" paper.

Index - a list of the 172 works in 20 "chi" 集 , with separate
tables at the beginning of each "chi".

Bound in 2 boxes 200 ts'ê (100 each).

Remarks - the item is new.

Accession No. 812   Index No. - 030-bhpf

Title   " Ku i ts'ung shu "
                古　逸　叢　書

Classification - C-338 雜家 一 叢書

Subject - (Gest No. 2) "Collection of 26 old and rare works."

References - 029-pffz 152   058-jffz 7/48   012-zafk 13/18

    Gest Nos. 2 and 2014.

Author - compiled and published by Li Shu-ch'ang 黎 庶 昌．

Edition - printed in Japan; dated Kuang-Hsü 10/1884.   Blocks;

    "fên" paper.

Index - a list of the 26 works, with a description of the original

    copy from which the reprint was made.

Bound in 1 box 50 ts'ê.

Remarks - a good edition; the item is complete and without defects.

Accession No. 813   Index No. - 077-amkp

Title   " Chêng-chio-lou ts'ung shu "
                正　覺　樓　叢　書

Classification - C-338 雜家 - 叢書
Subject - a collection of 29 miscellaneous reprints.

References - 029-pffz 190.

Author - not stated.

Edition - no notation; no date.   Blocks; "mao-pien" paper.

Index - none.

Bound in 1 box 36 ts'ê.

Remarks - an ordinary edition; complete and in good condition.

The University of Toronto Chinese Library

Accession No. 814 **Index No. -** 060-hehc 187-hoji

Title " Yü-ting P'ien tzǔ lei pien "
御 定 駢 字 類 編

Classification - C-348 類書

Subject - an encyclopaedia of 2 - character terms arranged under
12 main and 1 supplementary classifications.

References - 160-1j 163-ggcz 10/16 031-bgld 14/17 012-zafk 13/26
031-bgdf 136/19 Gest No. 815.

Author - compiled on order of Emperor K'ang-Hsi 康 熙 .

Edition - the "T'ung-wên-shu-chü" 同 文 書 局 ; dated Kuang-Hsü
"ting-hai" 13/1887. Lithographed on "fên" paper.

Index - a classified table of chapter headings for 240 chüan.

Bound in 1 box 48 ts'ê.

Remarks - a very fine edition; the item is complete and in perfect
condition.

Classification - C-260 譜録 - 器物

Subject - (Gest No. 1072-a) "illustrations of ancient sacrificial

　　utensils and explanation of the inscriptions thereon."

References - 160-1j   163-ggcz 9/9   031-bgld 12/14   012-zafk 12/1

　　031-bgdf 115/11   Gest Nos. 1072-a and 1865.

Author - prepared by an Imperial commission headed by Yün-lu 允　禄.

Edition - published in Japan on the basis of the "palace" edition;

　　dated Kuang-Hsü 14/1888.   Copper plates; "fên" paper.

Index - a list of chapter headings for 40 chüan, arranged according

　　to classes of utensils; separate lists for each chüan.

Bound in 22 ts'ê in 1 box with (b).

Remarks - this is a very fine edition; and the item is complete and

　　in perfect condition.   A very important work for references.

———•—•———

Accession No. 815-b   Index No. - 167-hh

Title   " Ch'ien lu "
                          錢　錄

Classification - C-263 譜錄 - 錢幣

Subject - (Gest No. 1738) "a description of Chinese coins and
    medals, principally the ancient ones."

References - Wylie's Notes page 147   160-1j   163-ggcz 9/9
    031-bgld 12/15   012-zafk 12/3   031-bgdf 115/25   (#)

Author - Imperially compiled.

Edition - uniform with (a).

Index - a general table of contents for 16 chüan.

Bound in 2 ts'ê in 1 box with (a).

Remarks - as under (a).

    (#) Gest Nos. 1072(b), 1738 and 1865 Toronto No. 418.

Accession No. 816   Index No. - 140-ikgf

Title   " <u>Wan shou shêng tien ch'u chi</u> "
               萬　壽　聖　典　初　集

Classification - B-287 政書 - 典禮

Subject - (Gest No. 1052) "a record of matters in connection with
    K'ang-Hsi's 60th birthday."

References - 163-ggcz 6/4   031-bgld 8/12   012-zafk 9/7
    031-bgdf 82/20   Gest No. 1052.

Author - compiled by an Imperial commission headed by <u>Wang Shan</u>
    王　掞.

Edition - a "palace" edition; (memorial) dated K'ang-Hsi 56/1717.
    Blocks; "k'ai-hua" paper.

Index - a general table of chapter headings for 120 chüan.

Bound in 4 t'ao 40 ts'ê (in 1 box).

Remarks - this is a very fine edition; and the item is complete
    and in perfect condition.

Accession No. 817   Index No. - 085-khbh

Title   " Han Wei Liu-ch'ao i pai san chia chi "
           漢 魏 六 朝 一 百 三 家 集

Classification - D-63 總集 一 詩文

Subject - a collection of 103 works consisting of prose and poetic

writings of 103 officials and scholars of the Han 漢 , Wei 魏 ,

Chin 晉 , Liu-ch'ao 六朝 and the short Sui 隋 dynasties.

References - 163-ggcz 16/9   031-bgld 19/30   012-zafk 19/13

031-bgdf 189/50   Gest Nos. 16 and 462.

Author - (編) Chang P'u 張 溥 .

Edition - a reprint by the "Hsin-shu-t'ang" 信 述 堂 ; dated

Kuang-Hsü "i-mao" 5/1879.   Blocks; "fên" paper.

Index - a list of the 103 works and the names of the authors, arranged

chronologically.

Bound in 1 box 100 ts'ê.

Remarks - an ordinary edition; the item is complete and without

defects.

The University of Toronto Chinese Library

Accession No. 818   **Index No.** - 096-zezl   137-ezlf

Title   " <u>Wang Ch'uan-shan i shu</u> "
王 船 山 遺 書

usually catalogued sub 船山遺書

En Toky 301

Classification - C-308 雜家 - 雜文

Subject - a collection of miscellaneous writings.

References - 029-pffz 132   012-zafk 13/13   Gest No. 11.

Author - (撰) <u>Wang Fu-chih</u> 王 夫 之 。

Edition - the "<u>Chin-liang-chieh-shu</u>" 金 陵 節 署 ; dated T'ung-Chih
4/1865.   Blocks; "mao-pien" paper.

Index - a list of the 58 works. (77 works with 19 unpublished)

Bound in 1 box 100 ts'8.

Remarks - this is an ordinary edition; and the item is complete and
without defects.

Accession No.   819   Index No. – 040-czfp

Title   " Shou-shan-ko ts'ung shu "
                         守 山 閣 叢 書

Classification – C-338 雜家 – 叢書
Subject – a collection of reprints of 110 works in all four classes

   of Chinese literature.

References – Wylie's Notes page 270   012-zafk 13/15   029-pffz 221.

Author – (輯) Ch'ien Hsi-tsu 錢 熙 祚 .

Edition – the "Hung-wên-shu-chü" 鴻 文 書 局 ; dated Kuang-Hsü

   "chi-ch'ou" 15/1889.   Lithographed on "fên" paper.

Index – a list of the 110 works arranged under four classes.

Bound in 1 box 100 ts's.

Remarks – this item is complete and in good condition.

Accession No. 820-a   Index No. - 030-bgfj

Title   " <u>Ku</u> <u>ching</u> <u>chieh</u> <u>hui</u> <u>han</u> "
               古 經 解 彙 函

Classification - A-137 羣 經 總 義   C-338 雜家 - 叢書

Subject - a collection of reprints of 23 works chiefly consisting

   of commentaries and explanations of the "Classics".

References - 029-pffz page 156   058-jffz 1/18   Gest No. 45.

Author - compiled by <u>Chung Ch'ien-chün</u> 鍾 謙 鈞.

Edition - the "<u>Yüeh-tung-shu-chü</u>" 粵 東 書 局 ; dated T'ung-Chih

   12/1873.   Blocks; "fên" paper.

Index - a list of the 23 works.

Bound in 35 ts'ê in 1 box with (b).

Remarks - this is a collection of useful reference works; and the

   item is complete and in very good condition.

Accession No. 820-b   Index No. - 042-zmj(fg)

Title   " <u>Hsiao hsüeh hui han</u> "
                小   學   彙   函

Classification - A-151 小 學   C-338 雜家 - 叢書

<u>Subject</u> - a collection of reprints of 14 works pertaining to the
        class of "Hsiao hsüeh",- dictionaries.

<u>References</u> - 029-pffz page 156   058-jffz 1/64   Gest No. 45.

<u>Author</u> - compiled by <u>Chung Ch'ien-chün</u> 鍾 謙 鈞 .

<u>Edition</u> - uniform with (a).

<u>Index</u> - a list of the 14 works; together with (a).

<u>Bound in</u> 33 ts'ê in 1 box with (a).

<u>Remarks</u> - as under (a).

The University of Toronto Chinese Library

Accession No. 821   Index No. - 073-hzab

Title   " Tsêng Wên-chêng kung shou shu jih chi "
曾 文 正 公 手 書 日 記

Classification - B-107 傳記 - 獨錄

Subject - reproduction of a holographic diary of Tsêng Kuo-fan 曾國藩
covering the period from the 21st year of Tao-Kuang to the 11th
year of T'ung-Chih (1841-1872).

References - none.

Author - Tsêng Kuo-fan 曾 國 藩 .

Edition - the "Chung-kuo-t'u-shu-kung-ssǔ" 中 國 圖 書 公 司; dated
Hsüan-T'ung 1/1909.   Lithographed on "fên" paper.

Index - none.

Bound in 1 box 40 ts'ê.

Remarks - a modern edition; the item is complete and as new.

Accession No. 822   Index No. - 106-dhhe

Title   " Huang-Ch'ao chang ku hui pien "
               皇 朝 掌 故 彙 編

Classification - B-277 政書

Subject - a record of governmental affairs and other related activities

of the Ch'ing Dynasty.

References - none.

Author - compiled by Sung Wên-wei 宋 文 蔚 and others.

Edition - the "Ch'iu-shih-shu-shê" 求 實 書 社 ; dated Kuang-Hsü

"jên-yin" 28/1902.   Type; "fên" paper.

Index - (內 編) a general table of contents for 60 chüan; (外 編)

same for 40 chüan.

Bound in 1 box 60 ts'ê.

Remarks - an ordinary edition; the item is complete and in good

condition.

———•———

Accession No. 823   Index No. - 069-1bb

Title   " Hsin Yüan shih "
                    新   元   史

Classification - B-12 正史
Subject - the officially approved and recognized new history of the

Yüan Dynasty.

References - Gest No. 974.

Author - (撰) Ko Shao-min 柯劭忞 .

Edition - the "T'ui-kêng-t'ang" 很 耕 堂 ; no notation as to the

date, but not earlier than A. D. 1922.   Blocks; "hsüan" paper.

Index - a detailed table of contents for 257 chüan.

Bound in 2 boxes 60 ts'ê.

Remarks - this is a very fine modern edition; and the item is new.

———————•———————

Accession No. 824   Index No. – 077-jcjc   077-lcjc

Title   " Li tai yü ti yen ko hsien yao t'u "
        歷 代 輿 地 沿 革 險 要 圖

Classification – B-187 地理－總志 B-232 地理－地圖
Subject – (Gest No. 2363) "a collection of maps giving the

political and administrative divisions of China from the

earliest times down to and including the Ming period;

together with notes."

References – Gest No. 2363.

Author – prepared by Yang Shou-ching 楊 守 敬.

Edition – the "Kuan-hai-t'ang" 觀 海 堂; printed between 1904-1911.

Blocks; "mao-pien" paper.

Index – a list of the separate groups, 47 in all, on of which has

not been printed.

Bound in 1 box 42 ts'ê.

Remarks – a modern edition; the item is new.

Accession No. 825   **Index No.** - 055-abbb

Title   " Nien-ssŭ shih san piao "
廿 四 史 三 表

Classification - B-187 地理－總志

Subject - a collection of 3 works consisting of various historical

tables,- genealogy; location of capitals; territorial occupation;

change of district names; dynastic names; etc.

References - none for the collection; for the 2d and 3d works, -

012-zafk 6/2   Toronto No. 287.

Author - (述) Tuan Ch'ang-chi 段 長 基 ; (編次) Tuan Chin-shu
段 摺 書.

Edition - the "Wei-ku-shan-fang" 味 古 山 房 ; (preface) dated
Kuang-Hsü 1/1875.   Blocks; "fên" paper.

Index - none.

Bound in 1 box 24 ts'ê.

Remarks - this is a useful reference work; and the item is complete.

The 3 works are, -

" Li-tai t'ung chi piao "   (077-jcfc; 077-lcfc)
歷 代 統 紀 表   13 chüan.

(#)

(#)　　" <u>Li-tai</u> <u>chiang</u> <u>yü</u> <u>piao</u> "　　　　(077-jcnh; 077-lcnh)
　　　　歷 代 疆 域 表　　　　　　　　　3 chüan

　　　　" <u>Li-tai</u> <u>yen</u> <u>ko</u> <u>piao</u> "　　　　　(077-jcez; 077-lcez)
　　　　歷 代 沿 革 表

332

Accession No. 826-a   Index No. - 076-hezh   037-zhif

Title   " Ch'in-ting Ta-ch'ing hui tien "
               欽 定 大 清 會 典

Classification - B-282 政書 - 通制

Subject - (Gest No. 3515) "a comprehensive description of the Chinese

   governmental system during the (first part of) Ch'ing or Manchu,

   dynasty."

References - Wylie's Notes page 70   163-ggcz 6/3   031-bgld 8/7

   012-zafk 9/5   031-bgdf 81/21   Gest Nos. 106-a and 3515 Toronto
   No. 550.

Author - Imperially compiled.

Edition - the "Shang-wu-yin-shu-kuan" 商務印書館; dated Kuang-Hsü

   "mou-shên" 34/1908.   Lithographed on "fên" paper.

Index - a table of contents for 100 chüan.

Bound in 10 ts'ê in 1 box with (b).

Remarks - this is an ordinary edition; and the item is complete.

Accession No. 826-b   Index No. - 076-heoh   037-zhif

Title   " Ch'in-ting hsü hsiu Ta-ch'ing hui tien shih li "
          欽 定 續 修 大 清 會 典 事 例

Classification - B-282 政書－通制
Subject - a comprehensive collection of historical events that have
    taken place in the various government offices during the
    (first part of) Ch'ing, or Manchu, Dynasty.

References - Wylie's Notes page 70   012-zafk 9/5   Gest No. 106-c.

Author - Imperially compiled.

Edition - uniform with (a).

Index - a detailed table of contents for 1,220 chüan.

Bound in 2 boxes 150 ts'ê; first box with (a).

Remarks - as under (a).

The University of Toronto Chinese Library

Accession No. 827   Index No. - 120-hkfd   120-hkfg

Title   " Wei-mo-ch'i so shuo ching "
       維 摩 詰 所 說 經
       " Wei-mo-ch'i ching "
       維 摩 詰 經

Classification - C-513 釋家
Subject - a Buddhist sutra.

References - Wylie's Notes page 205   160-1j   012-zafk 14/22
   Gest No. 1120(g).

Author - translated by Chiu-mo-lo-shih 鳩 摩 羅 什.

Edition - a manuscript written on "k'ai-hua" paper; dated Shun-Chih
   18/1661.

Index - none; 3 chüan.

Bound in 1 box 3 ts'ê; doubly interleaved.

Remarks - this is a very good manuscript; and the item is without
   defects.

Accession No. 828   Index No. - 042-zftc   042-zgtc

Title   " Hsiao ch'uang yen chi "
                   小　窓　(窗)　豔　紀

Classification - C-368 小説家
Subject - a collection of miscellaneous prose and poetic writings.

References - 012-zafk 14/16   031-bgdf 144/40   Gest No. 2529.

Author - (批選) Wu Ts'ung-hsien 吳　從　先　.

Edition - a Ming edition; (preface) dated "chia-yin" (? Wan-Li
    42/1614).   Blocks; bamboo paper.

Index - a detailed table of contents arranged according to classes
    of writing (not divided into chüan).

Bound in 1 box 8 ts'ĕ; doubly interleaved.

Remarks - this is a good edition; and the item is complete and
    without important defects.

The University of Toronto Chinese Library

Accession No. 829   Index No. - 018-eld

Title   " Ch'u t'an chi "
初　潭　集

Classification - C-328 雜家 - 雜纂

Subject - a collection of short notes and narrations, chiefly
dealing with the five human relationships; with commentaries.

References - 012-zafk 13/5   031-bgdf 131/20   Gest No. 704.

Author - (撰) Li Chih 李贄 .

Edition - the "Min k'o pên" 閩　刻　本; undated but of the Ming period.
Blocks; "mien" paper.

Index - a general table of contents for 30 chüan.

Bound in 1 box 8 ts'ê.

Remarks - this is a very good edition; and the item is complete and
in perfect condition.

Accession No. 830   Index No. - 167-zihi

Title   " Chin t'ang chieh chu "
                 金   湯   借   箸

Classification - C-33 兵家

Subject - a treatise on warfare; attack and defense; implements and
    weapons; etc.

References - (?) Wylie's Notes page 91   160-1j   012-zafk 10/15
    031-bgdf 100/25   Gest No. 3663.   (see Remarks)

Author - (輯著) Chou Chien 周 鑑 ; (較訂) Li Ch'ang-k'o
    李 長 科 .

Edition - a manuscript written on "mao-pien" paper; (preface) dated
    "Ch'ung-Chêng "mou-yin" 11/1638.

Index - a table of contents for 13 chüan.

Bound in 1 box 10 ts'ê; doubly interleaved.

Remarks - it is somewhat doubtful whether this item is the same as
    the one referred to in the above catalogues.   The title of the
    work referred to is 金 湯 十 二 籌 by Li P'an 李 盤 whose
    courtesy name 小 有 is the same as that of Li Ch'ang-k'o, one
    of the authors of this item.   It is probable that this item is
    (#)

The University of Toronto Chinese Library

(#)   reproduced upon the basis of the catalogued one with
some modifications and an additional chüan.

Although this manuscript claims to be the
original draft copy, it appears to have been written
fairly recently, but on old paper.

Accession No. 831   Index No.- 140-fzdz   140-fzhi   115-hi

Title   " Ching-ch'uan hsien-shêng pai pien "
               荆 川 先 生 稗 編

Classification - C-348 類書

Subject - (Wylie) "(by), who has endeavoured to embrace every subject,
     in a long series of articles extracted from the native literature.
     Beginning with the several subjects of the Six Classics given
     seriatim, he proceeds with Philosophical Writers, Fine Arts,
     Sciences, etc., after which the matters of the Six Supreme   (#)

References - Wylie's Notes page 186   163-ggcz 10/15   031-bgld 14/15
     012-zafk 13/24   031-bgdf 136/4.   Gest No. 2903.

Author - (撰) T'ang Shun-chih 唐 順 之.

Edition - no special notation; (preface) dated Wan-Li "hsin-ssŭ"
     9/1581.   Blocks; "mien" paper.

Index - a detailed table of contents for 120 chüan.

Bound in 8 t'ao 80 ts'$ (10 each).

Remarks - this is a very good edition; and the item is complete and
     with practically no defects except a few slight stains and some
     worm-holes.   -----------------

     (#) Boards are treated, concluding with disquisitions on History
     and Biography."

Accession No. 832-a   Index No. - 140-nf

Title   " Ts'ang shu "
                          藏   書

Classification - B-42 別史

Subject - an unofficial history of China from the latter part of
    the Chou Dynasty down to and including the Ming Dynasty;
    divided into two principal sections,- records and biographies.

References - 012-zafk 4/16   031-bgdf 50/45   Gest Nos. 793 and
    1703(a).

Author - Li Chih 李 贄 .

Edition - no particular notation; (preface) dated Wan-Li "chi-hai"
    27/1599.   Blocks; bamboo paper.

Index - a detailed table of contents for 68 chüan.

Bound in 2 t'ao 24 ts'ê (12 each).

Remarks - this item is complete and in generally good condition, -
    a few repaired defects.

Accession No. 832-b   Index No. - 120-onf   075-czon

Title   " Hsü ts'ang shu "
                        續   藏   書
                 " Li-shih hsü ts'ang shu "
                   李   氏   續   藏   書

Classification - B-42 別 史

Subject - a continuation and supplement to (a); and consisting of
         additional biographies.

References - 012-zafk 4/16   031-bgdf 50/46   Gest No. 793 and
         1703(b).

Author - Li Chih 李 贄 .

Edition - no particular notation; no date; but of the Ming period.
         Blocks; bamboo paper.

Index - a list of chapter headings for 27 chüan; a list of the
         biographies, arranged according to character of officials;
         separate lists at the beginning of each chüan.
Bound in 4 t'ao 40 ts'ê (10 each); doubly interleaved.

Remarks - the impression is blurred in some places.   The item is
         complete and in good condition with the exception of a few
         repaired defects mainly in the last ts'ê.

Accession No. 833   Index No. - 149-gzfc

Title   " <u>Shuo</u> <u>wên</u> <u>chieh</u> <u>tzǔ</u> <u>i</u> <u>chêng</u> "
               說　文　解　字　義　證

Classification - A-161 小學一字書

Subject - an explanation and commentary on the "<u>Shuo wên</u>" of

　　<u>Hsü Shên</u> 許　慎．

References - 163-ggcz 3/10   012-zafk 3/23   Gest No. 51.

Author - (學) <u>Kuei Fu</u> 桂　馥．

Edition - the "<u>Ch'ung-wên-shu-chü</u>" 崇　文　書　局 ; dated T'ung-Chih

　　9/1870.   Blocks; "mao-pien" paper.

Index - a list of the 540 radicals in 50 chüan.

Bound in 4 t'ao 32 ts'ê (8 each).

Remarks - this is a useful reference work.   The item is complete

　　and in good condition,- a few worm-holes.

Accession No.   834   Index No. - 010-dica   181-caec

Title   " Kuang-Hsü   Shun-t'ien   fu   chih "
                光   緒   順   天   府   志

Classification - B-194 地理 - 別志
Subject - a gazetteer of the Imperial prefecture in which the city
    of Peking is located.

References - 012-zafk 7/26   Gest No. 820.

Author - (纂) Hung Liang-p'in 洪 良 品 ; (輯) Miao Ch'üan-sun
    繆 荃 孫.

Edition - no particular notation; dated Kuang-Hsü "chia-shên"
    10/1884.   Blocks; "mao-pien" paper.

Index - a list of chapter headings for 130 chüan.

Bound in 8 t'ao 64 ts'ê (8 each).

Remarks - the item is complete and without defects.

Accession No. 835   Index No. - 076-hefg   073-fgkg

Title   " Ch'in-ting Shu ching t'u shuo "
               欽 定 書 經 圖 說 "

Classification - A-21 書

Subject - explanations of the text of the "Book of History";
    together with illustrations.

References - Gest No. 409.

Author - compiled by a board of editors headed by Sun Chia-nai
    孫 家 鼐 .

Edition - officially published; dated Kuang-Hsü 31/1905.
    Lithographed on "fên" paper.

Index - a general list of the main sections; separate tables at the
    beginning of each of 50 chüan.

Bound in 4 t'ao 16 ts'ê (4 each); singly interleaved.

Remarks - this is a fine edition; and the item is complete and
    without defects.

Accession No. 836   Index No. - 130-ezdb

Title   " Hu Wên-chung kung i chi "
               胡 文 忠 公 遺 集

Classification - D-43 列集一文
Subject - an individual collection of miscellaneous prose writings.

References - 012-zafk 18/31   Gest No. 441.

Author - (撰) Hu Lin-i 胡 林 翼.

Edition - the "Huang-hao-lou" 黃 鶴 樓; dated T'ung-Chih 6/1867.
   Blocks; "fên" paper.

Index - a detailed table of contents for 86 chüan.

Bound in 2 t'ao 24 ts'ê (12-12).

Remarks - an ordinary edition; complete and without defects.

The University of Toronto Chinese Library

Accession No. 837   **Index No.** – 040-ekh

Title   " Tsung ching lu "
宗　鏡　錄

Classification – C-513 釋家
Subject – a large thesaurus of Buddhist doctrine, in which the
various points of the system are discussed.

References – Wylie's Notes page 212   Gest No. 373   Toronto No. 805.

Author – compiled by the Buddhist priest Chih-chio 智覺 .

Edition – a reprint based upon the "palace" edition; (preface) dated
Yung-Chêng 12/1734.   Blocks; "fên" paper.

Index – none; 100 chüan.

Bound in 4 t'ao 24 ts'ê (6 each).

Remarks – this is a duplicate of Toronto No. 805.   The item is
complete and in good condition.

347

Accession No. 838   Index No. - 077-lcec   077-jcec   113-ecgn

Title   " Li-tai Shen-hsien t'ung chien "
               歷 代 神 仙 通 鑑

Classification - C-731 道家

Subject - a collection of biographical sketches of Taoist, Buddhist,
     and other immortals; with illustrations and commentatorial
     notes.

References - Wylie's Notes page 223   Gest Nos. 1068 and 3607.

Author - (述) Hsü Tao 徐 衢 ;（ 同訂) Chang Chi-tsung 張 繼 宗
     and Huang Chang-lun 黃 掌 綸 ·

Edition - the "Li-wu-fu-lou pi pen" 秫 屋 玞 樓 秘 本 ; (preface)
     dated K'ang-Hsi "jên-ch'ên" 51/1712.   Blocks; "mao-t'ai"
     paper.

Index - for 3 "chi" and 22 chüan.

Bound in 4 t'ao 24 ts'ê (6 each).

Remarks - this is a poor edition, and is from old worn blocks.
     The item is complete.

Accession No. 839   Index No. - 085-fdaj

Title   " Hung-Wu chĕng yün "
               洪 武 正 韻

Classification - A-166 小學 - 韻書

Subject - (Gest No. 1682) "a dictionary with the characters arranged
   according to the tones and (76) rhymes."

References - Wylie's Notes page 11 160-1j 163-ggcz 3/14 031-bgld 4/29
   030-iaff 5/25 012-zafk 3/28 031-bgdf 42/23 Gest Nos. 368 and
   1682.

Author - prepared by an Imperial commission headed by Yo Shao-fĕng
   樂 韶 鳳 .

Edition - a Ming edition; (postscriptum) dated Lung-Ch'ing 隆 慶
   1/1567.   Blocks; "mien" paper.

Index - a table of the 4 tones and 76 rhymes; in 16 chüan.

Bound in 1 t'ao 5 ts'ĕ.

Remarks - a good edition; the item is complete but with some worm-
   holes and stains.

Accession No. 840-a   Index No. - 077-lccz   077-jccz

Title   " Li-tai ming ch'ên chüan "

歷 代 名 臣 傳

Classification - B-117 傳記 - 總錄

Subject - a collection of biographical sketches of famous ministers
and officials from the Han Dynasty down to and including the
Yüan Dynasty.

References - none.

Author - (仝 訂) Chu Shih 朱 軾 and Ts'ai Shih-yüan 蔡 世 遠 .

Edition - no particular notation; dated Kuang-Hsü 23/1897.   Blocks;
"mao-pien" paper.

Index - a list of names arranged according to dynasties, for 35 chüan.

Bound in 3 t'ao 15 ts'ê; 3d t'ao with (b).

Remarks - the item is complete and in good condition.

Accession No. 840-b   Index No. - 077-lcic   077-jcic

Title   " Li-tai hsün li chuan "
              歷 代 循 吏 傳

Classification - B-117 傳記－總録

Subject - a collection of biographical sketches of loyal officials

    covering the period from the Han down to and including the

    Yüan Dynasty.

References - none.

Author - (仝 訂) Chu Shih 朱 軾 and Ts'ai Shih-yüan 蔡 世 遠.

Edition - uniform with (a).

Index - a list of names for 8 chüan arranged dynastically.

Bound in 4 ts'ê in the 3d t'ao of (a).

Remarks - as under (a).

Accession No. 840-c   Index No. - 077-lccn   077-jccn

Title   " Li-tai ming ju chuan "
                歷 代 名 儒 傳

Classification - B-117 傳記 - 總録

Subject - (Toronto No. 286) "collected biographies of noted scholars

   of the period from the Han 漢 down to and including the Yüan 元

   dynasty."

References - Toronto No. 286.

Author - (仝 訂) Chu Shih 朱 軾 and Ts'ai Shih-yüan 蔡 世 遠.

Edition - uniform with (a).

Index - a list of names, arranged chronologically; 8 chüan.

Bound in 4 ts'š in 1 t'ao with (d).

Remarks - as under (a).

Accession No.   840-d   Index No. - 077-lccz   077-jccz

Title   " Li-tai ming ch'ên chuan hsü pien "
           歷 代 名 臣 傳 續 編

Classification - B-117 傳記一總錄

Subject - a continuation and supplement to (a).

References - none.

Author - (仝 訂) Chu Shih 朱 軾 and Ts'ai Shih-yüan 蔡 世 遠.

Edition - uniform with (a).

Index - a list of names for 5 chüan arranged chronologically.

Bound in 2 ts'ê in 1 t'ao with (c).

Remarks - as under (a).

353

Accession No. 841   Index No. - 048-bzkb

Title   " Tso Wên-hsiang kung nien p'u "

左 文 襄 公 年 譜

Classification - B-107 傳記 - 獨錄

Subject - the biography and chronological record of Tso Tsung-t'ang

左 宗 棠 ·

References - 012-zafk 5/10.

Author - (纂) Lo Chêng-chün 羅 正 鈞 .

Edition - that of "Tso-shih" 左 氏 ; dated Kuang-Hsü "ting-yu"

23/1897.   Blocks; "mao-pien" paper.

Index - none; 10 chüan.

Bound in 1 t'ao 10 ts'ê.

Remarks - an ordinary edition; the item is complete and without

defects.

The University of Toronto Chinese Library

Accession No. 842   Index No. - 042-eb

Title   " Shang shih "
                      尚   史

Classification - B-42 列史

Subject - (Gest No. 1638) "a history of China covering the period
    from Huang Ti 黄帝 (2698 B C) to and including the Ch'in
    Dynasty 秦紀 (207 B C)."

References - Wylie's Notes page 30   163-ggoz 4/12   031-bgld 5/34
    031-bgdf 50/36   Gest No. 1638.

Author - (纂) Li Ch'ieh 李鍇 .

Edition - the "Yüeh-tao-lou" 悦道樓 ; dated Ch'ien-Lung "kuei-ssŭ"
    38/1773.   Blocks; "k'ai-hua" paper.

Index - a general table of the 8 main sections for altogether 72 chüan;
    a detailed list for all but the first section.

Bound in 4 t'ao 28 ts's (7 each).

Remarks - this is a fairly good edition; and the item is apparently
    complete and without defects.   The section on "Shih-chia"
    contains 12 chüan and not 13 as given in the general index.
    Possibly "13" is a misprint.

Accession No. 843   Index No. - 021-chfd

Title   " Pei-t'ang shu ch'ao "
                    北　堂　書　鈔

Classification - C-348 類書

Subject - an encyclopaedia under 19 main classifications with
          literary references in explanation.

References - 160-1j 163-ggcz 10/12 031-bgld 14/2 037-ahhg (hsü) 17/6
             106-gdkn 59/1 167-mhfm 17/1 012-zafk 13/20 031-bgdf 135/6.

Author - (撰) Yü Shih-nan 虞 世 南 ; (校 註) K'ung Kuang-t'ao
         孔 廣 陶 .

Edition - that of "K'ung-shih" 孔 氏 ; dated Kuang-Hsü "mou-tzŭ"
          14/1888.   Blocks; "fên" paper.

Index - a detailed table of contents for 160 chüan.

Bound in 4 t'ao 20 ts'ê (5 each).

Remarks - a fair edition; the item is complete and without defects.

Accession No. 844   Index No. - 162-gd

Title   " **T'ung ya** "
                              通　雅

Classification - C-308 雜家-雜文

Subject - a collection of dissertations on a large variety of
　　subjects arranged in the form of an encyclopaedia.

References - 160-1j 163-ggcz 10/5 031-bgld 13/12 012-zafk 12/21
　　031-bgdf 119/11 Gest No. 1400.

Author - (輯著) **Fang I-chih** 方以智 .

Edition - the "**Li-chiao-kuan**" 立教館 ; (preface) dated K'ang-Hsi
　　"ping-wu" 5/1666.   Blocks; "fên" paper.

Index - a general table of contents for 52 chüan.

Bound in **2 t'ao 20 ts'ê (10-10)**.

Remarks - this is a useful standard work; and the item is complete
　　and without defects.

Accession No. 845　　　　　Index No. - 030-czc　　030-czjk

Title　　　　　　　" Ming shan chi "
　　　　　　　　　　名　山　記

　　　　　　　　" Ming shan shêng kai chi "
　　　　　　　　　名　山　勝　槩　記

Classification - B-222 地理-遊記

Subject - a collection of notes and jottings written by ancient
　　scholars, up to the end of the Ming Dynasty, in description
　　of their travels over the famous mountains in China.

References - 012-zafk 8/23　031-bgdf 78/6.

Author - not stated.

Edition - a Ming edition; no date.　　Blocks; bamboo paper.

Index - a detailed table of contents for 48 chüan; with a separate
　　list at the beginning of each chüan.

Bound in 4 t'ao 32 ts'ê (8 each).

Remarks - this item is not quite complete.　Firstly, it is without
　　the 圖 and the 附錄 as mentioned in the catalogues.　Secondly,
　　chüan 43 is apparently missing, but there is no exact evidence
　　owing to the disagreement between certain parts of the table of
　　contents and the text of the book.　The last 3 pages of the last
　　ts'ê are handwritten.

358

Accession No. 846   Index No. - 106-dhgf   039-mghg

Title   " Huang Ch'ing ching chieh "
               皇　清　經　解
               " Hsüeh-hai-t'ang ching chieh "
               學　海　堂　經　解

Classification - A-137 羣經總義

Subject - a collection of 183 works, by various authors, chiefly

   consisting of explanations, discussions etc on the "Classics";

   with 2 additional works.

References - 160-lj   029-pffz 303   058-jffz 1/33   012-zafk 3/5

   Gest No. 33.

Author - (編 輯) Yüan Yüan 阮　元 and Yen Chieh 嚴　杰.

Edition - reprinted by Lao Ch'ung-kuang 勞　崇　光 ; dated Hsien-Fêng

   11/1861.   Blocks; "mao-pien" paper.

Index - a table of contents for 1,400 chüan; with 8 additional chüan.

Bound in 36 t'ao 360 ts'ê (10 each).

Remarks - a very important reference work.   The item is complete and

   in good condition.   About half of the original blocks were burned

   during the 7th year of Hsien-Fêng; and Lao supplied the deficiencies

   with newly cut blocks which bear the characters, - 庚 申 補 刋

   on the page-edges.

Accession No. 847   Index No. - 106-dhgf   120-odhg

Title   " Huang Ch'ing ching chieh hsü pien "
              皇　清　經　解　續　編
              " Hsü Huang Ch'ing ching chieh "
              續　皇　清　經　解

Classification - A-137 羣經總義

Subject - a supplementary collection of 209 classical works in
    continuation of the "Huang Ch'ing ching chieh". (Toronto
    No. 846)

References - 160-1j   029-pffz 306   058-jffz (hsü) chia/3
    012-zafk 3/6   Gest No. 34.

Author - (輯) Wang Hsien-ch'ien 王　先　謙.

Edition - the "Nan-ching-shu-yüan" 南　菁　書　院; (preface) dated
    Kuang-Hsü 14/1888.   Blocks; "mao-pien" paper.

Index - a list of the 209 works in 1,430 chüan.

Bound in 32 t'ao 320 ts'ê (10 each).

Remarks - this item is complete and in good condition.

360

Accession No. 848   Index No. - 072-hefh   054-fhc

Title   " Ching-Ting Chien-k'ang chih "
                景　定　建　康　志
               " Chien-k'ang chih "
                建　康　志

Classification - B-194 地理－別志

Subject - a description of the Chien-k'ang district during the
    period of Ching-Ting (Southern Sung), located to the south
    of the present Chiang-ning district in the province of
    Kiangsu; with chapters on topography; literature; famous
    mên; customs; mountains and rivers; illustrations; chronological
    tables; etc.
References - 163-ggcz 5/11 163-ggcz 7/9 012-zafk 6/4 031-bgdf 68/26.

Author - (撰) Chou Ying-ho 周 應 合 .

Edition - "Sun's" 孫 氏 reprint based upon the Sung edition; dated
    Chia-Ch'ing 7/1802.   Blocks; "mao-pien" paper.

Index - a table of contents for 50 chüan.

Bound in 4 t'ao 32 ts'ê (8 each); doubly interleaved.

Remarks - this is a good edition; and the item is complete and
    without a single defects.

Accession No. 849   Index No. - 142-gei

Title   " Ě shu pien "
                            蛾　術　編

Classification - C-308 雜家 - 雜文

Subject - a collection of dissertations on a large variety of
    classical and historical subjects.

References - 012-zafk 12/23.

Author - (撰) Wang Ming-shěng 王　鳴　盛.

Edition - the "Shih-ch'iai-t'ang" 世　楷　堂 ; dated Tao-Kuang
    21/1841.   Blocks; "mao-t'ai" paper.

Index - a detailed table of contents for 82 chüan.

Bound in 2 t'ao 24 ts'ê (12-12).

Remarks - an ordinary good edition; the item is complete and without
    defects.

Accession No. 850   Index No. - 024-gnmb

Title   " <u>Nan chiang i shih</u> "
                  南 疆 繹 史

Classification - B-52 雜史

Subject - (Wylie) "----- is an account of the unsuccessful efforts
    of the three last descendants of the Ming imperial family,
    Fǔh Wang, T'ang Wâng, and Yùng-ming Wâng, to reëstablish the
    falling dynasty."

References - Wylie's Notes page 33   012-zafk 4/26.

Author - (撰) <u>Li Yao</u> 李 瑤 .

Edition - no special designation; (preface) dated Tao-Kuang 10/1830.
    Blocks; "fên" paper.

Index - a table of contents for 卷 首 and 30 chüan.

Bound in 6 t'ao 36 ts'ê (6 each); doubly interleaved.

Remarks - this is a fairly good edition; and the item is complete and
    without defects except some stains and a few repaired worm-holes.
    Chüan 17 of the 摭 遺 is handwritten. There are two supplementary
    works as follows:-
    (#)

(#) " I shih hsü shih k'ao "   (120-mbfi)
     繹 史 邨 諡 攷   8 chüan

     " I shih ohih i "   (120-mbkl)
     繹 史 摭 遺   18 chüan

364

Accession No. 851   Index No. - 030-beji

Title   " Shih   hsing   yün   pien "
               史   姓   韻   編

Classification - B-117 傳記 - 總録   C-348 類書

Subject - (Gest No. 91) "Index of names of persons mentioned in the
    "Êrh shih ssŭ shih" 二 十 四 史 ,- the twenty-four dynastic
    histories, arranged according to rhymes -----."

References - 073-fzfh   大目/29   Gest No. 91   Toronto No. 289.

Author - (遺) Wang Hui-tsu 汪 輝 祖.

Edition - the "Chin-ling-shu-chü" 金 陵 書 局; dated T'ung-Chih
    "kêng-wu" 9/1870.   Blocks; "fên" paper.

Index - a table of contents for 64 chüan.

Bound in 4 t'ao 24 ts'ê (6 each).

Remarks - this is a very good edition; and the item is complete and
    in perfect condition.   A duplicate of Toronto No. 289.

Accession No. 852   Index No. - 055-azhb   007-zzzb

Title   " <u>Nien-i shih ssŭ p'u</u> "
                   廿 一 史 四 譜

                   " <u>Êrh-shih-i shih ssŭ p'u</u> "
                   二 十 一 史 四 譜

<u>Classification</u> - B-137 史鈔
<u>Subject</u> - an historical treatise dealing with four subjects, -
    (1) titles of the reign periods; (2) bestowal of ranks of
    nobility; (3) chief ministers; and (4) posthumous titles;
    covering a period from ancient times down to and including
    the <u>Yüan Dynasty.</u>
<u>References</u> - 012-zafk 5/29   Gest No. 92.

<u>Author</u> - (鈔) <u>Shên Ping-chên</u> 沈 炳 震 .

<u>Edition</u> - the "<u>Ch'ing-lai-t'ang</u>" 清 來 堂 ; dated T'ung-Chih
    "hsin-wei" 10/1871.   Blocks; "mao-pien" paper.

<u>Index</u> - a table of contents for 54 chüan.

<u>Bound in</u> 4 t'ao 24 ts'ê (6 each).

<u>Remarks</u> - this item is complete and without defects.

366

Accession No. 853   Index No. - 055-azbz   007-zzzb

Title   " <u>Nien-êrh</u> <u>shih</u> <u>yen</u> <u>hsing</u> <u>lüeh</u> "
               廿 二 史 言 行 略

               " <u>Êrh-shih-êrh</u> <u>shih</u> <u>yen</u> <u>hsing</u> <u>lüeh</u> "
               二 十 二 史 言 行 略

Classification - B-117 傳記 - 總録

Subject - a collection of biographical sketches taken from the
    official dynastic histories of China up to the <u>Yüan Dynasty</u>;
    arranged under 22 categories.

References - none.

Author - (輯) <u>Kuo Yüan-min</u> 過 元 旼 .

Edition - no particular notation; dated Chia-Ch'ing 15/1810.
    Blocks; "mao-pien" paper.

Index - a table of contents for 42 chüan.

Bound in 2 t'ao 16 ts'ê (8-8).

Remarks - the item is complete and in good condition.

The University of Toronto Chinese Library

Accession No. 854   Index No. - 031-hhzk

Title   " Kuo ch'ao wên hui "

國 朝 文 匯

Classification - D-73 總集-文

Subject - a comprehensive collection of prose compositions of all
the noted scholars of the Ch'ing Dynasty.

References - none.

Author - compiled by Shên Sui-fên 沈 粹 芬 .

Edition - the "Kuo-hsüeh-fu-lun-shê" of Shanghai 上海國學扶輪社;
dated Hsüan-T'ung 1/1909.   Lithographed on "fên" paper.

Index - a general list of writers' names for 甲 前 集 20 chüan;
甲 集 60 chüan; 乙 集 70 chüan; 丙 集 30 chüan; and 丁集
20 chüan; separate lists of writers at the beginning of each 集 ;(#)
Bound in 10 t'ao 101 ts'ê.

Remarks - an ordinary edition; the item is as new.

(#) a detailed table of contents at the beginning of each chüan.

Accession No. 855   Index No. - 067-zlcf

Title   " Wên miao ssǔ tien k'ao "
               文　廟　祀　典　考

Classification - B-287 政書-典禮

Subject - a treatise on the various matters connected with the
sacrifice to Confucius.

References - 012-zafk 9/9.

Author - (編輯) P'ang Chung-lu 龐　鍾　璐．

Edition - privately published; dated Kuang-Hsü "mou-yin" 4/1878.
Blocks; "mao-pien" paper.

Index - a table of contents for 卷 首 and 50 chüan.

Bound in 2 t'ao 12 ts'ê (6 each).

Remarks - the item is complete and without defects except some
slight worm-holes.

Accession No. 856   Index No. - 140-hndd

Title   " Hua yo ch'üan chi "
               華　嶽　全　集

Classification - B-207 地理－山川

Subject - a description of the "T'ai hua shan", the western of the

   "Five Sacred Mountains"; with wood-cuts, literary references,

   etc.

References - 012-zafk 8/7   031-bgdf 76/13   Gest No. 1216.

Author - said to be originally by Li Shih-fang 李 時 芳 ; this

   revised edition by Chang Wei-hsin 張 維 新 ·

Edition - no particular notation; (preface) dated Wan-Li "ting-yu"

   25/1597.   Blocks; "mien" paper.

Index - a table of contents for 13 chüan.

Bound in 2 t'ao 10 ts'6; doubly interleaved.

Remarks - this is a very good edition; and the item is complete and

   without defects.

Accession No. 857   Index No. - 112-ziqd

Title   " <u>Shih</u> <u>ch'ü</u> <u>pao</u> <u>chi</u> "
                石 渠 寶 笈

Classification - C-223 藝術 - 書畫

Subject - descriptions of ancient paintings and calligraphies
    stored in the various palaces during the period of
    Ch'ien-Lung.

References - 031-bgld 12/8   031-bgdf 113/21.

Author - compiled on order of <u>Emperor Ch'ien-Lung</u> by <u>Chi Yün</u> 紀 昀
    and others.

Edition - the "<u>Han-fên-lou</u>" 涵 芬 樓 ; dated "mou-wu" 1918.
    Lithographed on "fên" paper.

Index - for 44 chüan.

Bound in 6 t'ao 50 ts's (10-8-8-8-8-8).

Remarks - the item is complete and in good condition except for a
    few stains.

Accession No. 858   Index No. - 024-bhd   037-abib

Title   " Shêng-an chi "
                    升 庵 集

        " T'ai-shih Yang Shêng-an ch'üan chi "
         太 史 楊 升 庵 全 集

Classification - D-33 列集 - 詩文

Subject - an individual collection of prose and poetry.

References - 163-ggoz 15/7   031-bgld 18/25   012-zafk 16/22

     031-bgdf 172/1.

Author - (撰) Yang Shên 楊 慎．

Edition - the "Yang-cho-shan-fang" 養 拙 山 房 ; dated Ch'ien-Lung

     "i-mao" 60/1795.   Blocks; bamboo paper.

Index - a detailed table of contents for 81 chüan.

Bound in 2 t'ao 20 ts'ê.(10-10).

Remarks - this is a good edition; and the item is complete.

Accession No. 859   Index No. - 030-bke

Title   " Ku yüeh yüan "

古　樂　苑

Classification - D-38 總集一詩

Subject - a general collection of ancient verse and song covering a
period from the beginning of Chinese history down to the Sui
Dynasty.

References - 160-1j 163-ggcz 16/9 031-bgld 19/28 012-zafk 19/12
031-bgdf 189/33.

Author - (撰) Mei Ting-tsu 梅 鼎 祚 .

Edition - a Ming edition; (preface) dated "hsin-mao" 1591.
Blocks; "mien" paper.

Index - a detailed table of contents for 52 chüan.

Bound in 4 t'ao 20 ts's (4 each); doubly interleaved.

Remarks - this is a very fine edition; and the item is complete
and without important defects.　Page 10 in chüan 6 and page
13 in chüan 31 are missing.　There is a supplement entitled:-

" Ku yüeh yüan yen lu "   (030-bkec)

古 樂 苑 衍 錄

4 chüan

The University of Toronto Chinese Library

Accession No. 860   Index No. - 067-zccj   039-cj

Title   " **Wên ch'êng tzŭ hui** "
              文　成　字　彙

Classification - **A-161** 小學一字書

Subject - a dictionary of the Chinese language with the characters
         arranged under 214 radicals.

References - none.

Author - (音釋) **Mei Ying-tsu** 梅膺祚 .

Edition - the "**Ching-lun-t'ang**" 經綸堂 ; dated Chia-Ch'ing
         "kêng-shên" 5/1800.   Blocks; "mao-pien" paper.

Index - a table of the 214 radicals in 12 "chi" together with a
        leading and a concluding chapter.

Bound in 2 t'ao 14 ts'ê (7-7).

Remarks - an ordinary edition; the item is complete.

Accession No. 861   Index No. - 077-dgaf

Title   " Wu ching ch'i shu hui chieh "
            武 經 七 書 彙 解

Classification - C-33 兵 家

Subject - a collection of 7 ancient military works.

References - 029-pffz page 263.

Author - (纂 輯) Chu Yung 朱 墉 ; (重 訂) Kuo Ying 國 英 .

Edition - the "Ku-ching-ko" 古 經 閣 ; (preface) dated Kuang-Hsü
    2/1876.   Blocks; "fēn" paper.

Index - a list of the 7 works in 7 chüan together with a leading
    and a concluding chapter.

Bound in 2 t'ao 10 ts'ê (5-5).

Remarks - a modern edition; the item is new.

Accession No. 862   Index No. - 055-azbl   077-zzzb

Title   " Nien-i-shih t'an tz'ŭ chu "
               廿 一 史 彈 詞 註

               " Erh-shih-i shih t'an tz'ŭ chu "
               二 十 一 史 彈 詞 註

Classification - D-38 別集一詩

Subject - (Gest No. 2962) "a very brief synopsis of Chinese history
     in verse; the period covered being from the earliest times
     down to the close of the Yüan Dynasty."   This item includes
     the Ming Dynasty.

References - 012-zafk 16/22   Gest No. 2962.

Author - (編著) Yang Shên 楊 慎 ; (增定) Chang San-i 張三異

Edition - the "Kuan-chung-shu-yüan" 關 中 書 院 ; (preface)
     dated Tao-Kuang 12/1832.   Blocks; "fên" paper.

Index - none; 10 chüan; 明 紀 彈 詞 2 chüan; 類 聚 數 考 1 chüan.

Bound in 1 t'ao 8 ts'ê.

Remarks - this item is complete and in good condition.

Accession No. **863**   Index No. - **201-zziz   201-zzza   046-zzad**

Title   " <u>Huang wên-chieh Shan-ku hsien-shêng wên chi</u> "

黄 文 節 山 谷 先 生 文 集

" <u>Huang Shan-ku t'ai-shih wên chi</u> "

(#)   黄 山 谷 太 史 文 集

正 集

<u>Classification</u> - **D-33** 別集 - 詩文

<u>Subject</u> - an individual literary collection,- prose and poetry.

<u>References</u> - none to this particular edition; but see 012-zafk 15/16.

<u>Author</u> - (著) <u>Huang T'ing-chien</u> 黄 庭 堅 ; (校) <u>Fang Hang</u> 方 沆 .

<u>Edition</u> - a Ming edition; (preface) dated Wan-Li "kuei-mao" 31/1603.
   Blocks; bamboo paper.

<u>Index</u> - a detailed table of contents for 30 chüan.

<u>Bound in</u> 2 t'ao 10 ts'ê (5-5); doubly interleaved.

<u>Remarks</u> - the impression is taken from old blocks. The item is
   complete and without important defects.

(#)   " <u>Shan-ku chêng chi</u> "
            山 谷 正 集

Accession No. 864   Index No. - 039-ekf

Title   " Chi Han shu "
                          季 漢 書

Classification - B-42 別史

Subject - (Gest No. 847) "History opening with Annals of the last
    emperor of Han, Hsien-Ti 獻 帝 , and considering that the
    Shu 蜀 and not the Wei 魏 line should be the legitimate
    successors of the Han,-----."

References - 012-zafk 4/16   031-bgdf 50/50   Gest No. 847.

Author - (撰) Hsieh Pi 謝 陛 .

Edition - a Ming edition; no date.   Blocks; bamboo paper.

Index - none; 60 chüan; 答 問 1 chüan.

Bound in 2 t'ao 10 ts'ê (5-5).

Remarks - this is a good edition; and the item is complete but with
    a few repaired defects.

Accession No. 865   Index No. - 030-bm

Title   " Shih wei "
                         史 薈

Classification - B-137 史 鈔

Subject - extracts taken from the first 3 dynastic histories of
China, i.e., "Shih chi" 史 記 , "Han shu" 漢 書 , and
"Hou Han shu" 後 漢 書 ; with critical commentary.

References - none.

Author - (批 點) Wang Chia-chih 王 家 植 .

Edition - a Ming edition; (preface) dated Wan-Li 46/1618.   Blocks;
bamboo paper.

Index - a table of contents for 5 chüan.

Bound in 2 t'ao 10 ts'e (5-5); doubly interleaved.

Remarks - this item is complete and without defects.

Accession No. 866   Index No. - 050-ffhd

Title   " **Ti ching ching wu lüeh** "
         帝　京　景　物　畧

Classification - B-217 地理－雜記

Subject - **an archaeological and historical description of Peking and its environs.**

References - 012-zafk 8/18   031-bgdf 77/23.

Author - (修) **Liu T'ung** 劉　侗 and **Yü I-chêng** 于 奕　正 ；
      (定) **Fang Fêng-nien** 方 逢 年 ．

Edition - a Ming edition; (preface) dated Ch'ung-Chêng 8/1635.
    Blocks; bamboo paper.

Index - a table of contents for 8 chüan; separate lists for each
    chüan.

Bound in 2 t'ao 16 ts'ê (8-8); doubly interleaved.

Remarks - this is a good edition; and the item is complete and in
    fairly good condition.

Accession No. 867   Index No. - 119-fdhp

Title   " Yüeh-ya-t'ang ts'ung shu "
               粤 雅 堂 叢 書

Classification - C-338 雜家-叢書
Subject - a comprehensive collection of reprints.

References - 160-1j   012-zafk 13/15   029-pffz page 389
     058-jffz 7/18.

Author - (編刻) Wu Ch'ung-yao 伍崇曜 .

Edition - the "Yüeh-ya-t'ang"; (preface) dated Hsien-Fêng 3/1853.
     Blocks; "fên" paper.

Index - for 3 "pien" each containing 10 "chi"; a list of the various
     works in 30 "chi"; separate lists at the beginning of each "chi".

Bound in 30 t'ao 380 ts's.

Remarks - a clear - out small edition; the item is complete and
     without important defects.

381

Accession No.   868   Index No. - 005-agzd

Title   " <u>Chiu   chia   wên   ch'ao</u> "
                          九   家   文   抄

Classification - D-73 總集-文

<u>Subject</u> - a collection of selected prose writings of 9 noted
   scholars.

<u>References</u> - none.

<u>Author</u> - not stated.

<u>Edition</u> - no special notation; apparently of the Ming period.
   Blocks; bamboo paper.

<u>Index</u> - separate for the various works.

<u>Bound in</u> 4 t'ao 20 ts'ê (5 each); doubly interleaved.

<u>Remarks</u> - this item does not seem to be a complete work; and it is
   possibly a part of a certain "Ts'ung-shu" the title of which
   can not be found eitherfrom this item itself or from the
   catalogues.   The present title as given above is taken down
   only from the catalogue of books of the former owner,   (#)

(#) and is without authority elsewhere. The following is a
list of the 9 separate works:-

1. " Li I-shan wên ch'ao "   (075-cgzz)
李 義 山 文 抄   1 chüan
by Li Shang-yin 李 商 隱.

2. " Ts'ui Chung-fu wên ch'ao "   (046-hdbz)
崔 仲 鳧 文 抄   1 chüan
by Ts'ui Hsien 崔 銑.

3. " Hsü Wên-ch'ang wên ch'ao "   (060-gzzz)
徐 文 長 文 抄   1 chüan
by Hsü Wei 徐 渭.

4. " Wang Tao-k'un wên ch'ao "   (085-didz)
汪 道 昆 文 抄   1 chüan
by Wang Tao-k'un 汪 道 昆.

5. " Li Hsien-chi wên ch'ao "   (075-cpcz)
李 獻 吉 文 抄   1 chüan
by Li Mêng-yang 李 夢 陽.

6. " T'ang Jo-shih wên ch'ao "   (085-iezz)
湯 若 士 文 抄   1 chüan
by T'ang Hsien-tsu 湯 顯 祖.

7. " Wang Po-an wên ch'ao "   (096-zecz)
王 伯 安 文 抄   1 chüan
by Wang Shou-jên 王 守 仁.

8. " Li Yü-lin wên ch'ao "   (075-calz)
李 于 鱗 文 抄   1 chüan
by Li P'an-lung 李 攀 龍.

9. " Wang Yüan-mei wên ch'ao "   (096-zbcz)
王 元 美 文 抄   1 chüan
by Wang Shih-chêng 王 世 貞.

The University of Toronto Chinese Library

Accession No. 869-a   Index No. - 037-zmeg

Title   " <u>Ta-hsüeh chu su ta ch'üan ho tsuan</u> "
大學 註 疏 大 全 合 纂

Classification - <u>A-132</u> 四書-大學

Subject - commentaries on the advanced course of study for youths
under the <u>Chou Dynasty</u> educational system; a treatise on
government.

References - none to this particular edition.

Author - (纂) <u>Chang P'u</u> 張 溥 .

Edition - a Ming edition; (preface) dated Ch'ung-Chêng 9/1636.
Blocks; bamboo paper.

Index - none; 1 chüan.

Bound in 1 ts'ê in 1 t'ao with (b) and (c).

Remarks - this is a good edition; and the item is complete and in
perfect condition.

The University of Toronto Chinese Library

Accession No. 869-b   Index No. - 002-cheg

Title   " Chung-yung chu su ta ch'üan ho tsuan "
中 庸 註 疏 大 全 合 纂

Classification - A-133 四書－中庸
Subject - commentaries on the "Doctrine of the Mean".

References - none to this particular edition.

Author - (纂) Chang P'u 張 溥 .

Edition - uniform with (a).

Index - none; 1 chüan.

Bound in 2 ts'ê in 1 t'ao with (a) and (c).

Remarks - as under (a).

Accession No.   869-c   Index No. - 149-hgeg

Title   " Lun-yü chu su ta ch'üan ho tsuan "
           論 語 註 疏 大 全 合 纂

Classification - A-134 四書 - 論語

Subject - commentaries on the discourses of Confucius with his
     followers and others.

References - none to this particular edition.

Author - (纂) Chang P'u 張 溥 .

Edition - uniform with (a).

Index - none; 20 chüan.

Bound in 3 t'ao 8 ts'ê; lst t'ao with (a) and (b); 3d t'ao with (d).

Remarks - as under (a).

Accession No. 869-d   Index No. - 039-ezeg

Title   " Mĕng-tzŭ chu su ta ch'üan ho tsuan "
         孟 子 註 疏 大 全 合 纂

Classification - A-135 四書一孟子

Subject - commentaries on the discourses of Mencius on political,
    social and ethical subjects.

References - none to this particular edition.

Author - (纂) Chang P'u 張 溥 .

Edition - uniform with (a).

Index - none; 14 chüan.

Bound in 2 t'ao 7 ts'ĕ; 1st t'ao with (c).

Remarks - as under (a).

Accession No. 870   Index No. - 106-dhdh   169-dhzf

Title   " Huang Ch'ing k'ai kuo fang lüeh "
             皇　清　開　國　方　畧

Classification - B-22 編年

Subject - (Gest No. 848) "The record of the events in the history
    of the imperial house of the Ch'ing (Manchu) dynasty from
    A. D. 1583-1644;" together with additional matter related to
    the Manchu dynasty and its origin.

References - 160-1j   163-ggoz 4/9   031-bgld 5/25   012-zafk 4/11
    031-bgdf 47/54   Gest Nos. 848 and 1430.

Author - prepared by a commission headed by A Kuei 阿 桂 et al.

Edition - a manuscript written on "k'ai-hua" paper, based upon the
    Ch'ien-Lung 1786 palace edition.

Index - a list of "shou" and 32 chüan, arranged in chronological
    order.

Bound in 1 t'ao 16 ts's.

Remarks - a clear manuscript.   The item has no defects and is
    complete.

Accession No.   871   **Index No.** - 030-bfz

Title   " <u>Ku</u>   <u>ko</u>   <u>yen</u> "
                         古 格 言

Classification - C-328 雜家-雜纂

Subject - a collection of extracts of a homelitical nature taken
     from the "Classics" and other ancient works.

References - 012-zafk 13/10.

Author - (輯) <u>Liang Chang-chü</u> 梁 章 鉅 .

Edition - a reprint by <u>Jên Wei-chün</u> 任 位 俊 and <u>Jên Ch'ao-chün</u>
     任 超 俊 ; (postscriptum) dated Tao-Kuang "chia-ch'ên"
     24/1844.   Blocks; bamboo paper.

Index - none; 12 chüan.

Bound in 1 t'ao 4 ts'ê; doubly interleaved.

Remarks - a fair edition; the item is complete.

Accession No. 872   Index No. - 007-bgfc   007-bgfe

Title   " <u>Wu</u> ching p'ang hsün "
             五   經   旁   訓

             " <u>Wu</u> ching p'ang chu "
             五   經   旁   註

Classification - A-137 羣經總義

Subject - (Gest No. 2506) "a collection of commentaries on the

  '<u>Five Classics</u>'; that is the Canons of Changes, Poetry,

  and History; the Book of Rites; and the Spring and Autumn

  Annals."

References - Gest No. 2506.

Author - various for the several works.

Edition - the "<u>Li-tsung-shu-yüan</u>" 禮 宗 書 院 ; (preface) dated

  Ch'ung-Chêng 2/1629.   Blocks; bamboo paper.

Index - none.

Bound in 1 t'ao 8 ts'ê.

Remarks - this is a good edition; and the item is complete and

  without defects.

The University of Toronto Chinese Library

---·•·---

Accession No. 873   **Index No.** - 162-jccd   070-zamd

Title   " Hsün-chih-chai chi "
                遜 志 齋 集

        " Fang Chêng-hsüeh hsien-shêng Hsün-chih-chai chi "
        方 正 學 先 生 遜 志 齋 集

Classification - D-33 別集 - 詩文

Subject - an individual collection of prose and poetry.

References - 160-1j   163-ggcz 15/4   031-bgld 18/11   030-iaff 35/30

    106-gdkn 111/22 012-zafk 16/14 031-bgdf 170/5 Gest No. 2032

    Toronto No. 35.

Author - (撰) Fang Hsiao-ju 方 孝 儒 .

Edition - no particular notation; (preface) dated K'ang-Hsi "mou-yin"

    37/1698.   Blocks; bamboo paper.

Index - a detailed table of contents for 24 chüan.

Bound in 2 t'ao 16 ts'ê (8-8).

Remarks - this is an ordinary edition; and the impression is not a

    very good one.   The item appears to be complete.   The memorial

    at the beginning of the work is handwritten.   There are sup-

    plements as follows:-   a "shih-pu" 拾 補 ; a "wai-chi" 外 紀

Accession No. 874   Index No. - 024-zzgz

Title   " Shih i ching yin hsün "
　　　　　　　　　　十 一 經 音 訓

Classification - A-137 羣經總義

Subject - an explanation and commentary on 11 classical works.

References - 012-zafk 3/5.

Author - (撰) Yang Kuo-chên 楊 國 楨 .

Edition - no particular notation; dated Tao-Kuang "kêng-yin" 10/1830.
　Blocks; "mao-pien" paper.

Index - none.

Bound in 6 t'ao 26 ts'ê (5-4-4-4-4-5).

Remarks - this item is complete and without defects.

Accession No. 875   Index No. - 030-bfn

Title   " Ku shih kuei "
                          古 詩 歸

Classification - D-68 總集 - 詩

Subject - a collection of poems by ancient authors of the period
    from the earliest times down to and including the Sui Dynasty;
    with marginal notes and commentaries.

References - (詩歸) 012-zafk 19/11   031-bgdf 193/21
    Gest No. 788-a.

Author - (選定) Chung Hsing 鍾惺 ; T'an Yüan-ch'un 譚元春 .

Edition - a Ming edition; (preface) dated Wan-Li 45/1617.   Blocks;
    "mien" paper.

Index - separate lists of contents at the beginning of each of 15
    chüan.

Bound in 2 t'ao 16 ts's (8-8); doubly interleaved.

Remarks - this item is a part of the work entitled "Shih-kuei" 詩歸
    which is composed of 2 works,- the present item and the
    "T'ang-shih-kuei" 唐詩歸 .   It is a good item and has no
    defects.

The University of Toronto Chinese Library

Accession No. 876   Index No. - 076-heed   072-edkg

Title " Ch'in-ting Ch'un-ch'iu chuan shuo hui tsuan "
欽 定 春 秋 傳 說 彙 纂

Classification - A-101 春秋

Subject - a collection of commentaries on the "Ch'un-ch'iu" or the
"Spring and Autumn Annals", including the four famous
commentaries Tso-chuan 左 傳 Kung-yang 公 羊 Ku-liang 穀梁
and Hu-chuan 胡 傳 as well as comments from other great
scholars of the period from the Han to the Ming dynasty.

References - 163-ggoz 2/14   031-bgld 3/15   012-zafk 2/24
031-bgdf 29/2   Gest Nos. 879 and 2064.

Author - an Imperial commission headed by Wang Shan 王 掞 .

Edition - a "palace" edition; (preface) dated K'ang-Hsi 60/1721.
Blocks; "k'ai-hua" paper.

Index - a general table of contents for an introductory chapter in 2
sections; and 38 chüan.

Bound in 4 t'ao 24 ts'ê (6 each).

Remarks - this is a very fine edition; and the item is complete and
without defects with the exception of a few worm-holes.

Accession No. 877   Index No. - 076-heed   072-edbk

Title   " Ch'in-ting Ch'un-ch'iu Tso-chuan tu pên "
          欽　定　春　秋　左　傳　讀　本

Classification - A-101 春秋

Subject - an explanation of the "Tso-chuan" 左 傳 ,- a famous
     commentary on the "Ch'un-ch'iu".

References - 012-zafk 2/24.

Author - by Ying Ho 英 和 and others on Imperial order.

Edition - a "palace" edition; dated Tao-Kuang 2/1822.   Blocks;
     "fên" paper.

Index - none; 30 chüan.

Bound in 2 t'ao 16 ts'ê (8-8).

Remarks - a fairly good edition; complete and without defects.

Accession No. 878   Index No. - 072-edbk

Title   " Ch'un-ch'iu ssŭ chuan "
          春 秋 四 傳

Classification - A-101春秋

Subject - a collection of 4 commentaries on the "Ch'un-ch'iu",-
    the Hu-chuan 胡 傳 , Tso-chuan 左 傳 , Kung-yang 公 羊 and
    Ku-liang 穀 梁 .

References - 012-zafk 2/23   031-bgdf 30/6   Gest No. 556.

Author - not stated.

Edition - an undated Ming edition.   Blocks; "mien" paper.

Index - a general table of contents for 38 chüan.

Bound in 2 t'ao 8 ts's (4-4).

Remarks - this is a good edition; and the item is complete and
    without defects.

Accession No. 879   Index No. - 073-fgdk   073-fdk

Title   " Shu-ching chi chuan "
                      書 經 集 傳
                   " Shu chi chuan "
                      書 集 傳

Classification - A-21 書

Subject - (Gest No. 3658) "a commentary on the so-called 'Canon of
    History' (Wylie - 'Book of Government'); containing the
    historical remains of the Yü 虞 , Hsia 夏 , Shang 商 , and
    Chou 周 dynasties, and covering the period from about 2357 B.C.
    to 721 B.C."

References - Wylie's Notes page 3 163-ggcz 1/10   031-bgld 2/4
    037-ahhg 5/3 (hsü) 8/10 167-mhfm 2/6 030-iaff 1/25 012-zafk 1/16
    (#)
Author - Ts'ai Ch'ên 蔡 沉 .

Edition - a Ming edition; no date.   Blocks; "mien" paper.

Index - a general table of contents for 6 chüan.

Bound in 1 t'ao 6 ts'ê.

Remarks - a very good edition; the item is complete but with a few
    repaired defects.   The last page of chüan 6 is handwritten.

    (#) 031-bgdf 11/20   Gest Nos. 1731 and 3658   Toronto No. 761.

Accession No. 880   Index No. - 149-fgdk   149-fdk

Title   " Shih-ching chi chuan "
                   詩　經　集　傳
                   " Shih chi chuan "
                   詩　集　傳

Classification - A-31 詩

Subject - the standard commentary on the "Book of Odes".

References - Wylie's Notes page 3 106-1j   163-ggcz 2/2   031-bgld 2/15
      037-ahhg 7/2 (hsü) 2/13 12/6   167-mhfm 3/6   030-iaff 2/1   (#)

Author - (撰) Chu Hsi 朱 熹 .

Edition - a Ming edition; no date.   Blocks; "mien" paper.

Index - a detailed table of contents for 8 chüan.

Bound in 1 t'ao 4 ts's.

Remarks - this is a good edition; the item is complete. Manuscript
    pages:- chüan 2 pages 4 and 5; 3/36; 6/39; 7/3.

    (#) 106-gdkn 5/5   012-zafk 2/2   031-bgdf 15/18   Gest Nos.
        1731-c and 2960-c.

Accession No. 881   Index No. - 030-edkg   030-edgb

Title   " Chou-i chuan i "
                          周 易   傳   義

                  " Chou-i Ch'ǒng Chu chuan i "
                    周 易   程   朱   傳   義

Classification - A-11 易

Subject - (Gest No. 1148) "an exposition (commentary and
    explanation) of the Book of Changes".

References - 030-iaff 1/7   106-gdkn 2/12   012-zafk 1/2
    Gest No. 1148.

Author - (傳) Ch'ǒng I 程 頤 ; (本義) Chu Hsi 朱 熹 .

Edition - an undated Ming edition.   Blocks; "mien" paper.

Index - a general table of contents for 24 chüan.

Bound in 1 t'ao 6 ts'è.

Remarks - a good edition; the item is without defects and complete,
    with the exception of 2 pages missing in the section 周易篇義.

Accession No. 882   Index No. - 173-dgmc   113-mcdg

Title   " <u>Yün-chuang Li-chi chi shuo</u> "
                   雲 莊 禮 記 集 說

Classification - A-56 禮 -禮記

<u>Subject</u> - (Gest No. 2960-d) "the standard treatise and commentary
    on the "<u>Canon of Rites</u>".

<u>References</u> - Wylie's Notes page 6 160-1j   163-ggcz 2/8   031-bgld 2/34
    037-ahhg (hsü) 12/11   167-mhfm 4/12   030-1aff 2/25 106-gdkn 7/5
    (#)
<u>Author</u> - (撰) <u>Ch'ên Hao</u> 陳 澔 .

<u>Edition</u> - a **Ming** edition; no date.   Blocks; "mien" paper.

<u>Index</u> - a general table of contents for 30 chüan.

<u>Bound in</u> 1 t'ao 6 ts'ê.

<u>Remarks</u> - this is a good edition; and the item is complete and
    with no defects.   Page 5 of chüan 17 and page 17 of chüan
    26 are handwritten.

    (#) 012-zafk 2/14   031-bgdf 21/7   Gest Nos. 333, 716, 1731-d
    and 2960-d.

Accession No. 883   Index No. - 109-dhez   046-efdh

Title   " Hsiang-t'ai Yo shih pên Wu ching "
             相　臺　岳　氏　本　五　經

             " Yo k'o Hsiang-t'ai pên ku chu Wu ching "
             岳　刻　相　臺　本　古　注　五　經

Classification - A-137 羣經總義
Subject - a collection of the "Five Classics" with commentaries.

References - 058-jffz 1/7   029-pffz 286   Gest No. 401.

Author - (校刊) Yo K'o 岳　珂 .

Edition - a reproduction by the "Sung's Chüan-yü-lou" 宋氏卷雨廔
     of the Ch'ien-Lung 1783 reprint of Yo's Sung edition; dated
     "chia-tzǔ" 1924.   Process (?); white "mao-pien" paper.

Index - none; 5 works and 8 supplements in all.

Bound in 8 t'ao 44 ts'ê.

Remarks - this is a very good modern edition; and the item is
     complete and without any defects.   The five works are as
     follows:-

     (#)

(#)

1. " <u>Chou-i chu</u> "　　　　　(030-ede)
　周 易 註　　　　　　10 chüan　A-11

　　by <u>Wang Pi</u> 王 弼 .

2. " <u>Shang-shu</u> "　　　　　(042-ef)
　尚 書　　　　　　　13 chüan　A-21

　　by <u>K'ung An-kuo</u> 孔 安 國 .

3. " <u>Mao-shih</u> "　　　　　(082-zf)
　毛 詩　　　　　　　20 chüan　A-31

　　by <u>Chêng Yüan</u> 鄭 元 .

4. " <u>Li-chi</u> "　　　　　　(113-mc)
　禮 記　　　　　　　20 chüan　A-41

　　by <u>Chêng Yüan</u> 鄭 元 .

5. " <u>Ch'un-ch'iu ching chuan chi chieh</u> "　(072-edgk)
　春 秋 經 傳 集 解　　　30 chüan　A-101

　　by <u>Tu Yü</u> 杜 預 .

Accession No. 884 **Index No.** - 060-hnag 001-ag

Title " Yü-tsuan Ch'i ching "

御 纂 七 經

Classification - A-137 羣經總義

Subject - a collection of seven classics, with commentaries.

(see separate notes)

References - 029-pffz 348 058-jffz 1/13 Gest No. 31.

Author - Imperially compiled.

Edition - the "Ch'ung-wen-shu-chü" 崇文書局 ; dated T'ung-Chih

10/1871. Blocks; "fên" paper.

Index - none for the collection.

Bound in 23 t'ao 170 ts'ê.

Remarks - this is a fairly good edition; and the item is complete

and without defects.

Accession No. 884-a   Index No. - 060-hned   030-eddc

Title   " Yü-tsuan Chou-i chê chung "
               御 纂 周 易 折 中

Classification - A-11 易

Subject - (Gest No. 2096) "a dissertation on the "Book of Changes",
     based on the writings of 218 scholars from the Han to the
     Ming period, both included.

References - 163-ggcz 1/7   031-bgld 1/24   012-zafk 1/7   031-bgdf 6/3
     Gest Nos. 31-a and 2096   Toronto No. 554.

Author - an editorial commission headed by Li Kuang-ti 李 光 地 .

Edition - as under No. 884.

Index - a general table of contents for 卷 首 and 22 chüan.

Bound in 2 t'ao 12 ts'ê (6-6).

Remarks - as under No. 884.

Accession No. 884-b   Index No. - 076-hefg   073-fgkg

Title   " Ch'in-ting Shu-ching chuan shuo hui tsuan "
         欽 定 書 經 傳 說 彙 纂

Classification - A-21 書

Subject - (Gest No. 1695) "a commentary on the 'Book of History',
    based upon numerous works of a similar character."

References - 163-ggcz 1/12 031-bgld 2/10 012-zafk 1/18
    031-bgdf 12/22   Gest Nos. 31-b and 1695.

Author - an Imperial commission headed by Wang Hsü-ling 王 頊 齡 .

Edition - as under No. 884.

Index - a general table of contents for an introductory chapter in
    two sections; and 21 chüan.

Bound in 2 t'ao 12 ts'ê (6-6).

Remarks - as under No. 884.

Accession No.   884-c   Index No. - 076-hefg   149-fgkg

Title   " Ch'in-ting Shih-ching chuan shuo hui tsuan "
          欽　定　詩　經　傳　說　彙　纂

Classification - A-31 詩

Subject - a commentary on the "Book of Odes", based upon numerous
    works of a similar character.

References - 163-ggcz 2/3   031-bgld 2/21   012-zafk 2/4
    031-bgdf 16/18   Gest Nos. 778 and 1714.

Author - an Imperial commission headed by Wang Hung-hsü 王　鴻　緒.

Edition - as under No. 884.

Index - a general table of contents for an introductory chapter in
    two sections; 21 chüan; and a supplementary chapter in two
    sections.
Bound in 3 t'ao 18 ts'ê (6-6-6).

Remarks - as under No. 884.

Accession No. 884-d   Index No. - 076-heee

Title   " Ch'in-ting Chou kuan i su "

欽 定 周 官 義 疏

Classification - A-46 禮-周禮

Subject - a collection of commentatorial notes and disquisitions
on the "Chou Ritual".

References - 163-ggcz 2/5   031-bgld 2/27   012-zafk 2/9
031-bgdf 19/30   Gest No. 31-d.

Author - an Imperial commission headed by the prince Yün-lu 允 禄.

Edition - as under No. 884.

Index - a table of contents for 卷首 and 48 chüan.

Bound in 4 t'ao 28 ts'ê (6-7-7-8).

Remarks - as under No. 884.

Accession No.   884-e   Index No. - 076-hemm   009-mmgg

Title   " Ch'in-ting I li i su "
                   欽 定 儀 禮 義 疏

Classification - A-51 禮 - 儀禮

Subject - a collection of commentatorial notes and disquisitions

   on the "Decorum Ritual".

References - 163-ggcz 2/6   031-bgld 2/31   012-zafk 2/11

   031-bgdf 20/17   Gest No. 31-e.

Author - an Imperial commission headed by the prince Yün-lu 允 禄 .

Edition - as under No. 884.

Index - a table of contents for an introductory chapter in two

   sections; and 48 chüan.

Bound in 4 t'ao 32 ts'$ (7-8-8-9).

Remarks - as under No. 884.

Accession No. 884-f   Index No. - 076-hemc   113-mogg

Title   " Ch'in-ting Li chi i su "
                   欽 定 禮 記 義 疏

Classification - A-56 禮-禮記

Subject - a collection of commentatorial notes and disquisitions on
    the "Book of Rites".

References - 163-ggcz 2/8   031-bgld 2/35   012-zafk 2/14
    031-bgdf 21/17   Gest No. 31-f.

Author - an Imperial commission headed by the prince Yün-lu 允 禄.

Edition - as under No. 884.

Index - a general table of contents for 卷首   and 82 chüan.

Bound in 6 t'ao 48 ts'ê (9-7-8-7-9-8).

Remarks - as under No. 884.

Accession No. 884-g   Index No. - 076-heed   072-edkg

Title   " Ch'in-ting Ch'un-ch'iu chuan shuo hui tsuan "
欽 定 春 秋 傳 說 彙 纂

Classification - A-101 春秋

Subject - (Toronto No. 876) "a collection of commentaries on the
"Ch'un-ch'iu" or the "Spring and Autumn Annals", including
the four famous commentaries Tso-chuan 左 傳 Kung-yang 公羊
Ku-liang 穀 梁 and Hu-chuan 胡 傳 ,as well as comments from
other eminent scholars of the period from the Han to the Ming
dynasty."

References - 163-ggoz 2/14   031-bgld 3/15   012-zafk 2/24
031-bgdf 29/2   Gest Nos. 879 and 2064   Toronto No. 876.

Author - an Imperial commission headed by Wang Shan 王 掞 .

Edition - as under No. 884.

Index - a general table of contents for an introductory chapter in
2 sections; and 38 chüan.

Bound in 2 t'ao 20 ts'ê (10-10).

Remarks - as under No. 884.

Accession No. 885   **Index No. -** 128-gebd   060-hhzd

Title   " Shêng Tsu Jên Huang-ti chi "

聖 祖 仁 皇 帝 集

" Yü-chih wên chi "

御 製 文 集

Classification - D-33 列集-詩文

Subject - an individual literary collection,- prose and poetry.

References - Wylie's Notes page 234   163-ggcz 15/10   031-bgld 18/36

     012-zafk 17/1   031-bgdf 173/1   Gest No. 3508.

Author - the Emperor K'ang-Hsi 康熙 ; (編錄) of the 1st 2d and

     3d "chi" - Chang Yü-shu 張玉書 and others; of the 4th "chi" -

     Yün-lu 允祿 and others.

Edition - "palace" edition; dated K'ang-Hsi 53/1714; 4th "chi" dated

     Yung-Chêng 10/1732.   Blocks; "k'ai-hua" paper.

Index - (初集) a detailed table of contents for 40 chüan; detailed

     tables at the beginning of each chüan. (二集) same for 50

     chüan. (三集) for 50 chüan. (四集) 36 chüan.

Bound in 12 t'ao 98 ts'ê.

Remarks - this is a very fine edition; and the item is complete and

     without defects.

Accession No. 886   Index No. - 096-zfhm   162-mdc

Title   " Yü-ming-t'ang Huan hun chi "
               玉 茗 堂 還 魂 記

Classification – D-138 詞曲 – 南北曲

Subject – a Chinese play in 55 acts; with illustrations.

References – 012-zafk 20/35.

Author – (撰) T'ang Hsien-tsu 湯 顯 祖 :

Edition – the "Nuan-hung-shih" 暖 紅 室 ; date not given.
     Blocks; "fên" paper.

Index – a list of the 55 section headings (in 2 parts) for 2 chüan
     上 下 .

Bound in 1 t'ao 2 ts'ê.

Remarks – this is a very good edition; and the item is complete and
     without defects.

Accession No. 887   **Index No.** - 039-cn

Title   " Tzŭ chien "
           字 鑑

Classification - A-161 小學一字書

Subject - a dictionary of the Chinese characters arranged under 5
     tones and 206 rhymes.

References - Wylie's Notes page 13   160-1j   163-ggcz 3/12   031-bgld
     4/23   030-iaff 5/16   106-gdkn 15/21   012-zafk 3/21   031-bgdf 41/39
     Gest No. 346-3.

Author - (撰) Li Wên-chung 李文仲 .

Edition - that of "Chiang-shih" 蔣氏 ; dated Kuang-Hsü "chia-shên"
     10/1884.   Blocks; "fên" paper.

Index - separate at the beginning of each of 5 chüan.

Bound in 1 t'ao 1 ts'ê.

Remarks - the item is complete and in good condition.

Accession No. 888   Index No. - 169-km1

Title   " Kuan hsüeh pien "
              闢　學　編

Classification - B-117 傳記-總録

Subject - a collection of biographical sketches of noted scholars
   of the Sung, Chin, Yüan and Ming dynasties.

References - 031-bgdf 63/22.

Author - originally compiled by Fêng Ts'ung-wu 馮 從 吾 ;
   (續 編) Li Yüan-ch'un 李 元 春 .

Edition - the "Ch'uan-ching-t'ang" 傳 經 堂 ; (preface) dated
   Ch'ien-Lung "ping-tzǔ" 21/1756.   Blocks; "mao-pien" paper.

Index - a list of names for 4 chüan, chronologically arranged.
   (see "Remarks")

Bound in 1 t'ao 2 ts'ê.

Remarks - this item is undoubtedly incomplete.   The catalogue
   referred to above lists this work as in 5 chüan; but this
   item contains 4 chüan.   Although the table of contents and
   the text are in accord, they are simply made so to conceal
   the trace of the incompleteness.

Accession No. 889   Index No. - 162-1ebh   012-bhgh

Title   " Hsüan chu Liu-ch'ao T'ang fu "
               選 註 六 朝 唐 賦

Classification - D-68 總集 - 詩

Subject - a selection of compositions in the "fu" style written by
          scholars of the period of Liu-ch'ao and the T'ang Dynasty;
          with explanative notes.

References - 012-zafk 19/35.

Author - (選 註) Ma Ch'uan-kêng 馬 傳 庚 .

Edition - the "Sung-chu-chai" 松 竹 齋 ; dated Kuang-Hsü "ping-tzǔ"
          2/1876.   Blocks; "fên" paper.

Index - a table of contents not divided into chüan.

Bound in 1 t'ao 2 ts'ê.

Remarks - a modern edition; complete and as new.

415

Accession No. 890   Index No. - 046-zlfl   075-eecd

Title   " <u>Shan-hsiao-ko</u> <u>hsüan</u> <u>T'ang</u> <u>ta</u> <u>chia</u> <u>Liu</u> <u>Liu-chou</u> <u>ch'üan</u> <u>chi</u> "
山 曉 閣 選 唐 大 家 柳 柳 州 全 集

Classification - D-43 別集 -文
Subject - an individual collection of prose; with commentaries.

References - none.

Author - by <u>Liu Tsung-yüan</u> 柳 宗 元 ; (手 評) <u>Sun Tsung</u> 孫 琮 .

Edition - the "<u>Kuang-i-shu-chü</u>" 廣 益 書 局 ; undated, but fairly
recent.   Lithographed on "fên" paper.

Index - a table of contents for 4 chüan.

Bound in 1 t'ao 4 ts'ê.

Remarks - an ordinary modern edition; the item is new.

416

Accession No. 891   **Index No. -** 170-hhdf

Title   " T'ao Yüan-ming shih chi "
                   陶 淵 明 詩 集

Classification - D-33 別集 - 詩文

Subject - an individual literary collection,- prose and poetry.

References - 160-1j   167-mhfm 19/6   163-ggcz 12/2   031-bgld 15/4

   012-zafk 15/3   031-bgdf 148/32   Gest No. 1556   Toronto No. 339.

Author - T'ao Ch'ien 陶 潛 .

Edition - no notation; (postscriptum) dated Tao-Kuang "hsin-ch'ou"

   21/1841.   Blocks; "mao-pien" paper.

Index - a table of contents for 10 chüan.

Bound in 1 t'ao 1 ts'ê.

Remarks - the item is complete and in good condition.

Accession No. 892   Index No. - 031-cngc

Title   " Hui chiang t'ung chih "
             回   疆   通   志

Classification - B-192 地理－省志

Subject - a topographical and historical description of the Chinese
    Turkestan region,- the present province of Sinkiang.

References - none.

Author - (撰) Ho Ning 和 寗 .

Edition - no notation; (preface) dated Kung-Ho (Min-Kuo) 14/1925.
    Type; "mao-pien" paper.

Index - a detailed table of contents for 12 chüan.

Bound in 1 t'ao 4 ts'ê.

Remarks - an ordinary edition; complete and without defects.

The University of Toronto Chinese Library

Accession No. 893   Index No. - 030-cgh

Title   " <u>Ming li t'an</u> "
                          名　理　探

Classification - C-13 儒家

Subject - a work on logic,- being a translation from the original
   work in Latin entitled:- Commentarii Collegii Conimbricensis
   e Societate Jesu in universam dialecticam Aristotelis Stagiritae.

References - none.

Author - of original,- probably compiled by one or several Jesuits;
   of this translation,- (譯義) <u>Francois Furtado</u> 傅 汎 際
   and (達辭) <u>Li Chih-tsao</u> 李 之 藻 .

Edition - the "<u>Li-yün-shu-wu</u>" 勵 耘 書 屋 ; dated Min-Kuo 15/1926.
   Process (?); "fên" paper.

Index - a detailed table of contents for 5 chüan.

Bound in 1 t'ao 3 ts'ê.

Remarks - this is a good modern edition; and the item is complete
   and new.

419

Accession No.　894　　　　Index No. ‐ 009‐edfb　　174‐zid

Title　　　" <u>Yü Chung-hsüan kung wên chi</u> "
　　　　　　余　忠　宣　公　文　集
　　　　　　　　" <u>Ch'ing-yang chi</u> "
　　　　　　　　青　陽　集

<u>Classification</u> ‐ D‐33 別集－詩文

<u>Subject</u> ‐ an individual literary collection,‐ prose and poetry.

<u>References</u> ‐ 163‐ggcz 14/6　　031‐bgld 17/15　　012‐zafk 16/6
　　　　031‐bgdf 167/55.

<u>Author</u> ‐ (撰) <u>Yü Ch'üeh</u> 余　闕 . 1303-1358

<u>Edition</u> ‐ the "<u>Hung-t'ao-shan-fang</u>" 洪濤山房 ; dated Ch'ien-Lung
　　　　18/1753.　　　Blocks; "fên" paper.

<u>Index</u> ‐ a table of contents for 6 chüan.

<u>Bound in</u>　1 t'ao 4 ts's.

<u>Remarks</u> ‐ this item is complete but with a number of repaired
　　　　worm-holes.

Accession No. 895   Index No. - 067-zlg(zb)

Title   " Wên miao t'ung k'ao "
                      文   廟   通   考

Classification - B-117 傳記-總錄

Subject - a collection of biographical notes of Confucius, his
          disciples, and all the noted scholars through the various
          dynasties whose tablets have been set up by Imperial order
          in the Confucian temple for sacrifice.

References - 012-zafk 5/2.

Author - (撰) Niu Shu-mei 牛 樹 梅.

Edition - reprinted by the "Ch'ing-chiang-shu-yüan" 清 江 書 院 ;
          (preface) dated T'ung-Chih 11/1872.   Blocks; "fên" paper.

Index - a list of names in 6 chüan.

Bound in 1 t'ao 2 ts's.

Remarks - the item is complete and without defects.

Accession No. 896   Index No. - 030-bz

Title   " <u>Ku yen</u> "
                          古   言

Classification - C-308 雜家-雜文
Subject - (Gest No. 2819) "an individual literary miscellany."

References - 012-zafk 12/17   031-bgdf 125/1   Gest No. 2819.

Author - by <u>Chēng Hsiao</u> 鄭曉. 1479 - 1566

Edition - a Ming edition; (preface) dated Chia-Ching "i-ch'ou"
    44/1565.   Blocks; "mien" paper.

Index - none; 2 chüan 上 下 .

Bound in 1 t'ao 4 ts's; doubly interleaved.

Remarks - a very good edition; the item is complete but with a
    few repaired defects.

Accession No. 897   Index No. - 149-ofzc

Title   " **Tu shu jih chi** "
                        讀 書 日 記

Classification - C-13 儒家

Subject - (Toronto No. 189) "a collection of short essays of a
    philosophical nature."

References - 031-bgdf 98/6   Toronto No. 189.

Author - (撰) **Liu Yüan-lu** 劉 源 淥.

Edition - privately published; (preface) dated Yung-Chêng "kuei-ch'ou"
    11/1733.   Blocks; "fên" paper.

Index - a table of contents for 6 chüan; "pu pien" 2 chüan.

Bound in 1 t'ao 4 ts'ê.

Remarks - a duplicate of Toronto No. 189.   The item is complete.

Accession No.   898   Index No. - 076-heah   037-ahhg

Title   " Ch'in-ting T'ien-lu-lin-lang shu mu "
           欽 定 天 禄 琳 琅 書 目

Classification - B-342 目錄 - 經籍
Subject - the Imperial catalogue of the Sung, Yüan and Ming works
     stored in the T'ien-lu-lin-lang palace during the time of
     Emperor Ch'ien-Lung.

References - 160-1j 163-ggcz 6/6 031-bgld 8/19 012-zafk 9/15
     031-bgdf 85/16 Gest No. 674 Toronto Nos. 581 and 731.

Author - compiled on Imperial order by Yü Min-chung 于敏中
     and others.

Edition - the "Wang-shih" 王 氏 of Ch'ang-sha; dated Kuang-Hsü
     "chia-shên" 10/1884.   Blocks; "fên" paper.

Index - none; 10 chüan; 後 編 20 chüan.

Bound in 1 t'ao 10 ts'ê.

Remarks - a good modern edition; the item is complete.

Accession No. 899   Index No. - 055-azbl   007-zzzb

Title   " Nien-i-shih t'an tz'ŭ chu "
二十一史 彈 詞 註
" Ẽrh-shih-i shih t'an tz'ŭ chũ "
二 十 一 史 彈 詞 註

Classification - D-38 別集 - 詩

Subject - (Gest No. 2962) "a very brief synopsis of Chinese
history in verse; the period covered being from the
earliest times down to the close of the Yüan Dynasty."
This item includes the Ming Dynasty.

References - 012-zafk 16/22   Gest No. 2962   Toronto No. 862.

Author - (編著) Yang Shên 楊 慎 ; (增定) Chang San-i 張三異

Edition - the "Shu-yü-t'ang" 樹玉堂 ; (postscriptum) dated
Yung-Chêng 5/1727.   Blocks; bamboo paper.

Index - none; 10 chüan; 明 紀 彈 詞 2 chüan.

Bound in 1 t'ao 8 ts'ê; singly interleaved.

Remarks - the item is without important defects.

The University of Toronto Chinese Library

Accession No. 900   Index No. - 061-hedz

Title   " <u>Hsi-pao hsien-shêng ch'ih tu</u> "
              惜 抱 先 生 尺 牘

Classification - D-43 別集-文
Subject - an individual collection of personal letters.

References - 012-zafk 17/41.

Author - (撰) <u>Yao Nai</u> 姚 鼐 .

Edition - the "<u>Hai-yüan-ko</u>" 海 源 閣 ; dated Hsien-Fêng 5/1855.
    Blocks; "fên" paper.

Index - none; in 8 chüan.

Bound in 1 t'ao 2 ts'ê.

Remarks - the item is in perfect condition. The work referred to
    in the above catalogue is a more voluminous one; and the present
    item is a part of it, though a complete separate work.

Accession No. 901-a   Index No. - 072-edak

Title   " Ch'un-ch'iu chêng chuan "
               春　秋　正　傳

Classification - A-101 春秋

Subject - a commentary on the "Spring and Autumn Annals"; and
   containing disquisitive notes upon the comments by other
   famous commentators on the same work.

References - 163-ggcz 2/13   031-bgld 3/13   012-zafk 2/23
   031-bgdf 28/24.

Author - (撰) Chan Jo-shui 湛 若 水 .

Edition - the "Tzŭ-chêng-t'ang" 資 政 堂 ; dated T'ung-Chih
   "ping-yin" 5/1866.   Blocks; "fên" paper.

Index - none; in 37 chüan.

Bound in 2 t'ao 10 ts'ê (5-5).

Remarks - this item is complete and in very good condition.
   In the catalogue of books of the former owner, this work
   together with (b) and (c) are listed under a collective
   title,- 湛 文 簡 公 遺 書 三 種 . However, owing to
   the correctness of this title, the 3 works are catalogued
   separately.

The University of Toronto Chinese Library

Accession No. 901-b   Index No. - 128-gmfd   075-fdg

Title   " Shêng hsüeh ko wu t'ung "

聖 學 格 物 通

Classification - C-13 儒家

Subject - (Wylie) "-----, is a work after the model of the Ta hĕŏ
yen é,-----.   This is divided into six sections, under the
heads: Sincerity of Intention, Singleness of Aim, Personal
Cultivation, Family Adjustment, State Government, and
Pacification of the Empire.   The several points are   (#)

References - Wylie's Notes page 87   163-ggcz 7/6   031-bgld 9/20
037-ahhg 9/11   012-zafk 10/6   031-bgdf 93/22   Gest No. 2712
Toronto No. 621.

Author - (撰) Chan Jo-shui 湛 若 水 .

Edition - uniform with (a).

Index - a general table of contents for 100 chüan.

Bound in 4 t'ao 20 ts'ê (5 each).

Remarks - as under (a).

(#) elaborately illustrated by examples from history, with a
discussion of each paragraph by the author."

Accession No. 901-c   Index No. - 085-ized   099-zed

Title   " Chan Kan-ch'üan hsien-shêng wên chi "
　　　　湛 甘 泉 先 生 文 集
　　　　　" Kan-ch'üan chi "
　　　　　甘 泉 集

Classification - D-43 別集-文

Subject - a miscellaneous individual collection of prose compositions.

References - 012-zafk 16/22   031-bgld 176/18   Gest No. 1525.

Author - Chan Jo-shui 湛 若 水 .

Edition - uniform with (a).

Index - a table of contents for 32 chüan.

Bound in 2 t'ao 10 ts's (5-5).

Remarks - as under (a).

Accession No. 902   Index No. - 040-izzf

Title   " Han-shan-tzǔ shih chi "
              寒 山 子 詩 集

Classification - D-38 別集 - 詩

Subject - an individual literary collection,- poetry.

References - 163-ggcz 12/3   031-bgld 15/7   167-mhfm 19/10
            106-gdkn 68/1   012-zafk 15/4   031-bgdf 149/2.

Author - by the Buddhist priest Han-shan 寒 山 .

Edition - a Ming edition; (preface) dated Wan-Li "chi-mao" 7/1579.
         Blocks; "mien" paper.

Index - none; 1 chüan.

Bound in 1 t'ao 2 ts'ê; doubly interleaved.

Remarks - this is a very fine edition; and the item is complete
         and almost as new.

Accession No. 903   Index No. - 076-hebb   030-bbpe

Title   " Ch'in-ting ku chin ch'u êrh chin chien "
         欽 定 古 今 儲 貳 金 鑑

Classification - B-367 史評

Subject - (Gest No. 1319) "discusses the selection and appointment
    of the Imperial Heir Apparent, with special reference to
    historical examples."

References - 031-bgld 8/32   012-zafk 9/29   031-bgdf 88/27
    Gest No. 1319   Toronto No. 284.

Author - officially compiled.

Edition - a manuscript written on "fên" paper; dated Ch'ien-Lung
    51/1786.

Index - a table of contents for 6 chüan, arranged chronologically.

Bound in 1 t'ao 3 ts'ê; doubly interleaved.

Remarks - a fairly good edition; the item is complete and without
    defects.

431

DY

Accession No. 904   Index No. - 131-kzd   096-zkzz

Title   " Lin-ch'uan chi "
                        臨 川 集

                   " Wang Lin-ch'uan wên chi "
                     王   臨   川   文   集

Classification - D-33 別集-詩文
Subject - an individual collection of prose and poetry.

References - 160-lj 163-ggcz 13/5 031-bgld 15/41 030-iaff 27/13
        037-ahhg 10/22 106-gdkn 76/10 167-mhfm 20/18 012-zafk 15/15
        (#)
Author - (撰) Wang An-shih 王 安 石 .

Edition - the "Hsiao-fei-shan-kuan" 小 怌 山 館 ; dated Kuang-Hsü
     "kuei-wei" 9/1883.   Blocks; "fên" paper.

Index - a detailed table of contents (in 2 sections) for 100 chüan.

Bound in 2 t'ao 16 ts's (8 each).

Remarks - a good modern edition; the item is new.

    (#) 031-bgdf 153/42   Toronto No. 570 and 578.

The University of Toronto Chinese Library

—◆—◆—

Accession No. 905   Index No. - 085-hzkl   077-nbk

Title   " Ching t'u ch'uan têng kuei yüan ching "
             淨 土 傳 燈 歸 元 鏡
             " Kuei yüan ching "
             歸 元 鏡

Classification - C-513 釋家

Subject - (Gest No. 2880) "a Buddhist work; exhorting reformation,
     and return to and practice of the true and pure doctrine and
     teachings."

References - 012-zafk 14/27   Gest No. 2880.

Author - (撰) the priest Chih-ta 智達 ; (閱錄) Tê-jih 德 日 .

Edition - the "Lung-wang-miao" 龍 王 廟 ; (colophon) dated
     Ch'ien-Lung "chia-ch'ên" 49/1784.   Blocks; bamboo paper.

Index - a list of 42 items in 2 chüan 上 下 .

Bound in 1 t'ao 2 ts'ê.

Remarks - a good edition; the item is complete and without defects.

433

Accession No. 906   Index No. - 039-cbcz

Title   " Ts'un ku yo yen "
存 古 約 言

Classification - C-13 儒家

Subject - a work on ethics, with explanations.

References - 012-zafk 10/7   031-bgdf 96/38.

Author - (著) Lü Wei-ch'i 呂 維 祺 ; (訂) Fêng Ts'ung-wu
馮 從 吾.

Edition - a Ming edition; (preface) dated Ch'ung-Chêng "hsin-wei"
4/1631.   Blocks; bamboo paper.

Index - a list of the main section headings for 6 chüan.

Bound in 1 t'ao 2 ts's; doubly interleaved.

Remarks - the item is complete but with numerous repaired defects
on the page-edges.

The University of Toronto Chinese Library

Accession No. 907   Index No. – 120-gfcz

Title   " Ching shu tzŭ yin pien yao "
               經 書 字 音 辨 要

Classification – A-161 小學一字書

Subject – a vocabulary of the "Four Books" and the "Five Classics";
   with the characters arranged in the order as they appear in
   the respective works but with all duplicates omitted.

References – 012-zafk 3/25.

Author – (編 輯) Yang Ming-yang 楊 名 颺 ; (重 刻) Ch'ung Lun
   崇 倫 .

Edition – the "Ling-tê-t'ang" 令 德 堂 ; dated Tao-Kuang "ting-wei"
   27/1847.   Blocks; "fên" paper.

Index – none; in 9 chüan.

Bound in 1 t'ao 2 ts'ê.

Remarks – this is a useful reference work; and the item is complete
   and in good condition.

Accession No. 908   Index No. - 167-zzd

Title   " Chin shih so "

金 石 索

Classification - B-347 目録 - 金石

Subject - (Gest No. 1867) "this work illustrates and describes
   antiquities (metal, stone, clay etc.); for the most part
   from modern Shantung; but some Japanese mirrors and foreign
   tokens (religious) are also included. It stresses more
   especially the inscriptions on the various items   (#)

References - 160-1j 012-zafk 9/25 Gest Nos. 972 and 1867.

Author - (輯) Fêng Yün-p'êng 馮 雲 鵬 and Fêng Yün-yüan
   馮 雲 鵷 .

Edition - the "Shuang-t'ung-shu-wu" 雙 桐 書 屋; (postscriptum)
   dated Tao-Kuang 15/1835.   Blocks; "fên" paper.

Index - a general table of contents of 12 chüan,- 6 "chin" and
   6 "shih".

Bound in 2 t'ao 12 ts's (6-6).

Remarks - this is a very useful work; and the item is in good
   condition and appears to be complete (pages not numbered).

   (#) illustrated and described."

436

The University of Toronto Chinese Library

Accession No. 909-a   **Index No.** - 118-hz

Title   " <u>Kuan-tzŭ</u> "
                          管 子

Classification - C-43 法家

Subject - (Gest No. 3614) "a treatise on political philosophy,
    legislation, and related subjects."

References - Wylie's Notes page 92   160-1j   163-ggcz 7/9
    031-bgld 10/1   037-ahhg (hsü) 16/3   167-mhfm 14/1   (#)

Author - attributed to <u>Kuan Chung</u> 管 仲 , also known as <u>Kuan I-wu</u>
    管 夷 吾 , but doubtful. See 160-1j Giles B. D. 1006.
    (註) <u>Fang Hsüan-ling</u> 房 玄 齡 .

Edition - a Ming edition; undated.   Blocks; "mien" paper.

Index - a general table of contents for 86 sections in 24 chüan.

Bound in 2 t'ao 12 ts'ê (6-6).

Remarks - this is a very good edition; and the item is complete
    and without defects with the exception of a few repaired
    page-edges and some stains. The ninth ts'ê containing
    chüan 17-18-19 is a hand-written replacement.

(#)   030-iaff 16/1   106-gdkn 42/10   012-zafk 10/17
031-bgdf 101/1   Gest Nos. 325, 1659 and 3614
Toronto Nos. 469, 470 and 492.

Accession No. 909-b   Index No. - 178-hzz   178-hz

Title   " <u>Han Fei-tzŭ</u> "
                              韓 非 子
                              " <u>Han-tzŭ</u> "
                              韓 子

Classification - C-43 法家

Subject - (Gest No. 1559) "a collection of 55 miscellaneous essays
    on a variety of subjects, very few of which can properly be
    considered as pertaining to law or legislation, and some are
    closely related to Taoism and allied matters."

References - Wylie's Notes page 92 160-1j 163-ggcz 7/10 031-bgld
    10/2 030-iaff 16/2 106-gdkn 42/12 167-mhfm 14/9 012-zafk 10/17
    (#)

Author - <u>Han Fei</u> 韓 非 .

Edition - uniform with (a).

Index - a table of contents for 20 chüan.

Bound in 1 t'ao 8 ts'ê.

Remarks - a very good edition; the item is complete but with some
    stains, the more serious ones being at the end of the work.

    (#) 031-bgdf 101/7 Gest Nos. 1559 and 2384 Toronto No. 488.

The University of Toronto Chinese Library

Accession No. 910   Index No. - 031-dmch

Title   " K'un hsüeh chi wên "
                因 學 紀 聞

Classification - C-308 雜家 -雜文

Subject - a collection of critical discussions and observations
   on all the four classes of Chinese literature.

References - Wylie's Notes page 162   160-1j   163-ggcz 10/4
   031-bgld 13/11   030-iaff 18/30   037-ahhg 6/13-14   (#)

Author - by Wang Ying-lin 王 應 麟 .

Edition - the "Ma's Ts'ung-shu-lou" 馬 氏 叢 書 樓 ; dated
   Ch'ien-Lung "mou-wu" 3/1738.   Blocks; bamboo paper.

Index - a table of contents for 20 chüan.

Bound in 1 t'ao 6 ts'ê.

Remarks - this item is complete and without defects; a very good
   edition.

   (#)   106-gdkn 56/24   167-mhfm 16/14   012-zafk 12/20
      031-bgdf 118/43   Gest No. 452.

440

Accession No. 911   Index No. - 024-gchd   159-hdh

Title   " Nan-ts'un Cho kêng lu "
                南 村 輟 耕 録

Classification - C-368 小説家

Subject - a collection of essays and narrative notes, containing
    information regarding the overthrow of the Mongols (Yüan
    Dynasty); and other subjects of that period,- literature,
    poetry, painting, etc.

References - Wylie's Notes page 199   160-1j   163-ggcz 11/5
    031-bgld 14/32   030-iaff 21/15   106-gdkn 64/6   (#)

Author - by T'ao Tsung-i 陶 宗 儀 .

Edition - that of "T'ao-shih" 陶 氏 , based upon the Yüan edition;
    dated "kuei-hai" 1923.   Blocks; "fên" paper.

Index - a detailed table of contents for 30 chüan.

Bound in 1 t'ao 10 ts's.

Remarks - this is a very fine modern edition; and the item is
    complete.   This work is printed in blue ink.

    (#) 167-mhfm 17/19   012-zafk 14/5   031-bgdf 141/44
        Gest Nos. 139 and 246.

Accession No. 912-a   Index No. - 042-zfzc   042-zgzc

Title   " Hsiao ch'uang tzŭ chi "
                     小 窗 (窗) 自 紀

Classification - C-368 小說家

Subject - a collection of miscellaneous notes and writings on a
     variety of subjects.

References - 012-zafk 14/16   031-bgdf 144/40   Gest No. 2529 (a).

Author - (著) Wu Ts'ung-hsien 吳 從 先 .

Edition - no particular notation; (preface) dated Wan-Li "chia-yin"
     42/1614.   Blocks; bamboo paper.

Index - a detailed table of contents for 4 chūan, arranged according
     to classes of writings.

Bound in 1 t'ao 4 ts's.

Remarks - this is a fair edition; and the item appears to be
     complete and without important defects.

Accession No. 912-b   Index No. - 042-zftc   042-zgtc

Title   " Hsiao ch'uang yen chi "
                          小 窗 (窗) 豔 紀

Classification - C-368 小説家

Subject - a collection of miscellaneous prose and poetic writings.

References - 012-zafk 14/16   031-bgdf 144/40   Gest No. 2529 (b)
     Toronto No. 828.

Author - (批選) Wu Ts'ung-hsien 吳 從 先 .

Edition - uniform with (a).

Index - a detailed table of contents arranged according to classes
     of writings; not divided into chüan.

Bound in 1 t'ao 8 ts'ê.

Remarks - as under (a).

Accession No. 912-c   Index No. - 042-zfhc   042-zghc

Title   " Hsiao ch'uang ch'ing chi "

小 窓 (牕) 清 紀

Classification - C-368 小說家

Subject - a collection of miscellaneous notes and writings on a
variety of subjects.

References - 012-zafk 14/16   031-bgdf 144/40   Gest No. 2529 (c).

Author - (評輯) Wu Ts'ung-hsien 吳 從 先.

Edition - uniform with (a).

Index - none; not divided into chüan.

Bound in 1 t'ao 4 ts'ê.

Remarks - as under (a).

Accession No. 912-d   Index No. - 042-zfec   042-zgec

Title   " Hsiao ch'uang pieh chi "

小 窗 （ 宵 ） 別 紀

Classification - C-368 小說家.

Subject - a collection of miscellaneous notes and writings on a
variety of subjects.

References - 012-zafk 14/16   031-bgdf 144/40   Gest No. 2529 (d).

Author - (評選) Wu Ts'ung-hsien 吳 從 先 .

Edition - uniform with (a).

Index - a detailed table of contents for 4 chüan.

Bound in 1 t'ao 4 ts'ê.

Remarks - as under (a).

Accession No. 913   Index No. - 085-hdkb   085-jdkb

Title   " Han-fên-lou ku chin wên ch'ao "
            涵 (酒) 芬 樓 古 今 文 鈔

Classification - D-73 總集 - 文

Subject - a general collection of prose compositions of authors
    from ancient times down to and including the Ch'ing Dynasty.

References - none.

Author - (纂録) Wu Tsêng-ch'i 吳曾 祺 .

Edition - the "Shang-wu-yin-shu-kuan" 商務印書館 or The
    Commercial Press; dated Hsüan-T'ung 2/1910.   Type; "fên"
    paper.

Index - a list of the 13 main "classifications"; separate tables
    of contents at the beginning of each of 100 chüan.

Bound in 10 t'ao 100 ts'ê (10 each).

Remarks - the item is complete and in good condition.

Accession No. 914   Index No. - 163-gzlf

Title   " Ho shih i shu "
               郝 氏 遺 書

TS

Classification - C-308 雜家-雜文
Subject - an individual collection of works on miscellaneous
    subjects.

References - 029-pffz 331   Gest No. 3047.

Author - by Ho I-hsing 郝 懿 行.

Edition - an official publication; dated Kuang-Hsü 5 to 10/1879
    to /1884.   Blocks; "mao-pien" paper.

Index - a list of the 30 works.

Bound in 10 t'ao 84 ts's.

Remarks - an ordinary edition; the item is complete and without
    defects except a few worm-holes.

dup

Accession No. 915   Index No. - 060-hlbz   030-bzhn

Title   " <u>Yü-hsüan Ku wên yüan chien</u> "
御 選 古 文 淵 鑒

Classification - D-73 總集一文

Subject - a general collection of prose compositions by famous
scholars, officials etc., beginning from the time of the
<u>Tso-chuan</u>, down to the end of the <u>Sung Dynasty</u>; with
commentaries.

References - Wylie's Notes page 241 160-1j 163-ggcz 16/9 031-bgld
19/31 012-zafk 19/14 031-bgdf 190/1 Gest No. 170 Toronto No.
712.

Author - compiled on Imperial order by <u>Hsü Ch'ien-hsüeh</u> 徐 乾 學
and others.

Edition - the "<u>Chê-chiang-shu-chü</u>" 浙 江 書 局 ; dated T'ung-Chih
"kuei-yu" 12/1873.   Blocks; "mao-pien" paper.

Index - separate lists of contents for each of 64 chüan.

Bound in 4 t'ao 32 ts'ê (8 each).

Remarks - an ordinary edition; the item is complete and has no
defects.

448

Accession No. 916   Index No. - 085-jicp

Title   " P'ang-hsi-chai ts'ung shu "
             滂 喜 齋 叢 書

Classification - C-338 雜家-叢書
Subject - a collection of reprints of 54 works on various subjects.

References - 058-jffz 7/36   012-zafk 13/18   Toronto No. 511.

Author - (編) P'an Tsu-yin 潘 祖 蔭 .

Edition - the "P'an's Pa-hsi-chai" 潘氏 八 喜 齋 ; blocks cut at
     different times between T'ung-Chih and Kuang-Hsü; "fën" paper.

Index - a list of the 54 works.

Bound in 6 t'ao 48 ts'ê (8 each).

Remarks - this is a good edition; and the item is complete and
     without any defects.   The general table of contents is
     hand-written.

Accession No. 917   Index No. - 077-deih

Title   " Wu-ying-tien chü chên pan ts'ung shu "
        武 英 殿 聚 珍 版 叢 書

Classification - C-338 雜家 - 叢書

Subject - a collection of 54 reprints of works from all classes of
    Chinese literature.   (see "Remakrs")

References - Wylie's Notes page 255   160-1j   031-bgld 13/33
    058-jffz 5/8   Gest Nos. 566, 892 and 1666.

Author - compiled by an Imperial commission headed by Chi Yün 紀 昀 .

Edition - evidently the "Chiang-hsi-shu-chü" 江 西 書 局 ; date (?).
    Blocks; "fên" paper.   (see "Remarks")

Index - none.   (see "Remarks").

Bound in 10 t'ao 111 ts's (12-12-10-10-12-11-12-12-10-10).

Remarks - this is a reprint of a portion of the original collection
    of 138 works. This item is incomplete and it contains 48 works.
    The first 5 works and 1 in the middle are missing. Therefore all
    information as to the edition, the index and the date of publication
    is unavailable. The work 敬 齋 古 今 黈 in 2 ts's is from a
    different edition.

The University of Toronto Chinese Library

Accession No. 918   Index No. - 085-khpf

Title   " Han Wei ts'ung shu "
                    漢 魏 叢 書

Classification - C-338 雜家-叢書

Subject - a collection of 38 miscellaneous reprints by authors of
the Han 漢 Wei 魏 and the Liu-ch'ao 六朝 periods.

References - Wylie's Notes page 257 160-1j 031-bgld 13/31 012-zafk
13/12 029-pffz page 471 058-jffz 3/25 Gest Nos. 13 and 1662.

Author - (校刊) Ch'êng Jung 程榮 .

Edition - a Ming edition; (preface) dated Wan-Li "jên-ch'ên" 20/1592.
Blocks; bamboo paper.

Index - a list of the 38 works.

Bound in 6 t'ao 50 ts'ê (8-8-9-8-8-9).

Remarks - a good edition; the item is complete and in generally good
condition. There are a few defective pages and the last page of
the work 大戴禮記 is torn and partly missing. The work 商子
is from a different edition. Page 1 of the preface is missing.
A portion of the paper has been backed with old book-leaves; and
it was not done very skilfully.

451

Accession No.   919   Index No. - 005-jeaf

Title   " Ch'ien k'un chêng ch'i chi hsüan ch'ao "
           乾 坤 正 氣 集 選 鈔

Classification - D-73 總集-文

Subject - a collection of prose writings of noted scholars from
     ancient times down to the Ming Dynasty; being an abridgement
     of the original work entitled "Ch'ien k'un chêng ch'i chi".

References - none.

Author - selected by Wu Huan-ts'ai 吳 煥 采.

Edition - the "Ku-lien-hua-ch'ih" 古 蓮 花 池 ; dated Kuang-Hsü
     13/1887.   Blocks; "fên" paper.

Index - a list of the 97 works in 97 chüan.

Bound in 4 t'ao 32 ts'ê (8 each).

Remarks - a clear-cut edition; the item is complete.

Accession No.   920   Index No. - 046-hzfd

Title   " Ch'ung-wên shu chü hui k'o shu "
             崇 文 書 局 彙 刻 書

Classification - C-338 雜家-叢書
Subject - a collection of 33 miscellaneous reprints.

References - 058-jffz 7/34.

Author - the "Ch'ung-wên shu chü 崇 文 書 局 .

Edition - that of the author; dated Kuang-Hsü 3/1877.   Blocks;
    "fên" paper.

Index - none.

Bound in 8 t'ao 80 ts'ê (10-11-10-10-8-12-10-9).

Remarks - the item is complete and in good condition.

2
646

Accession No. 921   Index No. - 072-gzfp

Title   " Ch'ên-fêng-ko ts'ung shu "
               晨 風 閣 叢 書

Classification - C-338 雜家-叢書

Subject - a collection of 22 reprints of works on a variety of
   subjects.

References - 029-pffz 366   Gest No. 1123   Toronto No. 646.

Author - compiled by Shên Tsung-chi 沈 宗 畸.

Edition - that of the author; dated Hsüan-T'ung 1/1909.   Blocks;
   "fên" paper.

Index - a list of the 22 works.

Bound in   2 t'ao 16 ts'ê (8-8).

Remarks - an exact duplicate of Toronto No. 646; and the item is
   new.

Accession No. 922   Index No. - 170-iddz

Title   " Yang-ming hsien-shêng chi yao san pien "
陽 明 先 生 集 要 三 編

Classification - D-33 別集 - 詩文

Subject - an individual collection of miscellaneous writings

classified under 3 main headings,- mental philosophy; official

records (memorials etc); prose and poetry; with marginal notes.

References - 012-zafk 16/21.

Author - (撰) Wang Shou-jên 王 守 仁 ; (評 輯) Shih Ssŭ-ming

施 四 明 .

Edition - the "Chi-mei-t'ang" 濟 美 堂 ; dated Ch'ien-Lung "ting-wei"

52/1787.   Blocks; bamboo paper.

Index - a general table of contents for (理 學 集) 4 chüan;

(經 濟 集) 7 chüan; (文 章 集) 4 chüan. a detailed

list at the beginning of each chüan.

Bound in 2 t'ao 12 ts'ê (6-6).

Remarks - the item is complete and in good condition.

Accession No. 923   Index No. - 189-zedd   060-hhjd

Title   " Kao Tsung Shun Huang-ti Yüan-ming-yüan t'u yung "
           高 宗 純 皇 帝 圓 明 園 圖 詠
           " Yü-chih Yüan-ming-yüan t'u yung "
           御 製 圓 明 園 圖 詠

Classification - D-38 別集 - 詩

Subject - (Toronto No. 776) "a collection of poems written by the
       Emperor Ch'ien-Lung in description and praise of the Yüan-
       ming-yüan,- the Old Summer Palace which was burned during
       the reign of Hsien-Fêng by the foreign allied forces; with
       illustrations and commentaries.".

References - 012-zafk 17/1   Toronto No. 776.

Author - (註) O Êrh-t'ai 鄂 爾 泰 and others.

Edition - a manuscript written on "t'ai-hsi-lien" paper; no date.

Index - separate lists of contents for each of 2 chüan 上 下 .

Bound in 1 t'ao 2 ts'ê.

Remarks - this is a very fine manuscript and the item is complete
       and in perfect condition.

Accession No. 924   Index No. - 170-hkzd

Title   " T'ao-lou wên ch'ao "
                陶 樓 文 鈔

Classification - D-43 別集一文
Subject - an individual literary collection,-prose.

References - none.

Author - by Huang P'êng-nien 黃彭年.

Edition - privately published; dated "kuei-hai" 1923.   Blocks;
    "fên" paper.

Index - a detailed table of contents for 14 chüan.

Bound in 1 t'ao 6 ts'ê.

Remarks - a very good edition, printed in red ink; and the item is
    new.

Accession No. 925-a   Index No. - 140-mzhd   067-zhmd

Title   " Hsieh Wên-ch'ing chi "
                     薛 文 清 集

           " Wên-ch'ing Hsieh hsien-shêng wên chi "
             文 清 薛 先 生 文 集

Classification - D-33 別集 - 詩文

Subject - an individual literary collection,- prose and poetry.

References - 163-ggoz 15/4   031-bgld 18/14   012-zafk 16/16

     031-bgdf 170/29   Gest Nos. 695 and 1652.

Author - Hsieh Hsüan 薛 瑄 ; (校正編輯   ) Chang Ting 張鼎 .
                            1392 - 1446

Edition - the "Hsieh family" edition; dated Yung-Chêng "chia-yin"

     12/1734.   Blocks; "fên" paper.

Index - a table of contents for 24 chüan, arranged according to

     classes of writings.

Bound in 12 ts'ê in 1 t'ao with (b).

Remarks - this is a fairly good edition; and the item is complete

     and without defects.

458

Accession No. 925-b   Index No. - 149-ofh   140-mzhb

Title   " Tu shu lu "
                         讀　書　録
            " Hsieh Wên-ch'ing kung Tu shu lu "
              薛　文　清　公　讀　書　録

Classification - C-13 儒家

Subject - a collection of miscellaneous notes and jottings of a
     philosophical nature.

References - 160-1j   163-ggcz 7/5   031-bgld 9/18   012-zafk 10/5
     031-bgdf 93/8   Gest Nos. 719 and 1653.

Author - Hsieh Hsüan 薛　瑄 .

Edition - uniform with (a); but dated Ch'ien-Lung 11/1746.

Index - none; 11 chüan; 續　録 12 chüan.

Bound in 8 ts'ê in 1 t'ao with (a).

Remarks - as under (a).

Accession No. 926   Index No. - 085-eggc

Title   " Ho-nan t'ung chih "
河 南 通 志

Classification - B-192 地理-省志
Subject - gazetteer of the province of Honan.

References - 163-ggcz 5/12   031-bgld 7/15   012-zafk 6/7
031-bgdf 68/59   Gest No. 823.

Author - compiled by an editorial commission headed by
T'ien Wên-ching 田 文 鏡 and Wang Shih-chün 王 士 俊.

Edition - no particular notation; dated Kuang-Hsü "jên-yin" 28/1902.
Blocks; foreign paper.

Index - a general table of contents for 80 chüan.

Bound in 6 t'ao 48 ts's (8 each).

Remarks - this is not a good edition; and the impression is blurred
in many places, but the item is complete.

Accession No. 927   Index No. - 120-oegg

Title   " Hsü Ho-nan t'ung chih "
                 續 河 南 通 志

Classification - B-192 地理-省志
Subject - a continuation and supplement to the "Ho-nan t'ung chih".

References - Gest No. 823.

Author - compiled by an editorial commission headed by A-ssŭ-ha
         阿 思 哈 .

Edition - no particular notation; dated Kuang-Hsü 28/1902.
         Blocks; foreign paper.

Index - a general table of contents for 80 chüan.

Bound in 2 t'ao 16 ts's (8 each).

Remarks - a very ordinary edition; and the impression is difficult
          to read in places.   The item has no other defects and is
          complete.

Accession No. 928   Index No. - 096-zzcb   096-zzcd

Title   " Wang Wên-ch'êng kung ch'üan shu "
             王   文   成   公   全   書
             " Wang Wên-ch'êng ch'üan shu "
             王   文   成   全   書

Classification - D-33 別集 - 詩文

Subject - an individual collection of prose and poetry.

References - 163-ggcz 15/7   031-bgld 18/23   012-zafk 16/20
        031-bgdf 171/33   Gest No. 405   Toronto Nos. 456 and 491.

Author - (撰) Wang Shou-jên 王 守 仁 .

Edition - no particular notation; dated "i-wei" 1895.   Blocks;
    "mao-pien" paper.

Index - a detailed table of contents for 38 chüan.

Bound in 2 t'ao 24 ts'ê (12-12).

Remarks - this item is complete and in good condition.

Accession No. 929   Index No. - 030-bmhz   030-cgfo

Title   " K'o-i-t'ang i pai nien ming chia chih i "

可 儀 堂 一 百 廿 名 家 制 藝

Classification - D-73 總集-文

Subject - a collection of critical compositions on the "Four Books"
by scholars of the period from the Sung Dynasty down to and
including the K'ang-Hsi period of the Ch'ing Dynasty.

References - none.

Author - (論次) Yü Ch'ang-ch'ēng 俞 長 城 .

Edition - the "K'o-i-t'ang"; apparently of the Kuang-Hsü period.
Blocks; "mao-pien" paper.

Index - a list of the authors arranged chronologically; separate
detailed lists for each author.

Bound in 6 t'ao 38 ts's (6-6-6-6-6-8).

Remarks - this item is apparently complete and in good condition.

The University of Toronto Chinese Library

Accession No. **930**   Index No. - **170-hddd   066-dddd**

Title   " Lu Fang-wung ch'üan chi "
            陸　放　翁　　全　　集

            " Fang-wung ch'üan chi "
            放　　翁　　全　　集

Classification - **D-33** 別集－詩文

Subject - an individual miscellaneous collection, mainly prose and
        poetry.

References - 029-pffz 355.

Author - (著) **Lu Yu** 陸游 .   1125 1210

Edition - the "**Chi-ku-ko**" 汲 古 閣 ; no date; but of the Ming
        period.   Blocks; bamboo paper.

Index - none for the collection.

Bound in 4 t'ao 44 ts's (11 each).

Remarks - the edition is a good one; and the item is complete but
        worm-eaten in many places.   The defects have been repaired
        as far as possible.   The last ts's contains four manuscript
        pages.

Accession No. 931　　　　　Index No. - 030-bggk

Title　　　　　　　" Shih　t'ung　hsiao　fan "
　　　　　　　　　　史　　通　　削　　繁

Classification - B-367 史評
Subject - an historical critique; being an abridgment of the
　　　"Shih-t'ung".

References - 012-zafk 9/27　Toronto No. 260.

Author - (撰) Chi Yün 紀 昀 .

Edition - no particular notation; (preface) dated Ch'ien-Lung
　　　"jên-ch'ên" 37/1772.　　Blocks; "fên" paper.

Index - none; 4 chüan.

Bound in 1 t'ao 4 ts'ê.

Remarks - this is a fairly good edition; and the item is complete
　　　and without defects.

465

Accession No. 932   Index No. - 106-ahkk

Title   " Po chiang t'u chuan "
                百   將   圖   傳

Classification - B-117 傳記 - 總錄

Subject - (Toronto No. 252) "a collection of short biographical
    notes, together with illustrations, of 100 generals noted
    for their distinguished deeds during the period dating
    from the Chou 周 to the Ming 明 dynasty."

References - Toronto No. 252.

Author - Ting Jih-ch'ang 丁 日 昌 .

Edition - no notation; (preface) dated T'ung-Chih 9/1870.
    Blocks; "fên" paper.

Index - 2 separate lists of names; in 2 chüan 上 下 .

Bound in 1 t'ao 4 ts'ê; doubly interleaved.

Remarks - a duplicate of Toronto No. 252.   The item is complete
    and in good condition.

Accession No.   933   Index No. - 053-1ahk   053-1chm

Title   " Kuang po chiang chuan "
               廣   百   將   傳
               " Kuang ming chiang p'u "
               廣   名   將   譜

Classification - B-117 傳記-總錄
Subject - a collection of biographical sketches of more than 100
          famous generals of the period from the Chou 周 down to and
          including the Ming 明 dynasty; with critical notes.

References - 029-pffz 325   Toronto No. 297.

Author - (註斷) Huang Tao-chou 黃 道 周 .

Edition - the "Ch'ung-shan-t'ang" 崇 善 堂 ; (preface) dated
          Ch'ung-Chêng "kuei-wei" 16/1643.   Blocks; bamboo paper.

Index - a list of names for 20 chüan, arranged chronologically.

Bound in 2 t'ao 12 ts's (6-6); singly interleaved.

Remarks - an ordinary edition; and the item is complete.

Accession No. 934   Index No. - 001-azzh

Title   " Ch'i shih êrh hou chien "
七　十　二　候　牋

Classification - C-223 藝術-書畫

Subject - a collection of sketches to illustrate the 72 five day
    periods of the year.

References - Toronto No. 65.

Author - Ch'ien Chi-shêng 錢吉生．

Edition - the "Wên-mei-chai" 文美齋 ; (preface) dated Kuang-Hsü
    "mou-hsü" 24/1898.   Blocks; "fên" paper.

Index - at the beginning of each month.

Bound in 1 t'ao 2 ts'ê; doubly interleaved.

Remarks - an ordinary edition; the item is without defects.

Accession No. 935   Index No. - 149-eepz   140-pzdb

Title   " P'ing chu Su Wên-chung kung shih chi "

評 註 蘇 文 忠 公 詩 集

Classification - D-38 別集 - 詩

Subject - an individual collection of poetry; with commentary.

References - 012-zafk 15/16.

Author - Su Shih 蘇 軾 ; (評點) Chi Yün 紀 昀.

Edition - the "Han-mo-yüan" 翰 墨 園 ; (preface) dated Tao-Kuang
14/1834.   Blocks; "mao-pien" paper.

Index - a detailed table of contents (in 2 sections) for 50 chüan.

Bound in 2 t'ao 12 ts'ê (6-6).

Remarks - this item is complete and without defects.

469

Accession No. 936   Index No. - 149-gzfc

Title   " Shuo wên chieh tzŭ chu "
                          說　文　解　字　注

Classification - A-161 小學 - 字書
Subject - a commentary on the "Shuo wên chieh tzŭ"; with supplements.

References - 012-zafk 3/23   Gest Nos. 54, 350 and 384.

Author - (注) Tuan Yü-ts'ai 段 玉 裁 .

Edition - the "Ch'ung-wên-shu-chü" 崇 文 書 局 ; dated T'ung-Chih
    12/1873.   Blocks; "fên" paper.

Index - a general table of contents for 32 chüan including the
    六 書 音 均 表 ; 汲 古 閣 説 文 訂 1 chüan.

Bound in 2 t'ao 19 ts'ê (9-10).

Remarks - this is a good edition; and the item is complete and in
    perfect condition.

Accession No. 937   Index No. - 072-dkgz   201-zdib   201-zkgd

Title   " Ming Chang-p'u Huang Chung-tuan kung ch'üan chi "
         明 漳 浦 黄 忠 端 公 全 集

         " Huang Chung-tuan kung chi "
         黄 忠 端 公 集
(#)

Classification - D-33 別集-詩文
Subject - an individual collection of prose and poetry.

References - 012-zafk 16/15   Toronto No. 473.

Author - (撰) Huang Tao-chou 黄道周 ; (重編) Ch'ên Shou-ch'i
       陳 壽 祺.   1585-1646

Edition - no notation; dated Tao-Kuang 5/1825.   Blocks; "mao-pien"
    paper.

Index - a detailed table of contents (in 2 sections) for 50 chüan.

Bound in 2 t'ao 24 ts's (12-12).

Remarks - this is a good edition; and the item is complete.

    (#)   " Huang Chang-p'u chi "
              黄 漳 浦 集

471

Accession No. 938   Index No. - 085-jm

Title   " Tien hsi "
                          滇 繫

Classification - B-192 地理-省志
Subject - a "gazetteer" for the province of Yünnan.

References - 031-bgld 7/16   012-zafk 7/6   031-bgdf 68/66

    Gest No. 1728.

Author - (纂輯) Shih Fan 師 範 .

Edition - the "Yünnan-t'ung-chih-chü" 雲 南 通 志 局 ; dated

    Kuang-Hsü "ting-hai" 13/1887.   Blocks; "mien" paper.

Index - a general table of contents for 40 ts'ê, with detailed

    tables at the beginning of each.

Bound in 4 t'ao 40 ts'ê (10 each).

Remarks - this is an ordinary edition; the item is complete and

    in good condition.

Accession No. 939   Index No. - 075-1jdz   075-1jdf

Title   " <u>Yang-yüan hsien-shêng ch'üan chi</u> "
     揚   園   先   生   全   集
     " <u>Yang-yüan ch'üan shu</u> "
     揚   園   全   書

<u>Classification</u> - C-338 雜家－叢書
<u>Subject</u> - an individual collection of miscellaneous writings.

<u>References</u> - 029-pffz 440   031-bgdf 134/23.

<u>Author</u> - (撰) <u>Chang Li-hsiang</u> 張 履 祥 .
         1611-1674

<u>Edition</u> - the "<u>Chiang-su-shu-chü</u>" 江 蘇 書 局 ; dated T'ung-Chih
   "hsin-wei" 10/1871.   Blocks; "mao-pien" paper.

<u>Index</u> - a general table of contents for 54 chüan.

<u>Bound in</u> 2 t'ao 16 ts'ê (8-8).

<u>Remarks</u> - the item is complete and in good condition.

Accession No. 940   Index No. - 167-mhfm   040-dzbz

Title   " T'ieh-ch'in-t'ung-chien lou Sung Chin Yüan pên shu ying "
        鐵 琴 銅 劍 樓 宋 金 元 本 書 影

Classification - B-342 目錄 - 經籍

Subject - (Gest No. 1340) "lithographic reproductions of specimen
    pages from Sung, Chin , and Yüan dynasty editions in the
    library of the Ch'ü (瞿) family."

References - Gest No. 1340.

Author - none.

Edition - the "Ch'ü-shih" 瞿 氏 ; (preface) dated "jên-hsü" 1922.
    Lithographed on "fên" paper.

Index - none; 識 語 4 chüan.

Bound in 1 t'ao 9 ts'ê.

Remarks - a useful work; the item is complete and has no defects.

Accession No. 941   Index No. - 030-ghfb 170-hfbd 124-jed

Title   " T'ang Lu Hsüan-kung Han yüan chi "
               唐　陸　宣　公　翰　苑　集
               " Lu Hsüan-kung chi "
               陸　宣　公　集

          (#)

Classification - D-43 別集一文

Subject - an individual collection of prose writings,- memorials,
          announcements etc.

References - 163-ggcz 12/7 031-bgld 15/15 030-1aff 24/23 037-ahhg
          (hsü) 18/9 167-mhfm 19/20 012-zafk 15/8 031-bgdf 150/7 Gest
          No. 209.

Author - (撰) Lu Chih 陸　贄 ; (重 訂) Nien Kêng-yao 年 羹 堯 .

Edition - the "Chi-hsüeh-chai" 積　雪　齋 ; possibly of the Yung-Chêng
          period.   Blocks; bamboo paper.

Index - a detailed table of contents for 22 chüan.

Bound in   1 t'ao 6 ts's.

Remarks - this is a very good edition; and the item is complete and
          without defects.

          (#)   " Han yüan chi "
                            翰　苑　集

Accession No. 942-a   Index No. - 085-1jzz

Title   " Ch'ien-yüan &rh-shih-ssŭ chung "
           滑 圜 二 十 四 種

Classification - C-368 小説家
Subject - (Gest No. 1647-a) "en individual miscellany on a variety
    of unrelated subjects."

References - Gest No. 1647-a.

Author - by Wei Yüan-k'uang 魏 元 曠．

Edition - the "Wan-tsai-Hsing-lu-hsien" 萬 載 辛 録 軒 ; no date,
    but a modern edition.   Blocks; "fên" paper.

Index - a list of the 24 items.

Bound in 2 t'ao 12 ts'ê; 2d t'ao with (b).

Remarks - the item is complete and without defects.

Accession No. 942-b   Index No. - 085-ljdd

Title   ·   " Ch'ien-yüan ch'üan chi "
            滑 圜 全 集

Classification - D-33 別集-詩文

Subject - an individual literary collection,- prose and poetry.

References - Gest No. 1647-b.

Author - by Wei Yüan-k'uang 魏 元 曠 ·

Edition - as under (a).

Index - a general table of contents; "shih-ch'ao" 1 chüan; "shih-chi"
    12 chüan; "tz'ü" 4 chüan; "wên-chi" 14 chüan.

Bound in 6 ts'ê in the 2d t'ao of (a).

Remarks - as under (a).

Accession No. 943   Index No. - 085-hceo

Title   " Huai-an fu chih "
               淮 安 府 志

Classification - B-194 地理 - 列志

Subject - a "gazetteer" of Huai-an fu in Kiangsu province during
   the period of Ch'ien-Lung.

References - 012-zafk 6/17.

Author - (慕修) Yeh Ch'ang-yang 葉 長 揚 and Ku Tung-kao
   顧 揀 高.

Edition - the "Kung-chü" 公 局 ; dated Hsien-Fêng "jên-tzǔ" 2/1852.
   Blocks; "mao-pien" paper.

Index - a table of contents for 32 chüan.

Bound in 2 t'ao 16 ts'ê (8-8).

Remarks - an ordinary edition; the item is complete and without
   defects.

The University of Toronto Chinese Library

Accession No. **944-a**   Index No. - 096-zhif

Title   " <u>Yü</u> <u>t'ai</u> <u>hsin</u> <u>yung</u> "
                玉　臺　新　詠

<u>Classification</u> - D-68 總集-詩

<u>Subject</u> - a selection of poems written by scholars of the period

    prior to the <u>Liang Dynasty</u>.

<u>References</u> - 160-1j   163-ggcz 16/1   031-bgld 19/3   030-1aff 38/4

    037-ahhg 3/36   167-mhfm 23/4   106-gdkn 12/4   012-zafk 19/1

    (#)

<u>Author</u> - (編定) <u>Hsü Ling</u> 徐　陵 ; (批閱) <u>Yüan Hung-tao</u>

    袁　宏　道 ; (叅訂) <u>Shên Fêng-ch'un</u> 沈　逢　春 ·

<u>Edition</u> - a Ming edition; (preface) dated T'ien-Ch'i "jên-hsü" 2/1622.

    Blocks; bamboo paper.

<u>Index</u> - separate lists of contents at the beginning of each of 10

    chüan.

<u>Bound in</u> 6 ts'ê in 1 t'ao with (b); doubly interleaved.

<u>Remarks</u> - a good edition; the item is complete and in practically

    perfect condition.

    (#)   031-bgdf 186/7   Gest # # 194 - 1364 - 1365.

Accession No. **944-b**   Index No. - **120-ozhi**

Title   " **Hsü Yü t'ai hsin yung** "
　　　　　　　續　玉　臺　新　詠

Classification - **D-68** 總集 - 詩

Subject - **a supplement to (a).**

References - **012-zafk 19/14.**

Author - (續選) **Chêng Hsüan-fu** 鄭 玄 撫 ; (批閱) **Yüan Hung-tao**
　　　　袁 宏 道 ; (叅訂) **Shên Fêng-ch'un** 沈 達 春 .

Edition - **uniform with (a).**

Index - **separate lists for each of 4 chüan.**

Bound in **2 ts's in 1 t'ao with (a); doubly interleaved.**

Remarks - **as under (a).**

Accession No. 945   Index No. - 055-azbl   007-zzzb

Title   " Nien-i shih t'an tz'ŭ chu "
              廿 一 史 彈 詞 註

              " Erh-shih-i shih t'an tz'ŭ chu "
              二 十 一 史 彈 詞 註

Classification - D-38 列集-詩

Subject - (Gest No. 2962) "a very brief synopsis of Chinese history
    in verse; the period covered being from the earliest times down
    to the close of the Yüan Dynasty."   This item includes the
    Ming Dynasty.

References - 012-zafk 16/22   Gest No. 2962   Toronto No. 862 and 899.

Author - (編著) Yang Shên 楊 慎 ; (增定) Chang San-i 張 三 異.

Edition - the "Shih-li-t'ang" 視 履 堂 ; (postscriptum) dated
    Ch'ien-Lung 51/1786.   Blocks; "fên" paper.

Index - none; 10 chüan; 明 紀 彈 詞 2 chüan.

Bound in 1 t'ao 8 ts'ê.

Remarks - this item is complete and in good condition.

Accession No. 946   Index No. - 030-bzrz

Title   " Ku wên kuan chih "
               古　文　觀　止

Classification - D-73 總集-文

Subject - a collection of selected prose writings of scholars of
    the period from the Chou 周 dynasty down to and including
    the Ming 明 dynasty; with explanatory notes.

References - none.

Author - (鑒定) Wu Liu-ts'un 吳 留 村 .

Edition - the "Li-kuang-ming-chuang" 李 光 明 莊 ; no date, but a
    modern edition.   Blocks; "mao-pien" paper.

Index - a list of contents for 12 chüan.

Bound in 1 t'ao 6 ts's.

Remarks - an ordinary modern edition; the item is complete.

Accession No. 947   Index No. - 212-fikb

Title   " Kung Tuan-i kung tsou su "
龔 端 毅 公 奏 疏

Classification - B-72 詔令奏議-奏議
Subject - a collection of memorials.

References - 012-zafk 4/31.

Author - (著) Kung Ting-tzŭ 龔 鼎 孳 .

Edition - a reprint by the "T'ing-i-shu-wu" 聽彝書屋 ; dated
Kuang-Hsü "kuei-wei" 9/1883.   Blocks; "fên" paper.

Index - none; 8 chüan 附 錄 1 chüan; 沛 川 政 譜 2 chüan 上 下 .

Bound in 1 t'ao 5 ts'ê .

Remarks - a clear modern edition; the item is without defects.

dup

Accession No.   **948**   Index No. – **030-bfj**

Title   " <u>Ku shih yüan</u> "
                古　詩　源

Classification – D-68 總集-詩

Subject – (Toronto No. 779) " a collection of selected poems and
     songs of the period from ancient times down to the end of
     the <u>Liu-ch'ao</u>,– the six dynasties; with annotations."

References – Toronto No. 779.

Author – (選) <u>Shên Tê-ch'ien</u> 沈　德　潛．

Edition – reprinted by the "<u>Ssŭ-hsien-shu-chü</u>" 思　賢　書　局 ;
     dated Kuang-Hsü 17/1891.   Blocks; "fên" paper.

Index – none; in 14 chüan.

Bound in 1 t'ao 4 ts'ê.

Remarks – an ordinary modern edition; the item is new.

484

Accession No. 949   Index No. - 123-ggoe

Title   " Ch'un ching tzŭ ku "
                          羣 經 字 詁

Classification - A-137羣經總義

Subject - detailed explanations taken from various standard works
    on all the characters in 12 principal classical works; characters
    having appeared in the "Four-Books" being excepted.

References - 012-zafk 3/5.

Author - (撰) Tuan Ê-t'ing 段 諤 廷 .

Edition - that of "Yang-shih" 揚 氏 ; dated Tao-Kuang "chi-yu"
    29/1849.   Blocks; "mao-pien" paper.

Index - a list of the characters in 72 chüan.

Bound in   2 t'ao 13 ts'ê (6-7).

Remarks - an important reference work; the item is complete and
    in good condition with the exception of some worm-holes and
    a few defective pages.   The edition is an ordinary one.

Accession No. 950   Index No. - 070-zzlm   032-lm

Title   " Fang-shih mo p'u "
                 方 氏 墨 譜

Classification - C-260 譜録 - 器物

Subject - (Wylie) "----- is an extensive collection of engravings
    of cakes of ink,-----"

References - Wylie's Notes page 146   012-zafk 12/3   031-bgdf 116/14
    Gest No. 651.

Author - Fang Yü-lu 方 于 魯 .

Edition - a Ming edition; (preface) dated Wan-Li "ping-shên" 24/1596.
    Blocks; "mien" paper.

Index - separate lists of contents at the beginning of each of 6
    chüan.

Bound in 1 t'ao 8 ts'ê; doubly interleaved.

Remarks - this is a very fine edition; and the item is complete
    and without defects.

Accession No. 951   Index No. - 074-gjdz   074-gjd

Title   " Wang-hsi hsien-shêng ch'üan chi "
望 溪 先 生 全 集
" Wang-hsi chi "
望 溪 集

Classification - D-33 別集 - 詩文

Subject - an individual collection of prose and poetry; mainly the former.

References - 163-ggcz 15/18   012-zafk 17/19   031-bgdf 173/48
Toronto Nos. 55 and 701.

Author - Fang Pao 方苞 ; (重編) Tai Chün-hêng 戴 鈞 衡 .

Edition - no particular notation; (preface) dated Hsien-Fêng 1/1851.
Blocks; "mao-pien" paper.

Index - a table of contents for 18 chüan; 集 外 文 10 chüan;
集 外 文 補 遺 2 chüan; 年 譜 2 chüan.

Bound in 2 t'ao 14 ts'ê (8-6).

Remarks - an ordinary edition; complete and in good condition.

487

Accession No.   952   Index No. - 007-zgdf

Title   " Êrh   Ch'êng   ch'üan   shu "
                    二   程   全   書

Classification - C-338 雜家 - 叢書

Subject - a collection of 7 works of the 2 noted philosophers of
the Sung Dynasty,- Ch'êng Hao 程顥 and Ch'êng I 程頤.

References - 029-pffz page 3   058-jffz 9/1   012-zafk 13/11
Gest No. 853.

Author - (著) Ch'êng Hao 程顥 and Ch'êng I 程頤.

Edition - the "Liang-ch'êng-ku-li-ying-t'ang" 兩程故里影堂   ;
(preface) dated T'ung-Chih "hsin-wei" 10/1871.   Blocks;
"mien" paper.

Index - a list of the 7 works.

Bound in 2 t'ao 20 ts'ê (13-7).

Remarks - the edition is quite an ordinary one; but the item is
complete and has no defects.

Accession No.   953   Index No. - 011-blao

Title   " **Nei chien ch'ih tu** "
                          內   簡   尺   牘

Classification - D-43 列集 -文

Subject - **an individual collection of letters; with explanatory**
    notes.

References - 163-ggcz 13/11   012-zafk 15/21   031-bgdf 157/16
    Toronto No. 409.

Author - (撰) **Sun Ti** 孫 覿 ; (編 注) **Li Tsu-yao** 李 祖 堯 .

Edition - no notation; (preface) dated Ch'ien-Lung 12/1747.
    Blocks; bamboo paper.

Index - **a detailed table of contents for 10 chüan.**

Bound in **1 t'ao 8 ts'ê; doubly interleaved.**

Remarks - **this is a very good edition; and the item is complete.**

? dupl

Accession No. 954   Index No. - 060-1h1d

Title   " Fu-an i chi "
                       復 庵 遺 集

Classification - D-33 列集-詩文
Subject - an individual literary collection,- prose and poetry.

References - Toronto No. 213.

Author - Hsü Chüeh 許 珏 .

Edition - no notation; (preface) dated "jên-hsü" 1922.   Type;
    "mao-pien" paper.

Index - a general table of contents for 24 chüan.

Bound in 1 t'ao 8 ts'ê.

Remarks - the item is new.

Accession No. 955   Index No. - 072-dc

Title   " Ming   chi "
                       明   紀

Classification - B-22 編年

Subject - annals of the Ming Dynasty, beginning from the year

    A. D. 1351 (Yüan Dynasty) and going down to the end of

    that dynasty; including a record of the struggles of the

    three Ming princes against the Manchus.

References - 012-zafk 4/11   Gest No. 85.

Author - (纂) Ch'ên Hao 陳鶴 .

Edition - no particular notation; (preface) dated T'ung-Chih

    10/1871.   Blocks; "fên" paper.

Index - a table of contents for 60 chüan, arranged chronologically.

Bound in 2 t'ao 20 ts'ê (10-10).

Remarks - this item is complete and in good condition.

Accession No. 956   Index No. - 120-ckzd   104-ng

Title   " Chi Yin-t'ien hsien-shêng ch'ih shuo "
             紀 蔭 田 先 生 癡 説

Classification - C-308 雜家-雜文

Subject - (Gest No. 2853) "an individual collection of essays
    of a philosophical character; mainly based upon the personal
    life experiences of the author."

References - Gest No. 2853.

Author - (著) Chi Yin-t'ien 紀 蔭 田 .

Edition - the "Huai-ch'ing-t'ang" 懷 清 堂 ; dated Tao-Kuang
    "hsin-ssŭ" 1/1821.   Blocks; "mao-pien" paper.

Index - none; 8 chüan.

Bound in 1 t'ao 4 ts'ê; singly interleaved.

Remarks - a good edition; the item is complete and without defects.

Accession No. 957   Index No. - 031-bzbl

Title   " Ssŭ yen shih chêng "
                         四   言   史   徵

Classification - B-367 史評

Subject - a history of China written in verse, covering a period
    from ancient times down to the fall of the Ming Dynasty; with
    detailed explanatory notes.

References - 031-bgdf 90/27.

Author - (編 輯) Ko Chên 葛 震 ; (註 釋) Ts'ao Ch'üan 曹 荃 .

Edition - the "Chih-yüan" 芷 園 ; (preface) dated K'ang-Hsi
    "jêng-ch'ên" 39/1700.   Blocks; bamboo paper.

Index - a list of the successive reigns in 12 chüan.

Bound in 1 t'ao 12 ts'ê.

Remarks - this is a very good edition; and the item is complete
    and without defects except a few repaired worm-holes.

The University of Toronto Chinese Library

Accession No. 958-a   Index No. - 039-zfz(fg)

Title   " <u>Tzŭ p'in chin han</u> "
                  子 品 金 函

Classification - C-308 雜家-雜文

Subject - selections from the writings of some 50 authors, mostly
   philosophers; with marginal notes and commentaries.

References - none.

Author - (選) <u>Ch'ên Jên-hsi</u> 陳 仁 錫 .

Edition - a Ming edition; no date.   Blocks; bamboo paper.

Index - a table of contents in 4 chüan.

Bound in 4 ts'ê in 1 t'ao with (b) and (c).

Remarks - a fairly good edition; the item is apparently complete
   and without important defects.

494

Accession No. 958-b   Index No. - 067-zfd(fg)

Title   " Wên p'in fei han "
              文　品　帬　函

Classification - D-73 總集-文

Subject - selections from the prose writings of noted ancient
        scholars and officials; with commentary and marginal notes.

References - none.

Author - (選) Ch'ên Jên-hsi 陳 仁 錫.

Edition - uniform with (a).

Index - a table of contents for 3 chüan.

Bound in 3 ts's in 1 t'ao with (a) and (c).

Remarks - as under (a).

The University of Toronto Chinese Library

Accession No. 958-c   Index No. - 030-bfz(fg)

Title   " <u>Shih   p'in   ch'ih   han</u> "
               史   品   赤   函

Classification - D-73 總集-文

Subject - a collection of selected passages taken from standard
   historical works covering the period from the remotest times
   down to the end of the <u>Han Dynasty</u>; with a leading section
   on the writings of the various emperors of the same period.

References - none.

Author - (選) <u>Ch'ên Jên-hsi</u> 陳 仁 錫.

Edition - uniform with (a).

Index - a detailed table of contents for 4 chüan.

Bound in 4 ts's in 1 t'ao with (a) and (b).

Remarks - as under (a).

496

Accession No. 958-d   Index No. - 154-hff(fg)

Title   " Fu p'in hsi han "
                 賦 品 鳥 函

Classification - D-68 總集-詩

Subject - a collection of "fu" style compositions of noted
    ancient scholars.

References - none.

Author - (選) Ch'ên Jên-hsi 陳 仁 錫.

Edition - uniform with (a).

Index - a list of subject headings in 2 chüan.

Bound in 2 ts'ê in 1 t'ao with (e); (f); (g) and (h).

Remarks - as under (a).

Accession No. 958-e   Index No. - 149-ff1(fg)

Title   " Shih p'in hui han "
詩 品 會 函

Classification - D-68 總集 - 詩

Subject - a general collection of poetic writings of ancient
authors.

References - none.

Author - (選) Ch'ên Jên-hsi 陳 仁 錫.

Edition - uniform with (a).

Index - a detailed table of contents for 4 chüan.

Bound in 2 ts'ê in 1 t'ao with (d);(f); (g) and (h).

Remarks - as under (a).

Accession No. 958-f   Index No. - 073-ffc(fg)

Title   " Shu p'in t'ung han "
               書 品 同 函

Classification - D-73 總集-文

Subject - a collection of selected letters of noted scholars,
    arranged under 9 classifications.

References - none.

Author - (選) Ch'ên Jên-hsi 陳 仁 錫.

Edition - uniform with (a).

Index - a detailed table of contents for 2 chüan 上 下 .

Bound in 2 ts'ê in 1 t'ao with (d); (e); (g) and (h).

Remarks - as under (a).

Accession No. 958-g   Index No. - 030-hfb(fg)

Title   " Ch'i p'in yu han "
                    啟 品 有 函

Classification - D-73 總集-文

Subject - a collection of letters (congratulations, appreciations,
         requests, etc) of noted scholars.

References - none.

Author - (選) Ch'ên Jên-hsi 陳 仁 錫.

Edition - uniform with (a).

Index - a detailed table of contents for 2 chüan 上 下.

Bound in 2 ts'ê in 1 t'ao with (d); (e); (f) and (h).

Remarks - as under (a).

500

Accession No.   958-h   Index No. - 162-hfm(fg)

Title   " <u>I</u> <u>p'in</u> <u>i</u> <u>han</u> "
                           逸   品   譯   函

Classification - D-73 總集-文
Subject - a collection of miscellaneous prose writings of ancient
    authors.

References - none.

Author - (選) <u>Ch'ên Jên-hsi</u> 陳 仁 錫.

Edition - uniform with (a).

Index - a table of contents for 2 chüan.

Bound in 1 ts'ê in 1 t'ao with (d); (e); (f) and (g).

Remarks - as under (a).

Accession No. 959   Index No. - 140-pkhi

Title   " Su-lien yin mou wên chêng hui pien "

蘇 聯 陰 謀 文 證 彙 編

Classification - B-77 詔令奏議 - 公文

Subject - a collection of documents, statements and other materials
proved to be the evidences of a Soviet plot against the Chinese
Government, seized during a careful search of the Russian
Embassy and its adjoining premises at Peking by the metropolitan
Police Station on order of Marshal Chang Tso-lin in the year (#)

References - none.

Author - compiled and translated by a commission headed by
Chang Kuo-ch'ên 張 國 忱 .

Edition - published by the Metropolitan Police Headquarters, Peking;
(preface) dated Min-Kuo 17/1928.   Type; foreign paper.

Index - a list of the photographs; a detailed table of contents
under 11 classifications, (and supplements).

Bound in 2 t'ao 11 ts's (6-5).

Remarks - the item is without defects.

(#)   1927; together with English translation.

Accession No. 960   Index No. - 007-bild

Title   " Wu chung i kuei "
                         五 種 遺 規

Classification - C-328 雜家-雜纂
Subject - a collection of 5 works containing extracts from various
    standard works of a hortatory and ethical character.

References - 029-pffz 127.

Author - (編輯) Ch'ên Hung-mou 陳 宏 謀．

Edition - the "Chin-ling-shu-chü" 金 陵 書 局 ; dated T'ung-chih
    "mou-ch'ên" 7/1868.   Blocks; "mao-pien" paper.

Index - none; but the 5 works are given in the 2d preface.

Bound in 2 t'ao 10 ts'ê (5-5).

Remarks - this item is complete and in good condition.

Accession No.   961   Index No. - 007-b11d

Title   " Wu chung i kuei "
                          五　種　遺　規

Classification - C-328 雜家-雜纂
Subject - a collection of 5 works containing extracts from various
    standard works of a hortatory and ethical character.

References - 029-pffz 127   Toronto No. 960.

Author - (編輯) Ch'ên Hung-mou 陳宏謀.

Edition - the "Chin-ling-shu-chü" 金陵書局 ; dated T'ung-Chih
    "mou-ch'ên" 7/1868.   Blocks; "mao-pien" paper.

Index - none; but the 5 works are given in the 2d preface.

Bound in   2 t'ao 10 ts'ê (5-5).

Remarks - an exact duplicate of Toronto No. 960.

504

Accession No. 962   Index No. - 072-dehb

Title   " <u>Ming</u> <u>chi</u> <u>pai</u> <u>shih</u> <u>hui</u> <u>pien</u> "

明 季 稗 史 彙 編

Classification - B-52 雜史

Subject - (Gest No. 1482) "a collection of miscellaneous narratives
relating to the close of the <u>Ming Dynasty</u>, and mainly to the
period subsequent to the capture of Peking by the Manchus during
which period the last survivors of the Ming imperial line
attempted to restore the fallen dynasty to power."

References - Wylie's Notes page 33   029-pffz 268   Gest No. 1482.

Author - various.

Edition - the "<u>Liu-yün-chü-shih</u>" 留 雲 居 士 ; no date.   Blocks;
"mao-pien" paper.

Index - a list of the 16 works on the back of the title-page.

Bound in 2 t'ao 16 ts's (8-8).

Remarks - a good edition; and the item is complete but with a good
many defects on the page-edges and corners owing to the fragility
of the paper.

Accession No. 963   Index No. - 072-dnmf

Title   " Ming ju hsüeh an "
                           明　儒　學　案

Classification - B-117 傳記-總錄
Subject - a collection of biographies of scholars of the
Ming Dynasty.

References - 160-lj   163-ggcz 5/5   031-bgld 6/17   012-zafk 5/15
     031-bgdf 58/20   Gest No. 416.

Author - (著) Huang Tsung-hsi 黃 宗 義 .

Edition - the "Kuo-hsüeh-yen-chiu-hui" 國 學 研 究 會 ; dated
     Min-Kuo 1/1912.   Blocks; "mao-pien" paper.

Index - a list of names for 62 chüan.

Bound in 2 t'ao 32 ts'6 (16-16).

Remarks - the item is complete and without defects.

Accession No. 964   Index No. - 073-fdhf

Title   " Shu lin ch'ing hua "
                書 林 清 話

Classification - C-308 雜家-雜文

Subject - a comprehensive treatise and miscellaneous expositions
    on the printing of books and cutting of blocks during the
    recent dynasties in China.

References - Gest No. 432.

Author - (述) Yeh Tê-hui 葉 德 輝 .

Edition - the "Kuan-ku-t'ang" 觀 古 堂 ; dated "kêng-shên" 1920.
    Blocks; "fên" paper.

Index - a detailed table of contents for 10 chüan.

Bound in 1 t'ao 5 ts'ê.

Remarks - an important and useful reference work; and the item
    is new.

Accession No. 965   Index No. - 106-zdd   106-zdzd

Title   " Po-sha chi "
                              白 沙 集
                    " Po-sha-tzŭ ch'üan chi "
                      白 沙 子 全 集

Classification - D-33 別集－詩文
Subject - an individual literary collection,- prose and poetry.

References - 163-ggcz 15/5   031-bgld 18/15   030-iaff 36/11
      012-zafk 16/16   031-bgdf 170/36   Gest Nos. 700 and 1236.

Author - (撰) Ch'ên Hsien-chang 陳 獻 章 ． 1428 1500

Edition - the "Pi-yü-lou" 碧 玉 樓 ; dated Ch'ien-Lung "hsin-ch'ou"
      36/1771.   Blocks; "fên" paper.

Index - a detailed table of contents for 卷首 and 10 chüan;
      古 詩 教 解 2 chüan; 附 錄 1 chüan.

Bound in 2 t'ao 12 ts'ê (6-6).

Remarks - this is a very good edition; and the item is complete
      and as if new.

Accession No. 966   Index No. - 061-1zhp

Title   " Ai-jih-ching-lu ts'ang shu chih "
    愛 日 精 廬 藏 書 志

Classification - B-342 目錄－經籍
Subject - a descriptive catalogue of a collection of Chinese works.

References - 163-ggcz 6/7   031-bgld 8/20   012-zafk 9/18
  Gest No. 1010.

Author - by Chang Chin-wu 張 金 吾.

Edition - the "Ling-fên-ko" 靈 芬 閣 ; dated Kuang-Hsü 13/1887.
  Movable type; "mao-pien" paper.

Index - a list of classification headings for 36 chüan; 續志
  4 chüan.

Bound in 1 t'ao 10 ts'è.

Remarks - a good edition; and the item is complete.

Accession No. 967   Index No. - 009-zkid

Title   " Jĕn ching yang ch'iu "
          入　鏡　陽　秋

Classification - B-117 傳記-總録

Subject - a collection of short notes of a biographical character,
    containing stories of distinguished men and women of all
    dynasties, their outstanding characteristics being principally
    loyalty, faithfulness, filial piety, etc; each story with a
    pictorial illustration and a criticism.

References - none.

Author - (編) the Wu-wu-chü-shih 無 無 居 士 , i.e. Wang T'ing-no
    汪 廷 訥 .

Edition - a Ming edition; the "Huan-ts'ui-t'ang" 環 翠 堂 ; (preface)
    dated Wan-Li "kĕng-tzŭ" 28/1600.   Blocks; bamboo paper.

Index - a general table of 22 classifications under 4 main headings;
    a detailed classified list of names; 22 chüan.

Bound in 4 t'ao 24 ts's (6 each).

Remarks - this is a very fine and rare edition; especially the
    illustrations which easily lead us to think that the work of
    cutting the blocks must have been an extremely elaborate one.
    The item is complete and in good condition with the exception
    of some worm-holes and stains mainly at the end of the work.

Accession No. 968   Index No. - 042-zmde

Title   " Hsiao hsüeh chi chu "
                  小　學　集　註

Classification - C-13 儒家

Subject - a commentary on the "Lesser Learning",- a hand-book for
   the instruction of youth.

References - Wylie's Notes page 84   160-1j   163-ggcz 7/4   031-bgld
   9/11 012-zafk 10/3   031-bgdf 92/25   Gest Nos. 1478 and 3616.

Author - (撰) Chu Hsi 朱 熹 ; (集註) Ch'en Hsüan 陳 選 .

Edition - reprinted by Chang Hsüan 張 煊 ; (colophon) dated
   Ch'ung-Chêng 10/1637.   Blocks; "mien" paper.

Index - none; 6 chüan.

Bound in 1 t'ao 6 ts's; doubly interleaved.

Remarks - a good edition; the item is complete and without defects.

Accession No. 969   Index No. - 163-1zmq

Title   " Chêng-shih ying ch'an wu tai chi "
          鄭 氏 應 讖 五 代 紀

Classification - C-368 小說家

Subject - a story relating to the activities of Chêng Ch'êng-kung
     鄭 成 功 , the leader of a group of pirates occupying
     Formosa, who, being somewhat related to the fallen Ming Dynasty,
     made severe trouble with the Manchus by his attacks against cities
     in Fukien, but was suppressed during the reign of K'ang-Hsi.

References - none.

Author - (輯定) Chiang Jih-shêng 江 日 昇 .

Edition - a manuscript written on "mao-pien" paper; (preface) dated
     Chia-Ch'ing "hsin-yu" 6/1801.

Index - a table of contents for 50 chüan in 100 "hui" 回 .

Bound in 1 t'ao 10 ts'ê.

Remarks - an ordinary manuscript; the item is complete but with
     many stains.

Accession No. 970   Index No. - 106-ddgp   072-dgp

Title   " Huang Ming ch'ên tsao "
             皇 明 宸 藻

Classification - D-73 總集一文

Subject - a collection of Imperial edicts and other compositions
    written by the emperors of the Ming Dynasty from Hung-Wu to
    Lung-Ch'ing.

References - 012-zafk 19/8.

Author - (編) Yang Shên 楊 慎．

Edition - a Ming edition, having the appearance of being a part
    of   some "Ts'ung-shu"; no date.   Blocks; bamboo paper.

Index - a table of contents; complete in 1 chüan.

Bound in 1 t'ao 2 ts'ê; doubly interleaved.

Remarks - a very good edition; and the item is without defects
    and complete.

Accession No. 971   Index No. - 113-1hcz

Title   " Fu-t'ang-ssŭ jên hsiao ts'ao "
               福 堂 寺 人 小 草

Classification - C-368 小説家

Subject - a collection of miscellaneous notes and records in the
    Imperial palaces about the close of the Ming Dynasty.

References - none.

Author - (恭 纂) Liu Jo-yü 劉 若 愚 .

Edition - a manuscript written on bamboo paper; (preface) dated
    Ch'ung-Chêng 3/1630.

Index - a table of contents together with the preface for 21
    sections.

Bound in 1 t'ao 2 ts'ê.

Remarks - a work of very little importance and the item seems
    never to have been published.   No defects are noted except
    a few stains.

Accession No. 972   Index No. - 184-fakf

Title   " Yang chêng t'u chieh "
               養   正   圖   解

Classification - C-368 小說家

Subject - (Gest No. 2669) "a collection of historical incidents
    relating to exemplary upright conduct."

References - 031-bgdf 未 5   Gest No. 2669.

Author - by Chiao Hung 焦竑 .

Edition - no particular notation; no date.   Blocks; "fên" paper.

Index - a detailed table of contents, complete in 1 chüan;
    2 supplements.

Bound in 1 t'ao 6 ts's; doubly interleaved.

Remarks - a very good edition; and the item is complete and as if
    new.

Accession No. 973   Index No. - 118-hz

Title   " Kuan-tzŭ "
                     管　子

Classification - C-43 法家

Subject - (Gest No. 3614) "a treatise on political philosophy,
    legislation, and related subjects."

References - Wylie's Notes page 92   160-1j   163-ggcz 7/9
    031-bgld 10/1   037-ahhg (hsü) 16/3   167-mhfm 14/1   (#)

Author - attributed to Kuan Chung 管 仲 , also known as Kuan I-wu
    管 夷 吾 , but doubtful. (註) Fang Hsüan-ling 房 玄 齡 .

Edition - the "Shih-li-chü" 士 禮 居 ; based upon the Sung edition;
    (preface) dated Chia-Ch'ing "ping-yin" 11/1806.   Blocks;
    "fên" paper.

Index - a general table of contents for 86 sections in 24 chüan.

Bound in 1 t'ao 6 ts'ê; singly interleaved.

Remarks - a very good edition; the item is complete and in perfect
    condition.

    (#) 030-iaff 16/1   106-gdkn 42/10   012-zafk 10/17
        031-bgdf 101/1   Gest Nos. 325, 1659 and 3614
        Toronto Nos. 469, 470 and 492.

Accession No. 974   Index No. - 162-lgd

Title   " Hsüan i lin "
                        選 義 林

Classification - B-117 傳記-總錄

Subject - a collection of notes of a biographical character,
    containing records of martyrs, meritorious officials, etc
    of the Ming Dynasty.

References - none.

Author - (著) Liu Tung-tzŭ 劉 慟 于.

Edition - the "Chieh-en" 潔 巷 ; (preface) dated K'ang-Hsi "i-ch'ou"
    24/1685.   Blocks; bamboo paper.

Index - a table of contents for 5 chüan; and supplements.

Bound in 1 t'ao 6 ts'è.

Remarks - this edition is not one of the best; and the impression
    is blurred in many places.

Accession No. 975   Index No. - 119-fgkj

Title   " Yüeh hai-kuan Ch'ien-Lung yüan-nien chih shih-nien
         Fu-tu-yüan chun pu chuan kuan an-chüan "

         粵海關乾隆元年至十年撫都院准部轉關案卷

Classification - B-77 詔令奏議 - 公文

Subject - a collection of archives relating to the Canton Customs
    Service during the period from the 1st to the 10th year of
    Ch'ien-Lung.

References - none.

Author - not stated.

Edition - a manuscript written on "fēn" paper; dated Ch'ien-Lung
    10/1745.

Index - none.

Bound in 1 t'ao 1 ts'ê.

Remarks - the item is stained at the beginning and end with the
    result that the last page has been ruined and almost wholly
    missing.

Accession No. 976   Index No. - 037-znmo

Title   " Ta Tai Li-chi "
     大 戴 禮 記

Classification - A-56 禮 - 禮記

Subject - (Wylie) "Ritual of the Senior Taė."

References - Wylie's Notes page 6   160-1j under 禮記 163-ggcz 2/8
     031-bgld 2/37   037-ahhg 7/7 (hsü) 2/23; 2/24   030-iaff 2/29
     (#)

Author - (撰) Tai Tẹ 戴 德 .

Edition - a Ming edition apparently; undated.   Blocks; bamboo
     paper.

Index - none; in 13 chüan.

Bound in   1 t'ao 4 ts'ẹ; doubly interleaved with margins.

Remarks - there is no apparent evidence that this item is a Yüan
     impression upon the basis of the Sung edition, as stated in
     the catalogue of books of the former owner.   However, this
     edition is a fairly good one; and the item is complete and in
     very good condition.

520

Accession No. 977   Index No. - 106-dhcz   106-dhim   030-czzz

Title   " Huang-ch'ao ming ch'ên yen hsing wai lu "
           皇　朝　名　臣　言　行　外　録

           " Huang-ch'ao tao hsüeh ming ch'ên yen hsing wai lu "
           皇　朝　道　學　名　臣　言　行　外　録

           (#)

Classification - B-117 傳記-總録

Subject - a collection of biographies of famous officials of the
         Sung Dynasty.

References - 160-1j   163-ggcz 5/4   031-bgld 6/12   037-ahhg 5/46;
            (hsü) 15/2; 15/3   030-1aff 9/19   012-zafk 5/11   (##)

Author - Li Yu-wu 李 幼 武.

Edition - an early Ming edition apparently; no date.   Blocks;
         bamboo paper.   (See Remarks)

Index - none (See Remarks).

Bound in 1 t'ao 4 ts'ê; doubly interleaved with margins.

Remarks - this item is a small part of the complete work known as
         the "Ming ch'ên yen hsing lu" which is in 5 "chi" 集 .   This
         work belongs to the last "chi"; and contains say 6 chüan out
         of 17,- chüan 8 to chüan 13 though a few pages from chüan 7 are
         mixed up with chüan 13.   There is no apparent evidence that
         (###)

521

(#)　　" **Ming ch'ên yen hsing lu wai chi** "
　　　名臣言行録外集

(##)　　031-bgdf 57/30　　Gest Nos. 112 and 2479.

(###)　**this work is a Sung edition as stated in the catalogue**
　　　　of the former owner; and our observations seem to
　　　　indicate it to be of the Yüan or early Ming period,
　　　　though the exact date is not ascertainable due to the
　　　　incompleteness of the text.　The total number of pages
　　　　is 107, including 2 blank ones supplying 2 missing pages.

Accession No. 978   Index No. - 042-zhcc

Title   " Hsiao t'ien chi nien fu k'ao "
小 腆 紀 年 坿 攷

Classification - B-52 雜史

Subject - an historical record of the struggles of the 3 last
survivors of the Ming Imperial line against the Ch'ing
Dynasty with a view to restoring the fallen dynasty to
power; including matters regarding Chêng Ch'êng-kung
鄭 成 功, who with Formosa as the base, made unsuccessful
(#)
References - 160-1j   012-zafk 4/27.

Author - (譔) Hsü Tzŭ 徐 鼒.

Edition - the "Fu-sang-shih-chieh" 扶桑 使 廨 ; dated Kuang-Hsü
"ping-hsü" 12/1886.   Type; "fên" paper.

Index - for 20 chüan, arranged chronologically.

Bound in 1 t'ao 12 ts'ê.

Remarks - this item is complete and in good condition.

(#)   efforts toward the same object.

Accession No. 979   Index No. - 085-khbh

Title   " Han Wei Liu-ch'ao chêng shih wên hsüan "
汉　魏　六　朝　正　史　文　選

Classification - D-73 總集－文

Subject - a collection of selected prose compositions taken from
the official dynastic histories of the Han, Wei and the
Six Dynasties.

References - none.

Author - (輯 評) Ku Tsai-kuan 顧 在 觀 and others.

Edition - a Ming edition; (preface) dated Ch'ung-Chêng 8/1635.
Blocks; bamboo paper.

Index - a general table of contents for 24 chüan, with separate
detailed lists for each.

Bound in 1 t'ao 8 ts'ê.

Remarks - a good edition and the item is complete and has no defects.

Accession No. 980   Index No. - 031-bfce

Title   " Ssŭ-shu tzŭ ku "
                  四 書 字 詁

Classification - A-131 四書

Subject - (Toronto No. 786) "a comprehensive collection of
    explanations, taken from various sources, on a selection
    of characters from the "Four Books".

References - 012-zafk 3/13   Gest No. 786.

Author - (撰) Tuan Ê-t'ing 段 諤 廷 .

Edition - that of "Yang-shih" 楊 氏 ; dated Tao-Kuang "chi-yu"
    29/1849.   Blocks; "mao-t'ai" paper.

Index - an index of the characters arranged according to the radicals;
    a detailed table of contents for 78 chūan.

Bound in 2 t'ao 15 ts's (7-8).

Remarks - this is a duplicate of Toronto No. 786; and the item is in
    good condition with the exception of a few worm-holes.   The last
    page of the work is missing.

Accession No. 981   Index No. - 073-f1

Title   " Shu ying "
                         書 影

Classification - C-308 雜家－雜文

Subject - a miscellany on a variety of unrelated subjects.

References - 160-1j   012-zafk 12/34.

Author - the "Li-hsia-lao-jên" 櫟 下 老 人 , i.e. Chou Liang-kung
     周 亮 工 .

Edition - the "Yin-shu-wu" 因 樹 屋 ; (preface) dated Yung-Chêng
    3/1725.   Blocks; bamboo paper.

Index - none; 10 chüan.

Bound in 1 t'ao 10 ts'ê; doubly interleaved.

Remarks - this is a good edition; and the item is complete. Pages
    44 to 54 in chüan one are handwritten.

526

Accession No. 982   Index No. - 050-fzgd

Title   " Ti wang ohing shih t'u p'u "
帝 王 經 世 圖 譜

Classification - C-348 類書

Subject - tables and sketches illustrating the particular points
of the classical works with the "Chou Ritual" as a main topic;
including explanations taken from important works of other
classes.

References - 163-ggcz 10/13   031-bgld 14/7   030-iaff 20/5
012-zafk 13/21   031-bgdf 135/30.

Author - (撰) T'ang Chung-yu 唐 仲 友 .

Edition - a modern edition; no special designation; undated.
Blocks; "mao-pien" paper.

Index - separate lists of items at the beginning of each of 16 chüan.

Bound in 1 t'ao 6 ts's .

Remarks - the item is complete and in perfect condition.

Accession No. 983   Index No. - 048-bhjn

Title   " Tso sui lei tsuan "

左 粹 類 纂

Classification - C-348 類書

Subject - (Gest No. 1519) "an exegesis of selected outstanding
features of the "Tso-chuan"; arranged under 15 classified
headings, and divided into sub-groups according to dynasties
and states."

References - 012-zafk 13/23   031-bgdf 137/35   Gest No. 1519.

Author - (編集) Shih jên 施 仁 ; (批點) Sun Ying-ao 孫應鰲 .

Edition - no particular notation; (preface) dated Wan-Li "kuei-wei"
11/1583.   Blocks; "mien" paper.

Index - a table of contents for 12 chüan.

Bound in 1 t'ao 8 ts'ê.

Remarks - this edition is a good one; and the item is complete and
in generally good condition, but slightly stained.

Accession No. 984   Index No. - 030-cicg   140-fz

Title   " Ho chu ming chia p'i tien Hsün-tzǔ ch'üan shu "
         合   諸   名   家   批   點   荀   子   全   書

              " Hsün-tzǔ "
                荀   子

Classification - C-13 儒家

Subject - a philosophical work based on the doctrine of "original sin";

    together with commentary.

References - Wylie's Notes page 82   160-1j   163-ggcz 7/1   031-bgld 9/1

    037-ahhg 2/32   6/1   9/1   167-mhfm 13/1   030-iaff 15/2   (#)

Author - of the original work - Hsün K'uang 荀 況 ; (註) Yang Liang

    楊   倞 .

Edition - a Ming edition; no date.   Blocks; bamboo paper.

Index - a general table of contents for 20 chüan.

Bound in 1 t'ao 6 ts'ê; doubly interleaved.

Remarks - this is a good edition; and the item is complete but with

    a few defects and some stains.

    (#)   106-gdkn 39/1   012-zafk 10/1   031-bgdf 91/5   Gest Nos.

    339(6), 1650 and 3575   Toronto No. 53.

Accession No. 985   Index No. - 140-1edd   123-gfii

Title   " Wan Chi-yeh hsien-shêng Ch'ün shu i pien "
           萬 季 野 先 生 羣 書 疑 辨

Classification - C-308 雜家-雜文

Subject - a collection of dissertations and disquisitions on
   miscellaneous points of the classical, historical and other
   works.

References - none.

Author - (纂) Wan Ssŭ-t'ung 萬 斯 同 .

Edition - the "Kung-shih-t'ing" 供 石 亭 ; dated Chia-Ch'ing
   "ping-tzŭ" 21/1816.   Blocks; "mao-pien" paper.

Index - separate tables of contents at the beginning of each of
   12 chüan.

Bound in 1 t'ao 4 ts's.

Remarks - the item is complete and in perfect condition.

The University of Toronto Chinese Library

Accession No. 986   Index No. - 187-hdon

Title   " P'ien ya hsün chuan "
                 駢　雅　訓　纂

Classification - A-156 小學 - 訓詁

Subject - an analogic dictionary of 2-character phrases and terms
    arranged under 13 classifications; with detailed explanations
    taken from various works.

References - 163-ggoz 3/10   031-bgld 4/18   012-zafk 3/18
    031-bgdf 40/19.

Author - of original - Chu Mou-han 朱 謀 㙔 ; of this item -
    Wei Mao-lin 魏 茂 林 ·

Edition - the "Hou-chih-pu-tsu-chai" 後 知 不 足 齋　 ; dated
    Kuang-Hsü 12/1886.   Blocks; "fên" paper.

Index - a general table of contents; a list of chapter headings
    for 16 sections in 7 chüan.

Bound in 1 t'ao 6 ts'ê.

Remarks - a modern edition; and the item is in perfect condition.

Accession No. 987-a   Index No. - 149-hgde   149-hg

Title   " Lun-yü chi chu "
                          論 語 集 註
                         " Lun-yü "
                          論 語

Classification - A-134 四書 - 論語

Subject - (Gest No. 1498-c) "a commentary on the discourses of
   Confucius with his followers and others."

References - Wylie's Notes page 7   160-1j   163-ggcz 3/4
   031-bgld 4/3   167-mhfm 6/5   030-iaff 4/15   012-zafk 3/7
   (#)

Author - Chu Hsi 朱 熹 .

Edition - the "Pao-shu-t'ang" 寶 恕 堂 ; no date.   Blocks;
   "hsüan" paper.

Index - none; 10 chüan.

Bound in 1 t'ao 4 ts'ê.

Remarks - this is a very good edition; and the item is without
   defects and complete.

   (#)   031-bgdf 35/21   Gest No. 1498   Toronto Nos. 602-c
   and 768-c.

Accession No. 987-b   Index No. - 039-ezde   039-ez

Title   " **Mĕng-tzŭ chi chu** "
                 孟　子　集　註
                 " **Mĕng-tzŭ** "
                 孟　子

Classification - A-135 四書 -孟子

Subject - (Gest No. 1498-d) "a commentary on the discourses of
    Mencius on political, social, and ethical subjects."

References - Wylie's Notes page 8 160-1j 163-ggoz 3/4 031-bgld 4/3
    167-mhfm 6/5 030-iaff 4/15 012-zafk 3/7 031-bgdf 35/21 (#)

Author - Chu Hsi 朱熹 .

Edition - uniform with (a).

Index - none; 7 chüan.

Bound in 1 t'ao 7 ts'ĕ.

Remarks - as under (a).

    (#) Gest No. 1498 Toronto Nos. 602-d and 768-d.

533

Accession No. 988   Index No. - 118-hzne

Title   " Kuan-tzǔ tsuan ku "
                              管　子　纂　詁

Classification - C-43 法家
Subject - a treatise on political philosophy, legislation, and
    related subjects; with annotations.

References - 012-zafk 10/17.

Author - (纂詁) Yasui Hakari 安 井 衡 .

Edition - the "Yedo-sho-rin" 江 戸 書 林 ; (title-page) dated
    Kei-ō 1/1865.   Blocks; Japanese paper.

Index - none; 24 chüan; 考 謙 1 chüan.

Bound in 1 t'ao 10 ts's.

Remarks - a very good Japanese edition; the item is complete and
    without defects.

Accession No. 989   Index No. - 072-dcdz   072-dcd

Title   " Ch'ang-li hsien-shêng chi "
                昌   黎   先   生   集
               " Ch'ang-li chi "
                昌   黎   集

Classification - D-33 別集-詩文

Subject - an individual comprehensive collection of prose and
         poetry.

References - 012-zafk 15/8   167-mhfm 19/23   106-gdkn 67/7

     Toronto No. 106.

Author - (撰) Han Yü 韓愈 ; (編) Li Han 李漢 .

Edition - a reprint by the "Chiang-su-shu-chü" 江蘇書局;
          dated T'ung-Chih "chi-ssü" 8/1869.   Blocks; "fên" paper.

Index - a detailed table of contents for 40 chüan; 外集 10 chüan;
        遺文 1 chüan; 集傳 1 chüan.

Bound in 2 t'ao 10 ts'ê (5-5).

Remarks - the item is complete and in perfect condition.

Accession No. 990   Index No. - 048-bzkb

Title   " Tso Wên-hsiang kung tsou su "
            左　文　襄　公　奏　疏

Classification - B-72 詔令奏議-奏議

Subject - a collection of memorials, from the 11th year of
         Hsien-Fêng to the 11th year of Kuang-Hsü.

References - none.

Author - by Tso Tsung-t'ang 左 宗 棠 .

Edition - the "T'u-shu-chi-ch'êng-chü" of Shanghai 上 海 圖 書 集 成 局;
          dated Kuang-Hsü "kêng-yin" 16/1890.   Type; "fên" paper.

Index - (初 編) a detailed table of contents for 38 chüan;
        (續 編) a detailed list for 76 chüan;(三 編) for 6 chüan.

Bound in 2 t'ao 20 ts's (10-10).

Remarks - an ordinary edition; complete and without defects.

536

—•—

Accession No. 991   Index No. - 007-zzaz

Title   " Êrh-shih-chiu tzŭ p'in hui shih p'ing "
二　十　九　子　品　彙　釋　評

Classification - C-328 雜家-雜纂

Subject - selections from the writings of 29 philosophers; with
marginal notes and commentaries.

References - 031-bgdf 132/8.

Author - (參閱) Wung Chêng-ch'un 翁　正　春 ; (校正)
Chiao Hung 焦　竑 .

Edition - a Ming edition; no date.   Blocks; bamboo paper.

Index - none; 20 chüan.

Bound in 1 t'ao 8 ts'ê.

Remarks - an ordinary edition; and the item is complete and with
no defects other than stains. In the first ts'ê, chüan 2 and 3
are bound in wrong sequence. Not rebound, as it will mar the
writing on the page-edges.   In 031-bgdf the reviewer is rather
disparaging in his remarks regarding this work.

Accession No. 992   Index No. - 115-jej

Title   " Ku i hui "
                          穀 詒 彙

Classification - C-328 雜家-雜纂

Subject - a collection of homiletical writings and extracts taken
    from various ethical and hortatory works.

References - none.

Author - various.

Edition - no particular notation; no date, but appears to be of the
    Ch'ien-Lung period.   Blocks; bamboo paper.

Index - none; in 14 chüan.

Bound in 1 t'ao 10 ts'ê; doubly interleaved.

Remarks - this work is probably a part of some "ts'ung-shu"; as
    there is no index, preface or other similar section which an
    individual work usually contains.   A very good edition; the
    item is without defects and appears to be complete.

The University of Toronto Chinese Library

Accession No. 993   Index No. - 149-ofjc

Title   " Tu shu tsa chih "

讀 書 雜 志

Classification - C-308 雜家 - 雜文

Subject - a collection of disquisitions and commentaries on ten
standard philosophical and historical works.

References - 012-zafk 12/23   Toronto No. 476.

Author - (撰) Wang Nien-sun 王 念 孫 .

Edition - the "Chin-ling-shu-chü" 金 陵 書 局 ; dated T'ung-Chih
"kêng-wu" 9/1870.   Blocks; "mao-pien" paper.

Index - a list of the ten works; 餘 編 2 chüan.

Bound in 4 t'ao 24 ts's (6 each).

Remarks - this item is complete and in very good condition.

Accession No. 994   Index No. - 048-b1

Title   " Tso hsiu "
                      左　繡

Classification - A-101 春秋

Subject - a symposium of commentaries on "The Annals" of Confucius.

References - 031-bgdf 31/31   Gest No. 2957.

Author - (同編) Fêng Li-hua 馮李驊 and Lu Hao 陸浩.

Edition - the "Jui-yün-lou" 瑞雲樓 ; (preface) dated K'ang-Hsi
    59/1720.   Blocks; "mao-pien" paper.

Index - a general table of contents for a 首 and 30 chüan.

Bound in 2 t'ao 14 ts'ê (7-7).

Remarks - a very good edition; the item is complete and in practically
    perfect condition.

Accession No. 995   Index No. - 085-1jbd

Title   " Ch'ien-yüan yu p'ông shu wên "

　　　　　　　　潛　園　友　朋　書　問

Classification - D-73 總集-文

Subject - reproduction of a collection of autograph letters written
to Lu Hsin-yüan 陸 心 源 by his friends.

References - none.

Author - various; no notation as to the compiler.

Edition - privately published; no date, but fairly recent.
Process (?); "fên" paper.

Index - none; 12 chüan.

Bound in 1 t'ao 2 ts'ê.

Remarks - this item is in good condition and apparently complete.

541

Accession No. 996   Index No. - 115-efaz

Title   " Pi shu nien-i chung "
               秘 書 廿 一 種

Classification - C-338 雜家-叢書
Subject - a collection of reprints on 21 miscellaneous works.

References - 029-pffz 331   Gest Nos. 2327 - 2329.

Author - (校) Wang Shih-han 汪 士 漢 .

Edition - no particular notation, other than 本 衙 藏 板；
      (preface) dated K'ang-Hsi "chi-yu" 8/1669.   Blocks; bamboo
      paper.

Index - a list of the 21 works on the title-page.

Bound in 2 t'ao 12 ts's (6-6).

Remarks - a fair edition; the item is complete and in generally
      good condition,- some stains and a few minor defects.

Accession No. 997   Index No. — 007-bd

Title   " Wu ya "
                           五 雅

Classification — A-156 小學 — 訓詁

Subject — a collection of 5 standard analogic dictionaries.

References — 029-pffz 127   058-jffz 1/63.

Author — (輯) Lang K'uei-chin 郎 奎 金.

Edition — a Ming edition; (preface) dated T'ien-Ch'i "ping-yin"
    6/1626.   Blocks; bamboo paper.

Index — none.

Bound in 2 t'ao 12 ts's; doubly interleaved.

Remarks — a very good edition; the item is complete and without
    important defects except some repaired worm-holes on the
    page-edges of the last 3 ts's.

Accession No. 998   Index No. - 040-gcmf

Title   " Jung-chai sui pi "
                  容　齋　隨　筆

Classification - C-308 雜家-雜文

Subject - (Wylie) "is an extensive selection of extracts from the
national literature, with criticisms, published in five parts."

References - Wylie's Notes page 160   160-1j   163-ggcz 10/3
031-bgld 13/8   037-ahhg 16/13   030-iaff 18/27-28   167-mhfm 16/13
(#)

Author - (撰) Hung Mai 洪 邁 .

Edition - a Ming edition; (preface) dated Ch'ung-Chêng 3/1630.
Blocks; "fên" paper.

Index - a detailed table of contents for 16 chüan; (續筆) same
for 16 chüan; (三筆) 16 chüan; (四筆) 16 chüan; (五筆)
10 chüan.

Bound in 1 t'ao 9 ts's.

Remarks - a good edition; and the item is complete.

(#)   106-gdkn 56/3-10   012-zafk 12/19   031-bgdf 118/23.

The University of Toronto Chinese Library

Accession No. 999   Index No. – 128-g1lc

Title   " Shêng yü kuang hsün su i "
聖 諭 廣 訓 疏 義

Classification – C-13 儒家

Subject – an explanation of the "Shêng yü kuang hsün",– (Gest No. 1479)
"an expansion of the so-called 'Sacred Edict', being a collection
of short explanatory homilies on the sixteen maxims contained
therein."

References – none to this edition. To the original work,– Wylie's
Notes page 87 031-bgld 9/21 012-zafk 10/8 031-bgdf 94/2 (#)

Author – of original – the Emperor K'ang-Hsi 康 熙 of the expansion –
the Emperor Yung-Chêng 雍 正 . of this item – not stated.

Edition – the "Kuang-jên-shan-t'ang" 廣 仁 善 堂; dated Kuang-Hsü
16/1890.   Blocks; "mao-pien" paper.

Index – none.

Bound in 2 t'ao 16 ts'ê.

Remarks – the item is without defects and complete.

(#) Gest No. 1479 Toronto No. 96.

The University of Toronto Chinese Library

Accession No. 1000   Index No. - 042-zfec   042-zgec

Title   " Hsiao ch'uang pieh chi "
               小 窓 (窗) 別 紀

Classification - C-368 小説家

Subject - a collection of miscellaneous notes and writings on a
    variety of subjects.

References - 012-zafk 14/16   031-bgdf 144/40   Gest No. 2529(d)
    Toronto No. 912-d.

Author - (評選) Wu Ts'ung-hsien 吳 從 先.

Edition - a Ming edition; (preface) dated Wan-Li "i-mao" 43/1615.
    Blocks; bamboo paper.

Index - a detailed table of contents for 4 chüan.

Bound in 1 t'ao 8 ts'ê; doubly interleaved.

Remarks - the item appears to be complete and is in generally good
    condition.

The University of Toronto Chinese Library
. . . .

Accession No. 1001   Index No. A-137 024/3bg.

Title   " Shih San Ching "
               十 三 經

Classification - A-137   "Chün ching tsung i"
                                        羣 經 總 義
Subject -   Shih San Ching or the Thirteen Classics, including the "Yih-
       ching,""Shu ching","Shih ching," "Chou-li", "I li", "Li chi,"
       "Ch'un ch'iu", "Tso Chuan," "Ch'un Ch'iu Kung-yang Chuan",
       "Ch'un Ch'iu Kuh-liang Chuan,", "Hsiao Ching," "Lun Yü," "Meng Tzu"
       and "Erh ya".

References

Author -   Not stated.

Edition - dated the fifth year of T'ung Chih (1866)
           published by "Ching-ling Press." Lien-shih paper.

Index - none.

Bound in - 13 t'ao, 54 ts'e

Remarks   a very fine edition, the item is complete and in perfect con-
          dition.

547

The University of Toronto Chinese Library

. . . .

Accession No. 1002   Index No. 075/bzdR

Title -   "Chu Tzu Chüan Chi"
           朱 子 全 集

Classification - C-13- Ju-Chia 儒家

Subject - A Classified collection of memorials, letters and miscellan-
           eous
                  eous writings of Chu Hsi.

References -

Author -   ~~compiled by unknown persons.~~ Chu Hsi 朱熹

Edition - dated Hsien Feng Keng-Sheng, 1860
           Blocks, "mien-lien" paper
           published from the Tze-hsia-chow ancestral hall.

Index -   Nunxx A table of contents for 104 chuan

Bound in - 4 t'ao, 104 chuan in 40 ts'e

Remarks. - The item is complete and in good condition. This edition
           must not be confused with either the "Yu-Tswan Chu Tzu
           Ch'uan Shu" (1713) or "Chu Tzu Yu lei" (1270)

548

The University of Toronto Chinese Library

. . . .

Accession No. - 1003 ½   Index No. 007/09Raf.

Title -   "Wu Ching San Ch'uan Tu Pen "
            五 經 三 傳 讀 本

Classification- A-137- "Ch'ün Ching Tsung-i"
            羣 經 總 義

Subject-   A collection of commentaries on the Classics :-
            "Yi-ching," "Shu-ching," "Shih -ching," "Li-chi,"
            "Ch'un-ch'iu," "San-chuan"

References.

Author-   (Wan Ch'ing-ch'uan) not given in Catalogue (see p. 10)

Edition-   (Hsien-Feng,) (2/1852) ,published from the collection of the
           Lotus Peak Book Chamber of Mr. Wan of Hsün@yang.

Index -   None.

Bound in - 4 t'ao, 40 ts'e, "mien lien" paper.

Remarks.-

The University of Toronto Chinese Library

....

Accession No.   1004   Index No. 128/dʒ ed.

Title-   " Min-shih-hang-k'uan-shu wu-shih tsung"
                                k'uai   chung
              閩 士 行 快 書 五 十 種

Classification-   C-338- "Ts'ung Shu"
                          叢 書

Subjects   A collection of Reprints of Personal prose, verse, Poem
             written on various occasions.

References-

Author   Min Chin-hsien of Lien-chiang city (Fukien)
             閩 景 賢   連 江

Edition-   T'ien ch'i, ping yen   3/1626
             published by K'o wei-jan of Hsi Hu,
             Bamboo paper, blocks,

Index -   with a general table of contents at the beginning of the first
             Chuan.

Bound in-   1 t'ao, 12 ts'e , 50 Chuan.

Remarks.

550

The University of Toronto Chinese Library

. . . .

Accession No. - 1005?   Index No. 037/8巡2c

Title-   "Ta Hsüeh-hsü-shu-yen -ching -i"
          大 學 贖 衍 精 義

Classification -   A -132- Ta Hsüeh
                            大 學

Subject -   Concerning the right rule of an emperor.

References -

Author -   Liu Hung-mo of Ming Dynasty. 劉 洪 謨

Edition. -   The 2nd year of Ming Ch'ung Cheng 1629, Blocks, Bamboo paper

Index -   Index in the 1st ts'e including a brief summary of each chuan

Bound in -   1 t'ao, 18 chuan, 14 ts'e.

Remarks.

. . . .

Accession No.   1006   Index No. 187/-6dea

Title -   " Po Lü Liu-liang Ssu Shu Chiang-i "
                駁呂留良四書講義

Classification - A-131- "Ssu Shu "
                四書

Subject -   A memorial presented to the throne criticing Lü Liu-liang's
                exposition of the Ssu Shu.

References -

Author -   Chu Hsi and others. (Editors)
                朱軾等

Edition -   An official edition, blocks,
                Mao-pien paper.

Index -   None.

Bound in - 1 t'ao, 8 ts'e.

Remarks.

Accession No.   1007 ?   Index No. 030/66

Title -   "Shih   Wai "
                史   外

Classification - B-42-   "Pieh Shih"
                            别 史

Subject-   A record on the Biographies of famous personnel.

References -

Author -   Edited by
             Wong Yu-tien   of Ch'ing Dynasty   汪有典

Edition -   Family library edition, "Kwang Hsü" year (Ting-niu) 1877
             Blocks, mien-lien paper.

Index -   Index on first ts'e

Bound in -   1 t'ao, 8 chuan, 8 ts'e.

Remarks

The University of Toronto Chinese Library

·················

Accession No.   1008 ?.   Index No. 007/63de

Title -   " Wu Tzu Ching Szu Lu Fa Ming."
            五 子 近 思 錄 發 明

Classification - A-137. "Chung Ching Tsung I "
                  羣   經   總   義

Subject -   Concerning the way of Heaven, the pursuit of knowledge, the

             cultivation of personality. Concerning Law and discipline ,

             social obligation, self introspection etc.

References -

Author -   Shih heng Huang of Ch'ing Dynasty. 施 璜

Edition -   Home library edition, dated the year of K'ang Hsi, mao pien paper
            Blocks,

Index -   An index containg the general heading of each chuan.

Bound in - 1 t'ao, 14 chuan, 14 ts'e.

Remarks.-

554

The University of Toronto Chinese Library

....

Accession No.   1009 ✓   Index No. 075/㢆gK𝑓 RK

Title -   " Ch'uan Heng I Shu "
           權 衡 一 書

Classification - C-13- Ju-chia
                        儒家

Subject-   Concerning righteousness, instrospection, loyalty and responsibi-
            lity, knowledge, purity, chastity, perseverence.

References -

Author -   Edited by
            Wang Chih of Ch'ing Dynasty . 王植

Edition -   Ch'ung-ya Hall edition, dated the first year of Ch'ing Ch'ien-
            Lung, 6/1736. Blocks, Bamboo paper.

Index -   Consisted of main headings,

Bound in - 4 t'ao, 24 ts'e.

Remarks-

The University of Toronto Chinese Library

. . . .

Accession No.   1010   Index No. 040/dedd

Title -   " Sung Yüeh Chung Wu Wang Ching T'o Ch'üan Pien "
            宋   岳   忠   武   王   金   陀   全   編

Classification - B - 42-   "Pieh Shih."
            別 史

Subject -   Thegeneology of Yueh Fei; The record of Yueh Fei's campaign

             against rebels; and the death of Yueh-fei.

References-

Author -   Compiled by Yüeh Shih-ching, 岳 士 景 of Ch'ing

Edition - dated Ch'ien Lung year, Home library edition, Blocks - mien-lien

           paper

Index -   Index for both Cheng-p'ien 20 chuan and Shu-p'ien, 8 chuan.

Bound in -   Cheng-p'ien 20 chuan; Shu p'ien, 8 chuan in 4 ts'e.

Remarks-

Accession No. 1011✓   Index No. 037/a-22.

Title -   " T'ien Jang Yi Wen "
           天 壤 遺 文

Classification -   D-73- "Wen" 文

Subject - Consists of prose by sages; prose by heroes; prose by hermits.

References -

Author - Selected and commented on by Hsü T'ien-ch'ih, Ming. 徐天池

Edition - Private family
           Home library edition , white paper, date unknown.

 Index - An introduction to each chuan is given.

Bound in - 1 t'ao, 7 chuan, 7 ts'e.

Remarks - The item is rather old.

The University of Toronto Chinese Library

....

Accession No.   1012 ✓   Index No. 075/93dl.

Title -   " Liang Shih Yin P'u Szu Chung "
          梁   氏   印 譜   四   種

Classification - C-233- " Chuan K'o"
                          篆   刻

Subject -   " seals and seal cuttings"

References -

Author - Liang Teng-yung. of Ch'ing Dynasty. 清. 梁登庸

Edition - Ch'ien Lung Jen wu 1762, mien lien paper, blocks.

Index-   None.

Bound in -   1 t'ao, 6 ts'e.

Remarks - in good condition, seals in red.

558

The University of Toronto Chinese Library

. . . .

Accession No. - 1013   Index No. 189/33ch

Title -   "Kao shih ~~Tseng~~ Chan Kuo Ts'e"
           高 氏 戰 國 策

Classification - B-52-"Tsa shih"
                 雜 史

Subject-   Story of the contending states.

References -

Author -   Kao ~~Yeu~~ Yu commentary by of the Han. 高 誘

Edition - dated Ch'ien Lung ping tzu ~~wu~~ 1786 - Blocks, mien-lien paper.

Index -   Index of different states.

Bound in-   1 t'ao, 33 chuan , 6 ts'e.
            Appendix - shan shu ta chuan 3 chuan.

Remarks -   This is the oldest ~~Tseng~~ Chan Kuo Ts'e, but a part of Kao ~~Yew's~~ Yu's
            comments are now lost, and the edition published with his name
            has the missing parts supplied by Yao Hung of the Sung.

The University of Toronto Chinese Library

. . . .

Accession No. 1014   Index No. 085/K↓33

Title -   "Yü Yang Shan Jen Ching Hwa Lu "
          漁 洋 山 人 精 華 錄

Classification - D-68- "Shih "
                      詩

Subject -   A collection of verses of different styles.

References -

Author -   Compiled by Lin chi# of Ch'ing Dynasty
                林 佶

Edition   dated K'ang Hsi year, Home library edition, blocks, Bamboo paper.

Index-   A table of titles given.

Bound in - 1 t'ao, 10 chuan, 4 ts'e.

Remarks - Pring is not evenly clear on account of the rough surface of the
           paper used.

The University of Toronto Chinese Library

. . . .

33

Accession No.   1015 ✓   Index No. 086/missg

                 Tun-huang
Title -   " T-iun Hwang   Hsien Chih "
           燉   煌   縣   誌

Classification -   B- 194- "Pieh chih"
                    別   誌

Subject - History, geography, adminstration etc of Tun Huang Hsien (city)

References -

Author - Edited by
          Su Li-chi of Ch'ing: 清．蘇履吉

Edition -   The 11th year of Tao Kwang, 1831 , District magistrate office
            edition. Blocks, lien shih paper.

Index -. A list of contents is attached on the corner of xxxx the cover
          of each ts'e.

Bound in - 1 t'ao, 7 Chuan, 4 ts'e.

Remarks

561

The University of Toronto Chinese Library

....

Accession No. 1016?   Index No. 061/bddf

Title 忠告全書 Chung Kao Chüan Shu

Classification   C 308 Miscellaneous writings, discussions
                                  & expositions.
Subject a collection of essays exhorting
on the duties of an official.

References

Author Chang Wen-Chung of Yüan & others

Edition Tao Kwang 庚戌年?
         Block-print

Index none

Bound in   1 tao 4 tsé

Remarks

562

The University of Toronto Chinese Library

. . . .

|||

Accession No.   1017 ✓   Index No. 040/dh88

Title -   " Sung Ch'en Lung - Ch'uan hsien - sheng wen chi."
           宋　陳　龍　川　先　生　文　集

Classification -   D-73- "Wen"

Subject -   Personal correspondence and biographies.
             A criticism of the writings of Ch'en Lung-chuan of The Sung.

References -

Author -   ~~Criticized~~ By Wang ^tso~~cho~~ of the Ming. 王佐

Edition -   dated Ming, Ch'ung Cheng. Bamboo paper. Blocks,

Index -   provided.

Bound in   - 2 chuan in first chi, and 1 chuan in the second chi. Total
             2 ts'e.

Remarks - printing good, but the paper appears yellowish color.

The University of Toronto Chinese Library

. . . .

Accession No.   1018   Index No. 169/x/x/x 了 f g k

Title - "Kuang Ti Sheng Chih Tu Chih."
關　帝　聖　跡　圖　誌
　　　　　　蹟

Classification-   C-368-   "Hsiao shuo chia"
　　　　　　　　　小　説　家

Subject -   A Recorded history of Kwang Kung- his genealogy, his temples,
             his writings etc.

Author -   compiled by Wang K'ai-ling of the Ch'ing. 葛楷林

Edition -   2nd edition dated Tao Kuang Ping Sheng   1836.
             Hupei, Ching-i-shih, district officials Hupei edition.
                                Tao
             Blocks, mien lien paper.

Index -   Provided also with bibiography.

Bound in   1 t'ao, 10 chuan, 6 ts'e.

Remarks. -

The University of Toronto Chinese Library

. . . .

Accession No.　　1019　　　　　　　Index No. 030/69je

Title -　　"Shih Yüan T'ien Tz'u "　　　　　　填

史　院　填　詞

Classification -　D-143　詞曲 — 南北曲

Subjects -　Historical play.

References -

蔣士銓

Author -　Composed by Chiang Shih-ch'üan of the Ch'ing.

Index -　A title for each Act is given .

Bound in -　2 t'ao, 10 ts'e.

Remarks-　in good condition.

20

The University of Toronto Chinese Library

. . . .

Accession No.   1020   Index No. 046/зc

Title-   " Shan   Chih "
           山 志

Classification -   C-303 - "Tsa chia" 雜家
                   "Miscellaneous writers"

Subject -   A miscellaneous collection of notes on a variety of sub-
              jects, ancient and modern of moderate merit. The author
              is more famous for raising doubtful questions than for
              judgment in their solution.

References -

Author -   Wang Hung-chuan.

Edition - Tao Kwang, Blocks, mao pien paper

Index - None.

Bound in   2 Chi,:- First chi consists of 6 chuan,3 ts'e and the
              2nd chi consists of 6 chuan,3 ts'e.

Remarks

566

The University of Toronto Chinese Library

. . . .

Accession No. 1021 √   Index No. 070/38ßR

Title -   "Fang Yü lei chü"
          方 輿 類 聚

Classification - C-301 - "Tsa p'u" "Miscellaneous scientific works."
                  雜 譜

Subject- A classification of famous mountains, waters, and sites of
          China arranged according to the ~~No.~~ of words. ~~and to~~
          categories and (sequence)
          ~~categories.~~

References -

Author - Ch'ing, Fu+Sheng   *Fu Shen of The Ch'ing* 福中

Edition - Home library edition, printed by *The Yün* ~~Yung~~ Hsiang Hall-
           dated Tao Kuang year. Blocks, mien lien paper

Index -   Title of each chuan is given.

Bound in / 1 t'ao, 16 chuan, 4 ts'e.

Remarks. in very good condition.

The University of Toronto Chinese Library

. . . .

58

Accession No.   1022 ✓   Index No. 118/hacy

Title - "Ti Chiu Ts'ai Tzu"

第 九 才 子

Classification - C-387 - "T'ung Su Hsiao Shuo"

通 俗 小 說

Subjects -   Novel

References-

樵, 雲 山 人

Author-   Compiled by Ch'iao-yün-shan jen. ("The Man of the Woodcutter Cloud Mountain")

Edition -   T'ung Wen T'ang Edition, ~~dated~~ date unknown. Blocks

Mao-t'ai paper.

                                        hui
Endex - Title for each chuan and ~~H'oui~~ provided.
                                        ^

Bound in - 4 chuan, 4 ts'e, 1 t'ao

Remarks.

The University of Toronto Chinese Library

. . . .

Accession No. 1023 ✓ ¹⁶   Index No. 163/gcof

Title - "Chün <u>chai</u> ~~Tsai~~ Tu Shu Chih."

群 齋 郡 齋 讀 書 誌

Classification - B-337-"Mu-lu" (Catalogues.)

目 錄

Subjects- A ~~collection~~ Catalogues of books with brief introduction to
each book.

References -

Author - Edited by Ch'ao Kung-wu of the Sung . 宋, 晁公武

Edition - Home library edition, Blocks, date unknown, Bamboo paper.

Index   None

Bound in - 1 t'ao, 14 chuan, 6 ts'e.

Remarks -   in good condition.

The University of Toronto Chinese Library

. . . .

Accession No. 1024   ¹⁵   Index No. 163 /4.0.f.

Title -   "Lang Ch'ien Chi Wen."
          即 潛 紀 聞

Classification - ~~B-52-"Tsa shih"~~ C-308
                 ~~雜 史~~

                        of
Subject-   A collection ^ miscellaneous historical facts.

References - Toronto No. 1082

Author -   Ch'en K'ang-ch'i of the Ch'ing

Edition - Hsiao-ching-shan Fang edition, dated the 10th year of
          Kwang ~~shih~~ Hsü,   mao t'ai paper.

Index - Provided.

Bound in - 1 t'ao, 2 chi, 30 chuan, 8 ts'e.

Remarks.

The University of Toronto Chinese Library

. . . .

57

Accession No. ___ 1025 ✓   Index No. ᴏᴏ1/dgig

Title - "Shih Shuo Hsin Yü Pu"
世　説　新　語　補

Classification- C-368- Hsiao Shuo Chia (Essayists)

Subject- An appendix to the collection of minor incidents from the
          Hang to the Tsin dynasty inclusive.

References.-

                    宋、劉義慶   Sung Dynasty

Author - The original author is Liu Yi-ch'ing of the 6th cent. This
          appendix was written by Ho Liang-chün in the middle of the
          16th cent.

Edition - Ch'ien lung 1762. Mao-ch'ing library , Blocks,
          Mao t'ai paper.

Index-- provided.

Bound in - 1 t'ao, 20 Chuan, 8 ts'e.

Remarks.-

The University of Toronto Chinese Library

. . . .

Accession No. 1026. ✓   Index No. 046/Radi

Title - "Tsung Cheng Ho P'ien."
        Ch'ung
        崇 正 合 編

Classification- C-13-"Ju chia"
        儒 家

Subject -   A collection of writings dealing with the Classics, History,
            philosophy, education and the Religions of China.

References -

Author - Compiled by T'ang Yi-lun

Edition - Reprinted by Chou Chai-kao; dated Ta Ch'ing T'ung Chih
          7th year, 1868. Blocks, mao t'ai paper.

Index. provided with introductory notes, Bibliography, Biographies
        of the ancient scholars. Then followed by titles to each
        chuan.

Bound in   1 t'ao, 13 chuan, 5 ts'e.

Remarks:

The University of Toronto Chinese Library

. . . .

Accession No. 1027 ✓   Index No. 077/jdlb.

Title -   "Li K'o Ch'ao Yüan Chüan"
           歷 科 朝 元 卷

Classification-   D-95-   "Shih -wen"
                   試 文

Subject   A collection of Examination Essays and a brief biography of

           the writers.

References-

Author -   unknown.

Edition-   Official edition.   dated Kuang Hsü year,

                mien-lien paper, blocks.
Index -   None

Bound in-   1 t'ao, 2 ts'e.

Remarks-

University of Toronto Chinese Library

. . . .

Accession No.   1028 √   Index No. 124/je b t.

129

Title -   " Han ~~Wan~~ ~~Fong~~ Shu Lin Wen Cheng Tsung,"
           Yüan Feu
           翰 苑 分 書 臨 文 正 宗

Classification -   C-338 - "Ts'ung shu"
                    叢 書

Subject -   A collection of verses, essays, of resembling Chinese characters,

References -

Author -   Unknown.

Edition -   Kuang Hsü
            ~~Kwang shih~~ year edition, blocks, mien-lien paper.

Index -   None.

Bound In - 1 t'ao, 8 different subjects, 6 ts'e.

Remarks.-

574

The University of Toronto Chinese Library

. . . .

Accession No.　1029 √　　　　　　　Index No.　120/k898

Title -　　　" Kang Mu Yün Yen "
　　　　　　　綱 目 韻 言

Classification -　B-22 -　"P'ien nien"
　　　　　　　　　　　　編 年

Subject -　　　A collection of the history of the Chow; the Western Han, the
　　　　　　　　16 kingdoms, the T'ang , the 11 Kingdoms, The southern Sung ,
　　　　　　　　The Hsia, the Yüan etc.

References -

Author -　　　K'o　　k
　　　　　　　　Hao Hsiao-Kang of the Ch'ing 清、柯曉崗

Edition -　　　Tao Kwang year edition, published by Weng Hsin T'ang. Mao-pien
　　　　　　　　paper. Blocks.

Index -　　　　None.

Bound in -　　1 t'ao, 2 Ts'e.

Remarks.

The University of Toronto Chinese Library

· · · · · · · · · · · · · · · · ·

Accession No.   1030   Index No. 120/ogld

Title -   Hsü
"Shu Hsing Ying Chi"
續 心 影 集

Classification -   C-13-"Ju Chia"
儒 家

Subject -   dealing with the problems of reintrospection, family administra-
tion, the way of social contact and the spiritual awakening.

References -

Author -   Edited by
Shih
Li Shi-ling of the Ch'ing   清 李 士 麟

Edition -   Kuang Hsü
Kwang-shih Ping Tzu nien edition (1876),
published from Lang-chow, Kangsu prov. Government office,
Blocks, mien-lien paper.

Index -   a general table containing the main headings of the each chuan.

Bound in -   1 t'ao, 4 ts'e.

Remarks.

The University of Toronto Chinese Library

. . . .

Accession No. 1031 97 ✓   Index No. 085/Kfsf.

Title -   "Yü yang wen liieh" liao
             滇 洋 文 略

Classification - D-93 -   "Shih Wen P'ing " (Literary critiques.)
                          (Wen

Subject -   Poems, prose, history, and biographies.

References -

Author -   Wang Shih-cheng of the Ch'ing   王 士 禎

Edition -   K'ang Hsi year, mao-pien paper. Home library edition.

Index -   A table of content of each chuan in detail.

Bound in -   1 t'ao, 14 Chuan, 5 ts'e.

Remarks -

The University of Toronto Chinese Library

. . . .

Accession No.   1032   Index No. 066/889²·

Title -   " Chiao Chia P'ien " 教家編

Classification -   C-13- "Ju chia "

Subject -   Philosophy and the discipline and management or the establish-
               ment of a Family.

References -

Author -   Liang Hsien-tsu of the Ch'ing 清梁顯祖

Edition -   date unknown; Hsien Tao Hall edition.
             mao pien paper, Blocks,

Index -   provided.

Bound in -   1 t'ao, 2 chuan, 2 ts'e.

Remarks

The University of Toronto Chinese Library

. . . .

32

Accession No. - 1033.   Index No. 001/-333 b

Erh/   Title -   "Erh-shih-yih shih T'ang Tz'u"
                   二 十 一 史 彈 詞

        Classification -   D-38
                           R-52   "Tsa-chia" 別集 ── 詩
                                     雜 家

        Subject -   The historical events as recorded in the "Twenty-one Dynastic Histories" (History") are
                     arranged in phrases or in Poetic forms.

        References- 012-gofk 16/22 Gest No. 2962. Toronto No§/862
                     Gest No. 2962 ' Toronto No. 862 another edition

        Author -   Compiled by Yang Sheng of the Ming.

        Edition -   Kwang Chung College Edition. dated Ta'o Kwang year
                                                        Tao Kuang
                    T'ai-shih-lien paper.

        Index -   None.

        Bounded in   2 T'ao, 11 chuan, 8 Ts'e

        Remarks.-

The University of Toronto Chinese Library

. . . .

Accession No. 1034   Index No. 149-fgbi

Title 詩經去疑
       shih Ching Ch'ü Yi

Classification A31

Subject A

References

Author Edited by
        Wang Seu-shêng, Ch'ing Dynasty; 王遂升

Edition San Lo Chai (Studio of the Three Joys)
         Mao pien paper

Index

Bound in 1 tao, 8 chuan, 4 ts'e

Remarks

The University of Toronto Chinese Library

················

Accession No. 1035 ✓   Index No. 077/8cf8

34

Title -   "Li Tai Ti Wang Nien Piao"
            歷代帝王年表

Classification - B-52   "Tsa shih"
                 B-157   雜史

Subject -   Chronology of the emperors of the various dynasties of China.

References -

Author -   Edited by
            Ch'i Chao-Nan of the Ch'ing 清，齊召南

Edition -   Ta Ch'ing, Tao Kwang, 4th. year. 1824
            Shiao Lang Houng Hsien Kwang edition
            Huan Hsiao
            Blocks, Pai paper.

Index -   None.

Bound in - 1 t'ao, 3 chuan, 3 ts'e.

Remarks.

The University of Toronto Chinese Library

. . . .

Accession No.   1036   40   Index No.   072/da cg

Title -   " Ming Mo Chi Shih Pu i "
            明 末 紀 事 補 遺

Classification -   B- 32-

Subject -   An additional historical record to the Ming history.

References -

Author -   Edited by
             San Yü-shih of Nansha.   南沙 三餘氏

Edition -   T'ung Chih year
             Home library edition.
             Blocks, Bamboo paper.

Index -   None.

Bound in-   1 t'ao, 10 chuan , 8 ts'e.

Remarks -

The University of Toronto Chinese Library

....

Accession No.   1037   51   Index No.   037/eRc

I
Title-   "Yi Chien Chih."
                夷 堅 志

Classification -   C-368. "Hsiao Shuo Chia"
                小   說 家

Subject -   Miscellaneous narratives and legends

References -

Author -   Hung Mai of the Sung 宋、洪邁

Edition -   Reprinted Sung Edition
                Mao-tai paper.

Index -   A very complete index of contents provided.

Bound in-   1 t'ao, 20 chuan, 6 ts'e.

Remarks -

The University of Toronto Chinese Library

....

Accession No. 1038 ✓   Index No. 061/rgi

40

Title -   "Yi Hsing P'ien"

艷 行 編

Classification -   B-102-(Chuan chi)

Subject -   Biographies of some outstanding emperors and officials .

References -

Author -   *Edited by*
              Li Jung, of the Ch'ing   清 李 瀅

Edition   K'ang Hsi year

              Home library edition

              Bamboo paper

              Blocks.

Index -   provided.

Bound in-   1 t'ao, 8 chuan, 4 ts'e.

Remarks-

The University of Toronto Chinese Library

. . . .

Accession No. 1039 ✓ *49*   Index No. *149/c8b*

Title -   " Chi Shih *Chu* Tsu "
            記 事 珠

Classification- C-368   "Hsiao Shuo Chia"
                          小 說 家

Subject -   Miscellaneous narration, records etc,

References -

Author-   Chang Yi-ch'ien of the Ch'ing 清. 張以謙

Edition -   Kwang *Hsü* shih 1882
            published by *Sao Yie Shan* Shao Yieh San Fang, Shanghai

            Mao pien paper, Blocks.

Index -   Title of each chuan is given

Bound in - 2 t'ao, 10 Chuan , 10 t'se.

Remarks.-

The University of Toronto Chinese Library

. . . .

Accession No.   1040 ✓   Index No. 069/kykk

Title -   " Ssu
             " Shih Wen Ching Ts'ui "
             斯 文 精 粹

Classification - D - 73 - "Wen"

Subject -   A collection of literary composition by emperors or by outstan-
               ding persons on various subjects.

References -

Author-   Compiled by Ying + Chi-shan of the Ch'ing 严繼善

Edition-   29th year of Ch'ien Lung.
               Home library edition.
               Blocks, mao-t'ai paper
Index -   provided.

Bound in-   2 T'ao, 12 Ts'e.

Remarks.-

586

The University of Toronto Chinese Library

. . . .

Accession No.   1041   Index No.   639-92ic

Title -   Sun Tzu Ts'an Ch'ang T'ung.
                    孫 子 參 同

Classification -   C-33 - "Ping Chia" 兵家

Subject -   Military Strategy

Reference -

Author -   Edited by
                    Mei Kuo Cheng 梅國禎

Edition -   Home library edition,
                    Mao Pien paper, Blocks.

Index -   None

Bound In -   1 t'ao, 3 chuan, 6 tse.

Remarks -   each page is backed by a kind of oil paper which gives a
                                                                    be
                    peculiar smell. The original purpose might for the pre-
                    vention of worms and insects.

The University of Toronto Chinese Library

. . . .

Accession No. 1042   Index No. 118-ihk

Title   Chieh Fu Chuan 節婦傳

Classification B- 102

Subject A collection of Biographies of famous widows.

References

Author   Yang ~~Shih-fu~~ Hsi-fu of the ~~Tsing~~ Ch'ing 清, 楊錫紱

Edition Ch'ien Lung year. Home Library edition.
         Ho-lu-shih ~~ch'ang~~ ts'ang 'wei jen ~~chang~~ ts'ang edition
         Bamboo paper, blocks

Index   Provided

Bound in 1 t'ao, 16 chuan, 4 t'se.

Remarks

The University of Toronto Chinese Library

. . . .

Accession No. 1043   Index No.   140 / dzceh

Title   Chieh Tzu Yüan Hua Chuan
         芥 子 園 畫 傳 藝術一
Classification   C-223   Shu hua 書畫

Subject   On the history and the technique of painting.

References

Author   Lu ~~Tsai~~ Ch'ai   鹿柴

Edition   18th year of K'ang Hsi, 1679
          Blocks, bamboo paper

Index   provided.

Bound in   1 t'ao, 5 chuan, 5 ~~t'si~~ ts'e

Remarks

The University of Toronto Chinese Library

. . . .

Accession No. 1044   Index No.   ool/book

Title   San Pu Hsiu Tu Tsang
三不朽畫贊

Classification   B 102

Subject   Biographies with portraits and life stories

References

Author   Edited by
Chang T'ao-an of the Ch'ing   清．張陶巷

Edition   Printed in the 7th year of the Republic 1917
Reprinted in the 10th year of T'ung Chih

Kuo ko edition

Type, Lien shih paper

Index   A very complete index of names of famous men, arranged
according to the catagories of their virtues

Bound in 1 t'ao, 1 ts'e.

Remarks

The University of Toronto Chinese Library

. . . .

98

Accession No. 1045   Index No. 03⁹ / bzk

Title   Ku Wen I (or Yi)

古文翼

Classification D- 73

Subject   A selection of literature

References

Author   T'ang Chieh-Hsüan of the Ch'ing 唐介軒

Edition Dated T'ung Chih year, mao pien paper
Printed in the Yi-wen-t'ang (Hall of Talented Literature) of the Huang family.

Index   provided in each chuan

Bound in   1 t'ao, 8 chuan, 8 t'se ts'e

Remarks

The University of Toronto Chinese Library

....

Accession No. 1046   Index No. 072 /qZegf

Title 明季南畧 Ming Chi Nan ~~Lueh~~ Liao

Classification B-42 Pieh shih

Subject A history of the southern campaign during the later
Ming dynasty

References

Author Chi Lu-ch'i of the Ch'ing 清．計六奇

Edition 10th year of K'ang Hsi, Pan ~~hsun~~ sung chü shih edition,
Mao pien paper

Index A list of the headings of historical events

Bound in a t'ao, 18 chuan 12 ~~Tese~~ ts'e

Remarks

The University of Toronto Chinese Library

. . . .

Accession No. 1048   Index No. 042 / zhzd

Title Hsiao ~~chiang san~~ fang ch'ih ~~ta tu~~
        t'ang shan   chih

小 倉 山 房 尺 牘

Classification   D - 23   pieh chi

Subject An d individual collection of official and non-offical
         letters.

References

Author   Yüan ~~men~~ of the Ch'ing Dynasty 袁枚
              Mei

Edition dated ch'ien lung, Sui yüan edition

Index   none

Bound in 1 t'ao, 6 chuan, 2 t'se

Remarks

Not in Mei's catalogue ?

The University of Toronto Chinese Library
. . . .

Accession No. 1049 Index No. 067/3dfd

Title 文昌帝君陰隲文像註

wen ch'ang tang chün yin-chih wen
hsiang chu

Classification C-73+

C-378

Subject miscellaneous writings of Taoism

References

Author 大興趙如升九一甫輯著

Compiled by Chao Ju-sheng of
Ta-hsing district.

Edition 藜輝齋新鐫
江南金壇縣馮雲燦敬卯
Printed by Ping Yün Ching,

Index

Bound in 1 t'ao, 4 ts'ê

Remarks

594

The University of Toronto Chinese Library

. . . .

Accession No.   1050   Index No.   113 / mcme

Title   Li chi t'i chu ta ch'üan ho chuan ts'an
ho

Classification   A-56   禮記體註大全合參

Subject   Books of Rites

References

Author   edited by
         Fan Tza-teng of the Ch3ing   范子登

Edition   Wen Ch'engT'ang edition, bamboo paper

Index   provided

Bound in   1 t'ao, 4 vols, 4 t'se
                    (chuan 3)

Remarks

The University of Toronto Chinese Library

. . . .

Accession No.   1051   Index No.   120 / 齊魯

Title   Ching yü pi tu
             經 餘步讀
Classification   C- 13   Ju chia   儒家

Subject.   A collection of commentaries of the classics

References

Author   Compiled by Lei Hsiao-feng of The Ch'ing 清 雷 曉峯

Edition   Dated 8th year of Chia Ching,   Ch'eng Yü T'ang édition.
          Mao pien paper

Index   Main headings of each chuan are presented

Bound in   1 t'ao, 8 chuan, 4 ts'e.

Remarks

Accession No.   1052   Index No.   005/agbh

Title   Chiu Ching T'an

九　經　談

Classification   A - 137

Subject   On the nine classics

References

Author   ~~T'ai Tsien Yüan Cheng~~ of Japan.   日本，太田元貞
Tai Tien Yüan Chen

Edition   Szu-shu-fang of Japan

Index   None.

Bound in 1 t'ao, 10 chuan, and 4 t'se
          Japanese mien paper
Remarks

The University of Toronto Chinese Library

. . . .

Accession No. 1053   Index No. 053/1zzi

Title Kwang Ching Shih Yün Fu

廣 金 石 韻 府

Classification A-166

Subject Phonetic dictionaries

References

Author edited by 朱時望 Chu Shih-Wang of the Ming, reprinted by 周亮工 Chou Liang-kung of the Ch'ing.

Edition Ta yueh t'ang
        -yeh-

Index   None

Bound in   1 t'ao, 4 ts'e, mien lien paper.

Remarks

The University of Toronto Chinese Library

. . . .

Accession No. 1054   Index No.   051/bbh

Title   P'ing P'ing Lu

平 平 錄

Classification   C - 731

Subject   A collection of treatises about Tao and daily life problems.

References

Author   Yang Ch'eng-sun of the Ch'ing   清. 楊誠村

Edition   Wang Wen Ying, Tao Kwang year
                ʾyün

Index   provided

Bound in   1 t'ao, 10 chuan, 4 t'se
                Mao pien paper.   tsʾe
Remarks

599

The University of Toronto Chinese Library

....

Accession No. 1055   Index No.   102/zzic

Title   Chia Tze Hui Chi

甲 子 會 紀

Classification   B - 22

Subject   An annal, giving brief historical accounts to each
           period arranged chronologically from the eighth year
           pf Hwang-ti downward.

References

Author   Ch'ên   Edited by.   Ying-Ch'i of the Ming   明.陳應旂
          Sieh   chi

Edition   Ming Chia Ching year edition

Index   provided

Bound in 1 t'ao, 5 chuan, 4 t'se, bamboo paper, block

Remarks   colour of the paper has turned yellow.

The University of Toronto Chinese Library

....

Accession No.   1056   Index No.   (a) 044/eihh
                                                (b) 149/ofhh

Title   (a) Chü Yeh Lu T'sui Yü   居業錄粹語

        (b) Tu Shu Lu Ts'ui Yü   讀書錄粹語

Classification   C - 13

Subject   Treatise on various subjects

References

Author   (a)   Hu Cheng Tsai chü-jen, of the Ming

         (b) Hsieh Wen-Ch'ing

Edition (a) Tao Kwang Ping Ying Year edition. Printed by Chang Po-hang Shen

        (b)

Index   provided

Bound in   (a) 1 t'ao, 4 chuan, 6 t'se

           (b) same t'ao, 4 chuan, 4 tse.

Remarks   Mien lien paper, block

The University of Toronto Chinese Library

. . . .

Accession No. 1057   Index No. 009/dbge

Title   Ch'üan Shih Kung Tz'u

金　史宮詞

Classification   D - 113

Subject   A collection of poetical compositions

References

Author   Shih Meng-lan of the Ch'ing   史夢蘭

Edition   Home library edition, date unknown.

Index   provided

Bound in 1 t'ao, 20 chuan, 6 ts'e, Mao pien paper.

Remarks   in good condtion

The University of Toronto Chinese Library

. . . .

57

Accession No. 1058   Index No.   142/gi

Title   Shu Pi
           蜀碧
Classification   B - 42

Subject An unclassified historical writing dealing with the
         rebellion of Chang Hsien Chung in Szechuan province.

References

Author   *Edited by*
         P'eng Ch'ing-Chüan of the Ch'ing   清.彭馨泉

Edition   T'ien-lu-ko edition, Chia Ching year.

Index   giving only the references

Bound in   1 t'ao, 4 chuan, 2 ~~tze~~ *ts'e*
            Blocks, white paper
Remarks

The University of Toronto Chinese Library

. . . .

131
131

Accession No. 1059   Index No.   077/gcbf

Title   Li tai shih ~~luch~~ *liao* ku erh ~~t'su~~ *tz'u*

歷代史畧鼓兒詞

Classification   D - 147

Subject   Balla~~f~~ds on some historical events

References

Author   Chia Fu-Ch'i   賈鳧溪

Edition   Home edition, T'ung Chih 9th year.
Mao pien paper. One volume copied

Index   none

Bound in   1 t'ao, 2 t'se

Remarks

The University of Toronto Chinese Library

. . . .

Accession No. 1060   Index No. 030/bbmi

Title   Ku ching shih yi
         古 今 釋 疑

Classification   c - 308

Subject   Discussions and expositions on the classics, astronomy,
          divination, natural science etc.

References

Author   Fang Chung-li of the Ch'ing 方中履

Edition   ~~plate by~~ Boards of Hang Ch'ing Ko, date of publication not stated
           mien lien paper

Index   provided

Bound in   2 tao, 18 chuan, 10t'se

Remarks

605

The University of Toronto Chinese Library

....

Accession No. 1061   Index No.   166/b da

Title   Chung Pi Kan
           Ch'ung Ko Sung Pen T'ang Ying Pi Shih
           重刊 新 究 本 裳 陰 比 事

Classification   C - 43

Subject   A collection of strange criminal cases

References

Author   Edited by
           Kuei Meng-Hsieh, of the Sung   宋. 桂夢協

Edition   Chü Cheng & Fang Sung publication

Index   provided

Bound in   1 t'ao, 1 ts'e

Remarks

606

The University of Toronto Chinese Library

. . . .

Accession No.   1062   Index No.   075/czcd

Title   Li Ch'ang Chi Chi
         李 長 吉 集
Classification   C - lo3

Subject   A collection of lyrics

References

Author   Li ~~Hao~~ Ho, of the T'ang

Edition   Kwang ~~Hsü~~ 18th year. *Cut by Yeh Shih at Yang Ch'eng*
           mien lien paper.

Index   none

Bound in   1 t'ao, 2 tsce

Remarks

The University of Toronto Chinese Library

. . . .

Accession No. 1063   Index No. 075/fdg

Title 書 林 餘 話 Shu Lin Yü Hua

Classification   C - 13

Subject   Regarding the matter of printing according to the
writers of the Sung, Yüan and the Ming

References

Author   Narrated by
Yeh Teh-hui of the Ch'ing 清.葉德輝 Yeh Te-hui

Edition   Yeh Ch'i-yin press hsi yin (with metal type ?)
feng
nien lien paper

Index

Bound in   1 t'ao, 2 chuan, 2 ts'e.

Remarks

The University of Toronto Chinese Library

. . . .

27

Accession No.   1064   Index No.   018/mgk

Title   Chien Hsia Tsuan
           n   a
                 Hsia chuan
劍 俠 傳

Classification   B - 102 C-368 小說家

Subject Biographies of (magic) knights
                    legendary

References

Author   Sketched by Hsü Wei, of the Ming

Edition   Published by Wang Ling, in the year of Ch'ing Hsien Feng

Index

Bound in   1 t'ao 4 chuan, 2 t'se
              Mien Lien paper   tse
Remarks

Accession No. 1065   Index No.   009/nkdk

Title   Ju Hsing Chi Chuan

儒行集傳

Classification   C - 13

Subject   On the right conduct of a Confucian scholar

References

Author   Compiled by Hwang Tao-Chou of the Ming 明，黃道周

Edition   Home library edition, 4th year of T'ao Kwang

Index   1 t'ao, 2 chuang 2 tse

Bound in

Remarks

610

The University of Toronto Chinese Library

. . . .

Accession No. 1066   *117*   Index No.   030/bzzf

司馬氏書儀

Title   Ssu-Ma Shih Shu I

Classification   D - 43

Subject   Key to official letter writing

References

Author   Ssu-Ma ~~Kwang~~ *Kuang* of the Sung   司馬光

Edition   First year of Yung Cheng *1723 ?*

Index   provided in the form of classification

Bound in   1 t'ao, 2 ~~tse~~, Mao pien paper

Remarks

The University of Toronto Chinese Library

. . . .

41

Accession No. 1067   Index No.   010/bheb

Title 元 朝 秘 史
       Yüan C̶h̶o̶w̶ Pi Shih
          Ch'ao

Classification   B - 42

Subject Miscellaneous historical writings of Yüan Dynasty

References

Author   not stated

Edition   printed during the Kwang Ssu period, published by
          Kwang Ku-t'ang

Index   none

Bound in 1 t'ao, 10 chuan, 6 t'se, with two additional chuan.
          Lien-shih paper
Remarks

612

The University of Toronto Chinese Library

· ·

tung-su = popular

72

Accession No. 1068   Index No. / 001/bqaj

Title   三保太監西洋記通俗演義
        San Pao t'ai chien hsi yang chi t'ung su yen i
                                        su   yen

Classification   C - 387

Subject   Colloquial novels

References

Author   Lo Mou-teng of the Ming   明、羅懋登

Edition   published in Ming Wang Li Year (1537)
                              ting-yu

Index   provided

Bound in   20 chuan, 20 ts'e in 2 t'ao.
           bamboo paper
Remarks

The University of Toronto Chinese Library

. . . .

Accession No.   10699   48   Index No.   037/abhb
                1069

Title   T'ai Shih Hua Chü
               太 史 華 句

Classification   C - 308

Subject   Miscellaneous writings, discussions, and expositions
          on various subjects: astronomy, astrology and ~~chaomancy~~,
          geomancy,
          divination, folk-lore etc.

References

Author   Edited by
          Ling Ti-chih of Ming Dynasty 凌迪知

Edition   Ming edition, published in the reign of Ming Wan-li
          Ming mien paper

Index   provided

Bound in   1 t'ao, 8 chuan, 5 ts'e

Remarks

614

The University of Toronto Chinese Library

. . . .

Accession No.   1070   Index No.   167/zdic

Title   金 科 輯 要
          Chin Kuo Chi'i Yao
               K'o Chi

Classification   C - 43

Subject   Jurisprudence

References

Author   Kuei Kuan,
           Kuei-Kuan, Wu Ch'ang-H'ua   桂官,武昌侯
                    -hou

Edition   Printed in block from Chin K'uo Liu T'ung Ch'ü, Peking .
            mao pien paper   K'o

Index   provided

Bound in   2 t'ao, 18 chuan

Remarks

615

The University of Toronto Chinese Library

. . . .

Accession No. 1071 34   Index No. 010/63cj

Title
  Yüan chih shun, chen chiang chih

Classification B 194   元至順鎮江志

Subject The Chen-chiang Gazeteer of the chih Shun priod of Yüan Dynasty.

References

        no name
Author ch'ang Huang-sheng, Chen Ch'ing-nien

Edition

Index

Bound in 1 tao, 21 and 2 chuan, in 8 ts'e

Remarks

The University of Toronto Chinese Library
. . . .

Accession No. 1072   Index No. 060/f d h g

Title 律呂精義   Lü⁴ lü³ ching i

Classification c-228 音樂 Music

Subject

References

Author 鄭世子, 臣 載堉謹撰
Written by Cheng Shih-tzu.
Edition

Index

Bound in 2 t'ao*, 6 t₃'ê

Remarks

The University of Toronto Chinese Library

....

Accession No.   1073   Index No.   170/hhdd

94

Title   陶 淵 明 集
             T'ao ~~Yen~~ Ming Chi
             (Yüan)   Yüan

Classification   D - ~~38~~ 33

Subject   A collection of T'ao ~~Yen~~ Ming's verses
                            /yüan

References   Toronto No. 891

Author   T'ao Ch'ien of chin Dynasty 晉, 陶潛

Edition   Compiled by Yang Tzu-lieh, Hsian Feng year

Index   none

Bound in   1 t'ao, 10 chuan, 5 ts'e

Remarks

618

The University of Toronto Chinese Library

. . . .

119

Accession No. 1074   Index No.   0646/eddz

岳 忠 武 王 文 集

Title   ~~Yuch~~ Chung Wu Wang Wen Chi

Yüeh

Classification   D - 43

Subject   Biography of ~~Yuch~~ Fei, and also his petitions.

Yo

References

Author   Compiled by H̶wang Pang ^-ning of the Ch'ing 黄邦寧

? Edition   published by Ch'ing Feng Ko, Hsuan T'ung, Hsing Hai year.

Index   none

Bound in   1 t'ao, 10 chuan, 4 ts'e, mien lien paper

Remarks

The University of Toronto Chinese Library

. . . .

Accession No.   1075   Index No.   040/裒 (新)

Title   寶學考
         Shih Hsüeh K'ao

Classification   B - 117

Subject   Collected biographies

References

Author   *Yün Mao-ch'i*
          Yung Mou-Ch'i of the Ch'ing

Edition   Home library, bamboo paper

Index   provided

Bound in   1 t'ao, 4 chuan and 4 ts'e

Remarks

The University of Toronto Chinese Library

. . . .

Accession No. 1076   Index No.   031/bfcz

Title   四書代言
          Ssu Shu Tai Yen

Classification   A -131

Subject   Discussions on the Four Books (Ssu shu)

References

Author   Edited by
          Fang Ying Hsiang of the Ming   方應祥

Edition   Ming block, bamboo paper

Index   provided

Bound in   1 t'ao, 4 tuse.

Remarks

The University of Toronto Chinese Library

....

Accession No. 1077   28   Index No. 130/egte

Title Hu K 胡刻資治通鑑校字記
Hu k'o tzu chih tung chien chiao tzu chi

Classification B - 367

Subject a critical studies on the comparision of wording in different
versions of the Tze-Tze-Tung-Chien (資治通鑑)
Tzu chih tung chien

References

Author 清 熊羅宿著
Ch'ing, Hsiung Lo-hsiu of The Ch'ing

Edition Private Home edition
Mien lien paper

Index 1 t'ao,
5 4 chuan 4 t'ce

Bound in

Remarks

622

The University of Toronto Chinese Library

. . . .

Accession No. 1078   Index No. 042/zmdf

Title   Hsiao Hsüeh Chi ~~Chich Chu~~ *Chieh*   小學集解註
解

Classification   A - 151

Subject   Dictionaries

References

Author   *Edited by* 朱熹 Chu Hsi of the Sung, *with commentary of* Chang Po-hang *of The Ch'ing* 張伯行

Edition   Ch'ung Wen-Shu Chü, Hu-pei
Tsung Chih 6th. year
Mian lien paper

Index   none

Bound in   1 t'ao, 6 chuan, 3 t'ê

Remarks

The University of Toronto Chinese Library

. . . .

Accession No. 1079   Index No. 096/zfh

Title   Yü Ming T'ang Huan Hun Chi

玉茗堂 還 魂 記

Classification   D - 143

Subject   Librettos   戲本

References

Author   T'ang Hsien-Tsu   湯顯祖

Edition   Second edition, by Nuan H'ung-Shih, not dated
          Chieh lien paper

Index   Title of each Act and each scene

Bound in   1 t'ao, 2 tsê

Remarks

The University of Toronto Chinese Library

. . . .

Accession No.   1080   Index No.   003/cegh

Title   Tang Ch'ien Yü Lu

丹 鉛 餘 錄

Classification   C - 308

Subject   A collection of miscellaneous writings.

References   Wylie's notes on Chinese literature, p. 162

Author   Yang Yung Hsiu of the Ming   明、楊用修

Edition   The Ting Yu year of Ming Chia Ching preserved by Kao
Kao H'an-Sheng of the P'ing Shou   White paper   (1537)

Index   none

Bound in   1 t'ao, 3 chuan, 4 ts'e

Remarks

The University of Toronto Chinese Library

....

Accession No.   1081   Index No.   030/b5

Title   Shih Wei   史徵

Classification   B - 52

Subject   Miscellaneous historical writings

References

Author   Chang Ts'ai T'ien of the Ching   清、張采田

Edition   One of the series of collection from Tuo Chia Lo Hsiang
           kwan,   Mien Lien paper

Index   provided

Bound in   1 t'ao, 8 chuan, 4 ts'e.

Remarks

626

The University of Toronto Chinese Library

. . . .

Accession No. 1082   Index No.   163/flcf

69

Title   Lang Ch'ien Chi Wen   郎潛紀聞

Classification   C - 308

Subject   Miscellaneous writing on the past events

References   Toronto No. 1024

Author   Ch'en K'ang Ch'i of the Ch'ing

Edition   Printed in Kwang Hsü period

Index   A very brief index

Bound in   1 t'ao, 14 chuan, 2 tsê.

Remarks

The University of Toronto Chinese Library
. . . .

Accession No. 1084   Index No. 171/11

Title   Li Pien   隸辨

Classification   A - 161

Subject   Graphic dictionaries

References

Author   Ku Nan-Yüan of the Ch'ing   顧南　原   editor

Edition   Yü Yüan T'ang, printed in Chien Lung period

Index   None

Bound in   1 t'ao, 8 chuan, 8 ~~ch'e~~ ts'e
           Mao pien paper
Remarks

The University of Toronto Chinese Library

....

Accession No. 1085   Index No.   012/bohz

Title   Liu Yi Kang Mu   六藝綱目

Classification   A - 137

Subject   An outline of the six arts

References

Author   Narrator: 舒天民   Shu T'ien-Ming   Revised by Liu shih 劉氏 of Tung Wu

Edition 28th year of Tao Kwang

Index   None

Bound in   1 t'ao, 2 tse
           pai mien paper
Remarks

The University of Toronto Chinese Library

. . . .

Accession No. 1086   Index No.   019/ecif

Title   ~~Tsu~~ Tzu Pien ~~Lueh~~   *Chu*   *Liao*   助字辨略

Classification   A - 151

Subject   Dictionary on adverbs and prepositions

References

Author   Liu Ch'i of the Ch'ing   *Edited by*   劉淇

       Revised by Yang Shih of Ch'ang Sha

Edition   Ch'ing Chia Tzu year (1804)

       Mien lien paper

Index   provided

Bound in   1 t'ao, 5 chuan, 5 ts'e
        Mien lien paper

Remarks

The University of Toronto Chinese Library

．．．．．．．．．．．．．．．．．．．．．．．

95

Accession No.　1087　　　　　　Index No.　170/hkzd

Title　　T'ao Lou Wen Chao 陶樓文鈔

Classification　　D - 43

Subject　　A collection of essays

References

Author　Hwang P'ang-Nien of the Ch'ing 黃彭年
　　　　　edited by

Edition　printed by Wen K'uieh Tsai in Peking
　　　　　K'uei chai
　　　　　mien lien paper

Index　provided

Bound in　1 t'ao 14 chuan 6 t'se

Remarks　　Mien lien paper

631

The University of Toronto Chinese Library

. . . .

Accession No. 1088   Index No. 024/zggi

Title   Shih Chia Yü Lu Chai Yao   十家語錄摘要

Classification   C - 13

Subject   A collection of the work of ten scholars

References

Author   謝 蘭 生   Hsieh Lan-Sheng of the Ch'ing

Edition   Home library

Index   none

Bound in 1 t'ao, 3 chuan, 4 tsê

Remarks

The University of Toronto Chinese Library

. . . .

63

Accession No. 1089   Index No.   051/chhe 051-ciih

Title   年羹堯將軍兵法
         Nien Chiang Chün Ping fa

         Keng Yao
Classification   C 33

Subject   On military affairs

References

Author   Nien Keng Yao of the Ch'ing   清、年羹堯

Edition Pao Tsuan Lou edition. of the Chia Ching period.
         Mien lien paper.

Index provided in the first book

Bound in 1 t'ao 4 chuan 4 tse Mien lien paper.

Remarks

90

The University of Toronto Chinese Library

....

Accession No. 1090[9] Index No. 040-ca

Title 字枀
Tzu Hsi

Classification

Subject A 161

References

Author Hsia ~~Erh~~ Yüeh-chan of the Ch'ing 夏曰瑷

Edition Hsia Ching Hsien

Index

Bound in 1 t'ao, 15 chuan and 1 extra, 4 ts'e

Remarks

The University of Toronto Chinese Library

....

Accession No.   1091   Index No.   163/jhk(zh)

Title   鄉 黨 圖 考
         Hsiang Tang Tu Kou
                    Tu Kao

Classification   A - 71

Subject   On rituals and customs in Confucius time

References

Author   Chiang Yung of the Ch'ing   江永

Edition Chien Teh T'ang edition,
         Chien Lung Year

Index   provided

Bound in 1 tao, 10 chuan, 4 册
          Mao pien paper

Remarks
          In good condtion except the colour of the paper has turned
          red.

The University of Toronto Chinese Library

. . . .

15

Accession No. 1092   Index No.   010/bgdi

元 聖 武 親 征 錄

Title   Yüan Sheng Wu Ch'in Cheng Lu
Ch'in 親

Classification   B - 297 Military affairs

Subject   A record of the campaign of Yüan Sheng Wu.

References

Author   Edited by Ho Ch'iu-T'ao 何秋濤

Edition   Home Library

Index   none

Bound in   1 tao, 2 tsê, Lien shih paper.

Remarks

636

The University of Toronto Chinese Library

. . . .

Accession No.   1093   Index No.   149/ge

Title   説 鈴 事 鄉 贅 筆
         Shui Ling   or   Chuan Hsiang Chui Pi
         Shuo   Shun

Classification   C - 368

Subject   A record of news and strange events

References   none

Author   Tung Han of the Ch'ing 清 董含

Edition   Written ts style

Index   none

Bound in   1 t'ao, 3 chuan, 4 tu'e
           Bamboo paper
Remarks

The University of Toronto Chinese Library

. . . .

82

Accession No. 1094   Index No.   149/fhi$\frac{t}{}$

詩賦題典雅
Title ShihFu T'i Tien Ya

Classification   C - 13

Subject   Phraseology of Poetry

References

Author   Compiled by Chiu Ta Yu of the Ch'ing   邱大猷

Edition   Home Library Edition

Index   None

Bound in 1 tao, 5 chuan, 5 ~~冊~~ ts'e
          Bamboo paper
Remarks

The University of Toronto Chinese Library

. . . .

Accession No. 1095   13   Index No. 030/Logk

Title 古樂経傳
Ku lo ching chuan

Classification C-228 音樂 Music

Subject

References

Author 李光地註 Li Kuang-ti of the Ch'ing

Edition Home Library.

Index

Bound in 1 t'ao, 4 ts'ê
         5-chuan,

Remarks